Power & Inequality

POWER & INEQUALITY

A Comparative Introduction

GREGG M. OLSEN

OXFORD UNIVERSITY PRESS

8 Sampson Mews, Suite 204,
Don Mills, Ontario M3C 0H5
www.oupcanada.com

Oxford University Press is a department of the University of Oxford.
It furthers the University's objective of excellence in research, scholarship,
and education by publishing worldwide in

Oxford New York
Auckland Cape Town Dar es Salaam Hong Kong Karachi
Kuala Lumpur Madrid Melbourne Mexico City Nairobi
New Delhi Shanghai Taipei Toronto

With offices in
Argentina Austria Brazil Chile Czech Republic France Greece
Guatemala Hungary Italy Japan Poland Portugal Singapore
South Korea Switzerland Thailand Turkey Ukraine Vietnam

Oxford is a trade mark of Oxford University Press
in the UK and in certain other countries

Published in Canada
by Oxford University Press

First Published 2011

Library and Archives Canada Cataloguing in Publication

Olsen, Gregg M. (Gregg Matthew), 1956–
Power and inequality : a comparative introduction
/Gregg Olsen.
Includes bibliographical references.
ISBN 978-0-19-544400-1
1. Equality. 2. Power (Social sciences). I. Title.
HM821.O47 2010 305 C2010-903440-6

Cover image: Emin Kuliyev/Shutterstock

Printed and bound in Canada.

2 3 4 — 15 14 13

In memory of my parents,
Ralph and Joan Olsen

Contents

List of Figures

List of Tables

Preface and Acknowledgments

The only way to thoroughly understand nations is through a comparative lens. Cross-national and cross-temporal contrasts provide a broader context that allows us to more accurately interpret national findings. They also allow us to examine the varying impacts of global trends and developments, such as economic growth, stagnation, or integration, and to evaluate deterministic theories and arguments that celebrate, or decry, the futility of alternative socio-economic arrangements and policy approaches. And they can provide invaluable lessons. This is especially true in the area of social inequality. Students of social inequality are often aware of the warranted reputation, and long-standing status, of the Nordic lands as among the most egalitarian nations within the advanced capitalist world, even if they are not familiar with the details. Similarly, the Anglo-Saxon nations are generally acknowledged as central repositories of a broad range of inequalities. This study juxtaposes three Nordic lands (Finland, Norway, and Sweden) with three Anglo countries (Canada, the UK, and the US), closely highlighting marked variation along several key material and non-material indicators of inequality between, as well as within, these two families of nations.

Inequality is an inherent and defining feature of all capitalist societies, but it has been markedly diminished in the Nordic nations; poverty is not as widespread, severe, or intractable there, the middle classes are significantly larger, and far greater support is provided as a right of residency than in the Anglo-Saxon nations, among many others. Within the Anglo world, class polarization is most clearly evident in the US, where inequality, in its myriad forms, is typically highest and rising fastest, and the realization of the American dream appears least likely and increasingly out of reach for ever-growing numbers of the population. Of course, the achievements in the Nordic nations—especially reductions in material inequalities—will always be somewhat precariously situated and subject to some degree of retrenchment without a solid foundation of economic democracy. The gains made, and the periodic setbacks that have occurred, largely reflect shifts in the balance of power in these nations.

Although often cavalierly dismissed by some across the political spectrum, significant reductions in many forms of inequality in the Nordic nations are not inconsequential to the quality of life there, especially for those who were less well-off or marginalized. They also have the potential to empower, making the realization of farther-reaching changes more possible. Moreover, most of the achievements in the Nordic nations, such as the embedding of a wide range of rights and entitlements, and the construction of a comprehensive arrangement of inclusive and widely cherished social programs and supports, are central features of most visions of alternative egalitarian societies. It should also be stressed that many of these gains, including universal child care; generous parental leave programs; a dense network of rights and protections for children, women, gays, and people with disabilities; and high levels of female representation in parliament did not exist, or were not nearly as highly developed, during the oft-heralded 'golden age' of the 'Nordic model' in the 1970s. Despite significant setbacks in some areas, the dire forecasts predicting the imminent end of the Nordic approach that have been recurrently advanced over the past three decades have yet to materialize; during this same time frame the downtrodden and excluded in the Anglo nations have been routinely assured (usually from on high and by those who are rather well-off) that there are no alternatives to neo-liberalism, or that social measures that 'merely' humanize society are not worth pursuing, a kind of secular version of the notion that meaningful change will only come in the 'next life'. These views are critically assessed here.

The framework of this study has been a long time in the making, and I am happy to have the opportunity to acknowledge those who have, directly or indirectly, helped it along. First, I would like to express my gratitude to colleagues and friends who read and commented upon drafts of the manuscript (or parts thereof), provided valuable direction, or discussed the ideas presented herein with me. These include Bob Brym, Joan Durrant, Olle Lundberg, Rob Nestor, Julia O'Connor, Jonah Olsen, Michael Palamarek, Joakim Palme, and the anonymous reviewers for Oxford University Press. It would not be possible to individually acknowledge everyone whose ideas helped to shape the pages of this book. However, I would like to thank Barry Adam, Bernd Baldus, Bob Brym, Ralph Miliband, and Leo Panitch, whose work on inequality inspired me when I was their student many years ago and continues to do so today. The Institute for Social Research (SOFI) at the University of Stockholm has been an ideal research base for my comparative research for more than two decades; I thank SOFI, and all of my friends and colleagues there, for their ongoing support and hospitality. I would also like to thank everyone at Oxford University Press who helped to prepare this manuscript for publication, especially Katie Scott and David Stover, who made it an altogether enjoyable experience. I don't believe it could be possible to have a more congenial, helpful, and invariably supportive ally than David. My greatest debt is to my family, Joan and Jonah, for their enduring inspiration, support, and love. Sadly, the latter stages of this project coincided with the loss of my parents, Ralph and Joan Olsen. This book is dedicated, with much love and longing, to their memory.

Part I

Considering Inequality: Conceptualization and Comparison

1 Understanding Social Inequality: A Comparative Introduction

Introduction

Social inequality has been a pervasive and stubbornly unremitting feature of human society for millennia, with a profound and encompassing impact upon our daily lives. It has, consequently, also been a central and long-standing area of interest and concern in philosophy and across the social sciences and other branches of scholarly engagement. In sociology the study of inequality has been a pivotal issue since the inception of the discipline in the nineteenth century. Most of its founders and formative figures were occupied with it and, for some of them, it was a primary field of investigation. Embracing inequality as largely positive and inevitable, several of these thinkers initiated theoretical schools that have served to rationalize and legitimate many forms, and extreme levels, of social inequality, and their ideas have significantly shaped contemporary social policy. Those from other traditions have sought to challenge these dominant perspectives, viewing massive inequality, and attempts to rationalize it, as a product and reflection of the maldistribution of power in society. The central purpose of this volume is to explore discussions and debates concerning the character and inevitability of social inequality and to introduce some of the key issues, conceptual tools, controversies, thinkers, and theories that have informed and animated the literature and research on social inequality. It does this through the employment of a comparative and cross-national perspective, contrasting the varied conceptions of equality, forms and levels of social inequality, and ways inequality has been expressed and addressed across two groups of countries, the Anglo-Saxon and Nordic nations.

Cross-national Contrasts: The Anglo-Saxon and Nordic Nations

The past few decades have been marred by a disturbingly sharp rise in many forms of social inequality across the nations of the developed and affluent capitalist world. Yet, however ubiquitous this trend, there is marked cross-national variation in its character, extent, intensity, and acceleration. A central theme pursued in this book is that, while inequality is an inherent, defining feature of capitalism, this variation merits our attention and further exploration. Rising rates of poverty and homelessness, greater class polarization, declining levels of social mobility, and relentless attacks upon the welfare state and other long-standing social protections, entitlements, and rights have been observed virtually everywhere across the advanced capitalist world over the past few decades. But these trends are much more glaringly evident and deleterious in those nations, such as the US, that have most zealously embraced neo-liberalism. Although not immune from such developments, the Nordic lands, in contrast, still rank among the most egalitarian countries along most measures of inequality. Moreover, at least some forms of social inequality have continued to steadily decline across these northern European countries.

This cross-national variation challenges many classical and contemporary theoretical perspectives and accounts of social inequality. Their conclusions, so often echoed in the popular media today, suggest that, due to any of a wide range of 'irresistible' factors—including biological predispositions, the 'needs' of social systems, structural determinants, greater global integration, and other allegedly immutable economic forces and laws—social inequality ought to be fairly uniform across the advanced capitalist world. They also often maintain that there is little that can, or should, be done to redress this situation. This contention is assessed here through a close examination of social inequality from a cross-national perspective, juxtaposing three countries from the Anglo-Saxon world, Canada, the UK, and the US, with three Nordic nations, Finland, Norway, and Sweden (see Box 1.1). Particular focus is placed upon the nations that have been most and least successful in eliminating social inequality, both between and within these groups of nations.[1] Cross-national studies allow us to assess popular convictions and long-standing theories suggesting that high levels of inequality are inevitable. In short, there is far too much variation across human societies, from the past and the present, for us to accept this widely held idea. Neither should we embrace the best case examples presented here, or any others, as utopian or ultimate end points. No nation has ever eliminated the many expressions of social inequality, and there are many forms of inequality that the Nordic nations have not yet adequately addressed or even fully acknowledged. However, the cross-national contrasts presented here provide instructive direction, and a measure of hope, for more far-reaching change in the future.

Box 1.1 ⁂ The Anglo-Saxon and Nordic Nations: A Brief Overview

Given their colonial links to Britain, Canada and the United States clearly bear its imprint, with similar social structures and political and legal orientations based upon British common law. But there are some striking differences among these nations as well. The birth of the US as an independent, self-consciously distinct nation-state dates back to the American Revolution in 1776. Canada, in contrast, did not reject its British links. It did not emerge as a separate nation until the passage of the British North America Act (BNA Act) in 1867; its juridical ties to Britain remained in place until 1931; and its constitution was not patriated until 1982. Canada also maintained strong historical, institutional, linguistic, and socio-cultural ties to France. The Nordic lands, which include the four Scandinavian nations (Denmark, Norway, Sweden, and Iceland) and Finland, also have long-standing historical and political bonds. From 1397 until 1521 the three existing Scandinavian kingdoms were joined through the Kalmar Union, constituting the largest political realm in Europe during this period. Although each of them was to retain its own laws and privileges, Denmark, the predominant power among them, often ruled the union with an iron fist. After several attempts, Sweden finally gained permanent independence in 1521. Norway remained united with Denmark until 1814, when it was ceded to Sweden after Denmark's defeat in the Napoleonic Wars. (Norway's dependencies, however—Greenland, the Faroe Islands, and, until 1944, Iceland—remained part of Denmark.) In 1905 the Norwegian-Swedish union was peacefully dissolved. Finland, in turn, was a Swedish province from the 1150s until 1809, but ceded to Russia after Sweden's military defeat (1808–1809). Russia granted Finland privileged status as an autonomous, self-governing 'grand duchy' but became increasingly autocratic over time, leading to Finnish independence after the Russian Revolution in 1917. Finland is ethnically and linguistically distinct from Scandinavia; the Scandinavian languages have Germanic roots but Finnish belongs to the same language family as Estonian and Hungarian. As well, Finland is a republic, not a constitutional monarchy like the others. But its broad similarities, including its relatively low levels of inequality, highly developed welfare state, powerful labour movement, and well-entrenched social democratic traditions, are much more striking than its differences from Scandinavia. As in the other Nordic lands, a greater degree of cultural uniformity, and the dominance of Evangelical Lutheranism as the official and most widely (if dispassionately) embraced confession, have served to attenuate religious conflicts that have sometimes rent other parts of Western Europe. Until 1863 Swedish was the sole official language of Finland and it remains one of its two official languages today. The Swedish People's Party has been a fixture on the Finnish political scene since 1906. Sweden and Finland share yet another striking trait: their highly industrialized economies feature prominent high-tech industries.

A second closely related theme advanced here is that this cross-national variation is linked to the constellations of power in these countries. Where labour movements, women's groups, civil rights activists, and various other actors are well-organized, significant gains have been made that can lead to further attempts to redress social inequalities, especially when these groups work in tandem. The stronger, more egalitarian traditions and conditions in northern Europe, and the strikingly and consistently higher levels of inequality along most dimensions across the Anglo-Saxon world, reflect the strength of countervailing forces from below in each of these nations. This is not to deny the very real constraints and biases of social contexts and structures, such as capitalism, patriarchy, and racism, but to acknowledge their social roots and the room for human agency to challenge and transform them. As the German social theorist and political revolutionary Karl Marx (1934 [1852]:10) famously suggested, people make their own history, but under circumstances and conditions directly encountered and transmitted from the past, not ones they have chosen themselves. These themes and goals are addressed through an exploration and synthesis of central theoretical and empirical research on social inequality.

The Rise and Stall of Equality: Cross-national Variations on a Theme

Throughout much of the twentieth century, several long-standing forms of social inequality were directly addressed and significant inroads made toward their redress across the advanced capitalist world. In the first few decades, these efforts sought to extend what are sometimes referred to as 'first generation' rights, opportunities, and entitlements—those primarily associated with equality before the law and political equality.[2] These included the extension of suffrage as well as the eradication of property laws, poll taxes, literacy and language requirements, and countless other practices that had been deliberately and effectively employed to restrict the political and civil liberties of some groups and curtail their eligibility for full citizenship. Over the next few decades the emphasis shifted to economic and social concerns and 'second generation' rights. This period was characterized by a general improvement in wage levels, working conditions, and standards of living for most families and the introduction and development of the 'Keynesian welfare state'—a broad array of income transfers; social services; and other social, fiscal, and regulatory policies and protections. These achievements, in large part, reflected the struggles and growing vitality of national labour movements, women's organizations, civil rights protest, and other groups and their ability to challenge and resist the power of the dominant classes and corporations, as well as their organizations, interests, and ideologies, in a period of economic growth. Of course, significant cross-national variation in the strength of these countervailing forces, and in the consequent 'balance of power', resulted in equally significant cross-national variation in the character and impact of their efforts, victories, and gains in the decades following World War II. But notable reductions in inequality could be readily observed across virtually all of the nations of the advanced capitalist world. And while certainly not eradicated or silenced, racist, sexist, and other justifications of social inequality that sought to deny the equal worth of all people and sanction the mistreatment of some groups were increasingly discredited and in retreat in many quarters.

By the 1970s, as capitalism went into crisis yet again, many of these trends and impulses toward greater equality stalled or began to be reversed. A reorientation toward neo-liberalism was propelled further and faster as Keynesian socio-economic orthodoxy soon came under sustained attack for its inability to effectively deal with widespread economic stagnation. Ardently advanced by 'New Right' ideologues, and most prominently embraced by President Reagan in the US and Prime Minister Thatcher in the UK, this free-market fundamentalism quickly metastasized, spreading to Australia, Canada, and New Zealand, and well beyond the borders of the Anglo world. It entailed sweeping reforms that greatly extended the scope of the market, including privatization, deregulation, greater corporate tax breaks and freedoms, and an abandonment of previous commitments to full, or at least high, employment levels. It was also characterized by more direct and sustained attacks upon organized labour, significantly eroding its bargaining power. Inflation-fighting, public spending cuts, and the contracting out of many public sector social services became commonplace. Many social programs were eliminated or severely cut back—particularly those measures targeted at people most in need and least able to resist—rendering them less accessible and much more frugal. Escalating levels of poverty and homelessness, widening chasms separating the rich from the poor, and the restructuring of the welfare state were especially evident in the US. Indeed, by the mid-1970s the US had already assumed its unrivalled position as the 'inequality capital' of the advanced capitalist world, a title it has vigorously maintained and defended for over three decades. Moreover, inequality in the US persisted even when the US economy recovered and entered a period of almost unprecedented prosperity.

It is ironic that the most virulently anti-Marxist nation in the world today has most closely realized Marx's predictions about class polarization and inequality. Indeed, Marx could not have envisioned the staggering level of affluence of American multi-billionaires, such as Bill Gates, Warren Buffett, and Paul Allen, whose collective wealth by 2004 exceeded $113 billion. That year a minimum net worth of $900 million was required to secure a place on the *Forbes* list of the 400 wealthiest people in the US, and the combined net worth of this group was $1.13 trillion (Forbes 2005). At the same time, every large American city has its own internal 'Third World' where the poor and the homeless struggle just to survive on the margins. While these developments have been most prominent and extreme in the US, they have become increasingly familiar across much of the developed capitalist world.

The rise of neo-liberalism and the shift in the balance of power has involved a significant change in the way inequalities are viewed and legitimated. There has been a resurgence of previously discredited and dormant explanations and theories seeking to justify the high and rising levels of inequality in society. In the last few decades of the twentieth century, Herbert Spencer's notion of the 'survival of the fittest' resurfaced, and it became more acceptable once again to rationalize and even acclaim growing economic disparities. This time around, however, these ideas have become more closely conflated with notions of 'freedom' and 'individual rights'. Those at the bottom, it is commonly argued, are there because they are 'naturally' or culturally inferior or deficient, as reflected by lower IQs, slothfulness, and propensities toward immoral and deviant behaviour. Today, as in Victorian England, the homeless and the poor are often ignored or held in contempt. Echoing nineteenth-century arguments against Poor Laws and other supportive measures, demands are made that those most in need prove that they are 'truly deserving'—and even then, they may be denied support. In a period characterized by high unemployment, cuts to both labour market training programs and unemployment insurance, reduced services and spaces in health care facilities, severe shortages in affordable housing, and declines in housing assistance, governments cynically criminalize those forced to live on the streets. They seem even *more* oblivious to their hardships and daily struggles to find food, a place to store their few belongings, and shelter for the night. Many large North American cities have passed strict new laws, or selectively enforce existing ones, to sweep the homeless out of sight. To this end some municipalities have removed park benches in areas where homeless people sleep, forced them out of makeshift homes, and dismantled their cardboard and tent cities on the outskirts of major urban centres across North America. Panhandling is increasingly restricted to certain zones and must be sanctioned through the purchase of a licence; those who sit or lie in public spaces are charged with obstructing sidewalks; subways are closely monitored and policed. Abuse of the homeless, whose numbers have been rapidly multiplying virtually everywhere over the past two decades, is now routine.

It is argued here that social inequality is created, reproduced, institutionalized, legitimated, and perpetuated by the people who hold the most resources in society. In capitalist societies it is those who own and manage the largest corporations and economic and financial institutions—the 'capitalist class'—that wield the most power. This economic power translates into political and ideological power. By definition, the power of this class greatly exceeds that of any other 'actor' or group in society. But a comparative examination of social inequality suggests that alternative power sources can be mined and imbalances in power constellations altered. This is reflected in marked variation across most forms of social inequality that we observe when the Anglo-Saxon and Nordic lands are contrasted.

The levels and depth of poverty are much less severe in Sweden, Norway, and Finland—even if there has been a disturbing rise in these nations over the past two decades—than in Canada, the UK, and the US. Income and wealth are more evenly distributed in the Nordic nations, resulting in significantly larger middle classes. And, contrary to the dominant media myth of the US as the 'land of opportunity', there is greater social mobility from the lower socio-economic ranks to the higher ranks in the Nordic nations. Moreover, these countries have typically introduced and supported more far-reaching, progressive legislation, securing the rights to various forms of protection, provision, and participation for many groups—including children, gays and lesbians, people with disabilities, and women—that are often marginalized or denied the same kind of benefits, opportunities, and considerations widely enjoyed in society by more powerful or established groups. These nations have all constructed comprehensive networks of regulatory laws, income support programs, and social services, which are typically accessed as entitlements by all on the basis of citizenship or even residency. They were, for example, among the first nations to legislatively protect children from corporal punishment and endorse same-sex 'unions', and their levels of female political representation in parliament have long been among the highest on the planet. While certainly not immune from neo-liberal attack or cutbacks over the past two decades, their more comprehensive welfare states have been more resistant than those in the Anglo-Saxon nations and remain highly developed and very supportive by international standards. It is absurdly utopian to envision a capitalist society without significant inequalities, but it is imperative, and gainful, to observe that they can be markedly reduced, and that such achievements *may* pave the way for further reform. However insufficient the gains, rights, and social programs introduced in the Nordic lands—no matter how much remains to be done—similar measures would be essential to any alternative socio-economic system.

The Organization of this Book

This volume is divided into three sections. Central ideas and themes are introduced in Part I. Chapter 1 clarifies the meaning of key terms, such as structured inequality, stratification systems, and power, which are widely employed but often take on very different meanings across the various disciplines and myriad studies that address social inequality. This chapter concludes with a detailed account of the strengths of the comparative approach in studies of social and political inequality.

Egalitarians, by definition, believe that people are, or should be, equal in some sense, but there is considerable dissent over the interpretation of these claims. Chapter 2 focuses on the strikingly varied meanings often applied to **equality** and examines some of the most contentious debates among egalitarians today concerning who and what it is that should be equal, how we should go about creating greater equality, and how far we should go to do so. Much of the discussion in this chapter has a more philosophical bent, addressing conceptions of fairness, equity, and justice. I identify and elaborate upon four ideals of equality that are conventionally recognized in the literature: **intrinsic equality**, **equal opportunity**, **equality of condition**, and **equality of outcome**. Here I argue that, while they are often presented as discrete, or even somewhat contradictory, all four of these ideals are indispensable and closely interrelated in their most encompassing and meaningful interpretations; that is, the *full* realization of each ideal is ultimately dependent upon recognition of the three others. For example, it is commonly argued by many today that equal opportunity is, or ought to be, provided for everyone, but not equality of condition or equality of outcome. Unlike equal opportunity, many suggest, the realization of these two latter ideals would require some form of unfair and coercive government 'interference' in the marketplace. But, apart from sidestepping the highly coercive nature of capitalist markets themselves, and the very central role that states have played in the operation of 'free' markets via the priority they place upon property rights, the dissociation of equal opportunity from these other ideals is not possible. The fulfilment of equal opportunity—the dominant and most widely embraced equality ideal today—in any meaningful form requires the eradication of numerous informal and cultural obstructions that exclude and marginalize some people and groups, not just the removal of formal, direct, and explicitly discriminatory barriers. It also requires the provision of a wide range of government services, programs, and other redistributive measures that create more equal conditions and 'starting points' for the economically and socially disadvantaged. And, while equal opportunity requires certain basic rights for everyone so that all may compete in the 'race' for positions and rewards in society, it does not address what happens to people after the 'race' is over. The desperate living conditions, exclusion, and humiliation of the people who 'lose' in the race is not a concern; they have simply received their 'just desserts', rendering any notion of intrinsic equality rhetorical. This chapter also indicates how these four ideals have been expressed across the Anglo-Saxon and Nordic worlds, a discourse that is explored in greater detail in two chapters of the next section.

Part II moves from discussion of equality to focus squarely upon **inequality**, a multi-dimensional and exceedingly complex concept comprising an almost limitless range of interrelated aspects and issues. However, an exhaustive, detailed examination and discussion of the myriad manifestations of social inequality and social well-being within the Anglo-Saxon and Nordic worlds is not our purpose here. Nor would such an account be remotely possible given the overwhelming breadth and complexity of this field of study; there are far too many aspects to consider, even within any single nation. My goal is much more modest. This section of the book provides an overview of a few selected central indicators and axes of inequality to illustrate how they can vary—often quite remarkably—across the nations under scrutiny.

Most accounts of social inequality in contemporary capitalist societies focus upon **material** indicators of social inequality, and have been especially preoccupied with the distribution of income or wealth in society. This is understandable. Inequality is an abstract concept and very difficult to quantify, while the distribution of income and wealth can be readily measured with a considerable degree of precision. Moreover, income and wealth can enable people to access many other goods in capitalist societies, provide them with numerous opportunities, and help them to realize their goals. Chapter 3 begins with a critical review of widely reported accounts of national progress and achievement that focus almost exclusively upon economic growth and per-capita GDP. While economic growth *may* lead to greater equality, this will not happen unless there are mechanisms in place, such as developed welfare states, social and fiscal policies, and strong unions and other organized groups, to address inequality. This chapter then provides a cross-national presentation and discussion of some central material measures of inequality, including the distribution of income and wealth, poverty levels, social mobility patterns, and health and political inequalities.

National and cross-national accounts of social inequality typically address economic and other related 'material' dimensions of inequality while neglecting other important, **non-material** forms of inequality that relate to the dignity, respect, recognition, and valuing of people and groups. Chapter 4 provides an introduction to some key non-material aspects of inequality. It shows these forms of inequality are addressed across the Anglo-Saxon and Nordic worlds through networks of rights, entitlements, protections, and programs provided for—or withheld from—their national residents, or certain groups of them.

Finally, Part III provides a critical review of some of the dominant theories that have been advanced to explain the existence, prevalence, and persistence of social inequality today. These theories are organized into four broad traditions that emphasize (1) socio-biological factors, (2) social systems and structures, (3) culture, ideologies, and values, and (4) power. For the most part, the first three schools of thought have largely served to rationalize and legitimate existing forms and levels of social inequality. These highly influential and widely embraced perspectives are critically reviewed in Chapter 5 in light of the cross-national evidence on inequality examined in the previous chapters. Chapter 6 examines the theoretical traditions that challenge the idea that high levels of inequality are 'normal' and inevitable in society. Power is highlighted in this chapter here as a particularly important factor that, while often left unaddressed today, lurks behind the other three theoretical traditions and is better able to explain significant cross-national variability. Thus, for example, it is sometimes suggested that women's inferior position and status in society is a function of 'natural' differences between males and females, a contention that is routinely and vehemently challenged by sociologists and other social scientists. However, even if it could be proven that there are important biological or 'extra-socio-cultural' differences between women and men that predispose each group toward certain occupations and pursuits, why are those viewed as best suited to the natural talents, strengths, and abilities of women so often deemed less important and typically unpaid or underpaid? And how can these natural or 'essential' differences lead to such striking cross-national variation in the involvement of women in certain spheres, such as politics—long considered a male strength and preserve—between the Anglo and Nordic worlds?

Other theories maintain that inequality exists and endures because certain positions and roles that are crucial for society's survival and development must provide very high levels of material and non-material rewards to entice the 'best and brightest' people to fill them. But who gets to determine which roles and occupations are the most 'functionally important' and the nature and level of these rewards? And how is it possible that remuneration and rewards for these same 'crucial' roles and positions can vary so dramatically cross-nationally?

Cross-national variation in different forms of inequality is sometimes explained as largely a product or reflection of widely differing values, ideologies and cultures across countries. Surveys routinely indicate that Americans *are* more tolerant of high levels of inequality than people in most other advanced capitalist nations, and more likely to believe that those at the bottom of society are largely the authors of their plight. And Americans *are* among the least inclined to support state intervention through comprehensive social programs, social and fiscal policies, and other regulations, which are widely viewed as 'un-American'. In the Nordic lands labour unions are seen as important actors that have long played a central and largely positive role. But in the US, the fragmented and comparatively weak labour movement is commonly viewed as a threat to the American way of life. National values, ideologies and cultures, and the institutions they are embedded within are clearly crucial considerations in any account of the character and level of inequality across nations. However, these 'culture and institutional trajectories' are too often accepted as primordial, as if they unconsciously emerge holus-bolus from out of the blue and for all time, like the goddess

Athena in Greek mythology, who springs from the head of her father Zeus as a fully grown adult in glittering armour and ready for battle. The central issues that must be addressed here are why it is that cultures and dominant ideologies vary as much as they do cross-nationally and how these differences are maintained. It is important to understand how attitudes toward state intervention; unions; the 'proper sphere' for women; children's rights; and other national values, ideologies, and cultures are shaped, reproduced, perpetuated, and institutionalized by those with power, and how these ideas can and have been challenged in other nations. I argue that differences in the 'balance of power' across nations provide a key part of the answer to these questions. It is also crucial to recognize that national values and cultures are multi-vocal, fluid, and contested, and thus open to change when the power balance is shifted.

Social Inequality and Power: Key Concepts and Terms

Despite their centrality to the discipline of sociology, and to discussions of inequality in particular, many of the most central terms and concepts commonly employed are often used in strikingly different ways by sociologists and other researchers working in this broad area. 'Social inequality', 'stratification', 'structured inequality', 'stratification systems', and 'power', for example, are among the key concepts that have often been variously interpreted and defined. It is useful to clarify their meaning for this volume at the outset.

Structured Inequality and Stratification Systems

Social inequality refers to the unequal access people have to a wide range of material and non-material resources, supports, provisions, and opportunities that are widely viewed as valuable and desirable in society and are consequential to our lives. It also refers to the asymmetrical distributions that this unequal access fosters and perpetuates across many sites (such as the family, the economy, the workplace, and the state) and spheres (economic, political, and social). Studies of material inequalities typically narrowly focus upon the dispersion of income and wealth, and our chances of improving our socio-economic positions. But they may also highlight our differing capacities to access a wide range of services and other social, cultural, and socio-economic goods and resources that shape our living conditions. For example, they may focus upon differences in the availability, nature, and security of our conditions of employment and working environments, including the amount of autonomy and control we have over our labour and workplaces, how much time we have away from our work, and how these factors impact upon our health and longevity.

Non-material inequalities are asymmetrical distributions of symbolic or less tangible rewards, such as respect, honour, status, and prestige. They include our differing capacities to benefit from a wide range of rights, entitlements, and other social protections from exploitation, oppression, discrimination, marginalization, and social exclusion.[3] Our access to these material and non-material goods significantly affects our level of comfort and security and our opportunities for growth and fulfilment, or what the Greek philosopher Aristotle referred to as 'human flourishing' (*eudaimonia*).[4] Many centuries later the German sociologist and political scientist Max Weber (1864–1920) referred to this broad constellation of social, economic, and political conditions as our 'life chances'. Today we more commonly talk about our general 'well-being' or 'welfare', and its dependence upon our access to these material and non-material resources. Our ability to access these resources is closely linked to power, another crucial aspect of social inequality.

Social stratification typically refers to the hierarchical arrangement or ordering of groups or strata in society—most commonly likened to the layers or bands of rocks studied by geologists, the rungs of a ladder, or the steps of a pyramid—that stand in a relationship of advantage and superiority, or disadvantage and subordination, according to some particular inequality metric or indicator. However, the conceptualization, construction, and character of these discrete ranked groupings can vary greatly. Some researchers, for example, simply take one key indicator of inequality and chart its distribution across ordered, statistical, or numerical aggregates of equal size in a society, most commonly deciles or quintiles.[5] Researchers using this approach can usefully illustrate how equally or unequally income, wealth, or some other valued good is distributed within a particular society or across nations. They can also track trends and patterns, indicating how these dispersions change over time. They often correlate their findings with the distribution of other central indicators of social inequality, such as levels of education or health status. Other stratification researchers identify and arrange strata on the basis of social roles or positions, such as occupation, sector, or some other socio-economic category (such as blue-collar worker/white-collar worker, or upper class/middle class/working class/lower class, and so on), denoting the varying levels of income, wealth, privilege, esteem, opportunities, protections, or other resources that may be enjoyed by each of them.

Both of these stratification traditions have been invaluable. However, these accounts often emphasize description over analysis, highlighting where people end up rather than why, where, and how they began.[6] While carefully documenting the dispersion of material and non-material goods among the various groups or strata that they identify in society, they sometimes neglect, or minimize, the *relational* aspect of social inequality—how some groups gain at the expense of others—and how those at the top of the hierarchies are able to use their position, influence and power to maintain and legitimate their power and privilege.

These observations are less true of a third stratification approach that constructs **status groups**, or strata, on the basis of certain physical, biological, and/or cultural characteristics—such as sex, race, ethnicity, age, sexual orientation, and ability—which often serve as bases or foundations for their unequal treatment.[7] For example, women, members of particular ethnic groups or 'races', immigrants, children, gays and lesbians, and people identified as having disabilities are among the groups most commonly ranked lower, provided with fewer opportunities and inferior resources, denied full citizenship rights, and disempowered. Of course, the biological and sociocultural differences among people that are identified are not the real source of their inferior, disadvantaged positions. But this differentiation, which itself is largely socially constructed, encourages or allows for the emergence of structured inequality. The identified differences among people are given social meaning, and the groups or strata that are established are rewarded according to their ranking. The creation of these hierarchies and the unequal treatment of the strata they create are imposed 'from above' and legitimated through ideological means by those with power.[8]

All human societies generate social relationships that determine 'who gets what and why', typically culminating in some level and forms of social inequality in society, even though its patterns, contours, and intensity can vary significantly over time and place. The unequal distributions and conditions, and the gradations or strata that emerge from these social relationships—one manifestation or form of inequality—reflect this process. In simple foraging societies, for example, social inequalities are relatively minimal and organized along only a few axes, such as sex or age. Moreover, these societies have not typically established strict formal means enabling those who are advantaged to directly pass on their superior social position over generations. Karl Marx and Friedrich Engels, among others, characterized them as early ('primitive') forms of communism. Most of these tribal communities—the form of society in which humans have spent more than 90% of their social life—were highly egalitarian from a comparative perspective.[9] Marshall Sahlins (1972, 2006), the noted American anthropologist, famously referred to this form of human community as 'the original affluent society'. It has more recently been described by two eminent Canadian anthropologists as 'the oldest and perhaps the most successful human adaptation' (Lee and Daly 2006:1). Rather than developing ideologies and laws to defend and rationalize inequality, members of such societies often used cultural means to resist inequality and promote collective egalitarian values.[10] In more complex agrarian and industrial societies, by contrast, social inequality is much more structured and systemic. **Structured inequality** exists when the social relationships that generate inequality harden and become institutionalized; the social inequalities are patterned and predictable. Directly and indirectly, overtly and covertly, structured inequality encourages and authorizes the inter-generational transmission of advantage and the reproduction and legitimation of the dominant, advantaged groups.[11] However, inequality can be structured and legitimated in a variety of ways.

Sociologists conventionally identify four central forms of structured, patterned inequality, or **stratification systems**, that have emerged in advanced, complex societies based upon castes, slavery, estates, or class which, in turn, are shaped by, and interlock with, other axes of inequality, such as race/ethnicity, sex/gender, sexual orientation, age, and ability. Of course the institutions, and the cultural norms, procedures, practices, laws, and ideologies that constitute and legitimate them, have varied greatly from one type of stratification system to the next, but all of them have sought to organize and stabilize the existing social structures and patterns of inequality. Inequalities become institutionalized and firmly established in socio-cultural and political practices, social structures, and ideologies that serve to sustain and legitimate the power, privilege, and advantage of those at the top of society and the subordinate status and starkly inferior conditions of those at the bottom. In this way they become 'internalized', expected by society's members, and viewed as 'normal', even if they are not always or necessarily accepted as entirely just. Although not often acknowledged, this is no less true of modern class-based systems of stratification than of those from the past. Thus many people today agree that 'the rich get richer and the poor get poorer' and that 'it is not what you know but who you know' while simultaneously demonstrating an apparently insatiable fascination with the 'lifestyles of the rich and famous'. While many people in the lower socio-economic groups do not vote because they believe that 'nothing will change', they often harbour little resentment toward those at the top and maintain a lively hope that they can climb up the socio-economic ladder to reach the pinnacle. In capitalist society those at the top of the hierarchy, and best placed to transmit and legitimate their position of advantage, superiority, and dominance, are those who possess key social assets, especially property and great wealth. These positions are disproportionately held by white men, reflecting the complex intersection of class, sex, and race and other bases or axes of social inequality.

Central Axes of Inequality and their Social Construction

Class, sex/gender, and race/ethnicity have long been recognized as central axes of inequality in modern capitalist society. Each of these has served as a foundation for the creation of groups with differential access to highly valued material and non-material resources in society. And each of them has been studied extensively in sociology and across the social sciences. The first generation of studies often focused upon gender and race or ethnicity as separate bases of inequality, or simply added race and sex to class analysis. However, there has been a shift over the past two decades, with researchers seeking to understand class, race, and sex as interlocking systems of inequality with a common foundation. They have also increasingly addressed other social inequality fault lines, including age, nativity, sexual orientation, and ability.[12]

Class

Class is a pivotal component of structured inequality in capitalist societies. It is also among the most highly contested and has been conceptualized, defined, and measured in a wide variety of ways. Most contemporary researchers view class as a distributional and gradational concept. For them, and in popular discourse, classes are objectively defined in terms of material resources related to living standards or lifestyles, typically indexed by income, wealth, and/or other related distributional measures.[13] Marx and Weber, two of sociology's most central and influential theoreticians, in stark contrast, conceptualized class relationally, emphasizing class conflict and power over distribution.

Weber distinguished four distinct classes in his schema: (1) an **upper class** composed of the owners of large-scale productive assets, (2) a **propertyless upper class** composed of high-salaried administrators and managers, (3) a **petit bourgeoisie**, composed of business-people, shopkeepers, farmers, and other smaller-scale property owners, and (4) a **working class**. He highlighted the very different living conditions and 'life chances' afforded to each of them.[14] But he also stressed the 'market situation' of the people in each of these classes—the kind and quantity of resources that each of them possessed and brought with them to market exchanges. These assets largely determined their living standards and opportunities. Ownership of large-scale productive property typically provided much greater wealth, opportunities, and power than alternative forms of resources. But other classes (or the various occupational groups within them) could rely upon alternative means to increase their rewards and greatly enhance their life chances while closing off these opportunities and benefits to 'outsiders'.

Social closure, a central element of Weber's discussion of inequality, refers to the varying ability of groups to maximize the advantages and privileges of their own members by restricting access to other people defined as 'external' to their group. Social exclusion has been especially effective when based upon readily identifiable, visible characteristics, such as 'race' or sex, but others, including nativity, ethnicity, sexual orientation, and age, have also been effectively employed. Occupational closure is a specific instance of social closure in which the members of a group use credentials, licensing, certification, or association to raise the rewards of their members by creating and channelling demand for their services and/or engineering an artificial scarcity of people with the ability to perform them (Weeden 2002).

Marx placed even greater emphasis upon the relational dimension of class in his account of social inequality. Although he acknowledged several class groupings, Marx maintained that there were only two *central* classes in capitalist society, the **capitalist class** (or bourgeoisie), which owns the 'means of production', and the **working class** (or proletariat), which has only its labour power to bring to the market. Class inequality is rooted in this maldistribution of the productive assets in society. Exclusive, or nearly exclusive, ownership of the central means of production confers great wealth and power upon the capitalist class, allowing it to dominate market exchanges. However, Marx goes considerably further than Weber here, identifying a second way that the capitalist class gains at the expense of the working class. Separated from the means of production, workers are also separated from any means of subsistence; consequently, they are forced to sell their labour power in order to survive. Both theorists emphasize the exclusion of the working class from ownership of property and other productive assets. But Marx also stresses the fact that this exclusion renders the working class structurally dependent upon the capitalist class, which is able to set the terms of exchange and, as a result, largely determine the working and living conditions of workers. The power and wealth of the capitalist class that stems from ownership of the means of production enables it to exploit and oppress others in society (Wright 2002).

Marx also highlighted the relationship between economics, politics, and culture. The dominant ideas in any epoch, he argued, were those of the ruling class and they would serve to obfuscate and legitimate social inequality. Marxist class analysis provides invaluable insights here; the gains made through the redistribution of income and the provision of greater opportunities for workers via fiscal and social policy cannot, alone, bring about a truly egalitarian society. Nor will such gains ever be entirely secure without some form of democratic control over the economy—considerations that are especially relevant in the Nordic lands today and present a much more daunting challenge in a period of ever-increasing global integration. Demands for greater economic democracy, like those for universal political suffrage centuries earlier, will be castigated as subversion and fiercely resisted by those who gain the most from the existing social order. This is particularly true in the US where even those who call for the creation of a national health care system, government intervention to address child poverty, or many other social programs long-established and cherished in the rest of the advanced capitalist world, are often denounced as socialist or communist.

Gender, Race, and Other Socially Constructed Groups

It might be argued that class inequality differs from forms of inequality constructed along other fault lines in that the very existence of class distinctions, however defined or conceptualized, is *necessarily* based upon an unequal distribution of some socio-economic good, whether income, wealth, standard of living, 'life chances', or following Marx, ownership of productive property. The differences between men and women, 'blacks' and 'whites', heterosexuals and homosexuals, the 'able-bodied' and the 'disabled', or adults and children, in contrast, are not *necessarily* linked to inequality. For these groupings, inequality is not viewed as *the* only defining characteristic. Common ownership and democratic control of the means of production and the provision of similar kinds and levels of rewards, resources, and privileges to everyone across all classes would largely eradicate or nullify existing class systems. Providing equal or equitable benefits, rights, opportunities, and resources across the groups along each of these other axes of inequality might make the distinctions among them socially, economically, and politically insignificant, but the differences among the people that constitute them would not disappear; anatomical, physical, socio-cultural, and other distinctions would remain. However, it would become much clearer that the identification of discrete, immutable groups along such fault lines is a social construction.

Inequality among such groups in society is made possible through the process of **differentiation**. Of course, simply identifying differences among people does not in itself create inequality, or necessarily lead to inequality. Some physical differences among people, such as eye colour, hair colour, and 'handedness' (left/right) have rarely resulted in structured hierarchy. Even skin colour, or the identification of sex/gender role differences—perhaps the two most dominant and prevalent bases for unequal treatment in society—have not always led to marked inequality. In some hunting and gathering societies, such as the nomadic !Kung San tribes of the Kalahari, for example, sex role differentiation exists, but both male and female roles are highly valued. While hunters are usually men—and the meat they provide typically considered the most prestigious food—female gatherers have also been greatly appreciated as the providers of a significantly larger portion of the tribe's total food intake. They are also highly respected for their skills in both discriminating among hundreds of indigenous edible and poisonous species of plants, as well as reading animal tracks to aid men in the hunt (Draper 1975). Among other hunting and gathering societies, such as the Iroquois in North America, positions of power, such as chief and other political offices, were typically held by older males. But they were elected to, and could be dismissed from, these positions by the women of their matrilineal clans. And they were typically advised by women on matters of policy (Trigger 1990).[15] Several other foraging societies, such as the Agta and the Batak in southeast Asia and the Paliyans in southwest India, have also been characterized by considerable gender equality across many spheres (Endicott 2006).

Acknowledgement of differences among people, whether biological or social, does not necessarily culminate in high levels of inequality. However, when the differences that have been identified among people lead to the construction of discrete and fixed groups—sometimes involving binary groupings (e.g., heterosexual/homosexual, non-disabled/disabled, male/female) or many more categories (e.g., ethnic groups, religious groups, age-based groups, and so on)—the stage is set for inequality to play a starring role. Social inequality takes root when the groups that have been identified are ranked and rewarded accordingly, with privilege, prestige, opportunity, and power increasing progressively toward the top of these hierarchies and material deprivation, marginalization, devaluation, and abuse increasing progressively toward the bottom. It is often pointed out that these hierarchies are socially created. The social construction of the groups and categories themselves is less commonly considered.

The social construction of status groups is perhaps most easily seen with the creation of distinct categories based upon age. The establishment of a precise age when a person is no longer a child, or has become elderly, are clearly somewhat arbitrary decisions, but they are widely employed to confer rights to some people and deny them to others. The social roots of such categories are reflected in the wide variation in such definitions over time and place. Indeed, it is often pointed out that the very idea of 'childhood' itself is a relatively modern invention. Not so long ago children typically worked side by side with their parents in the fields and, prior to their recognition as children through the establishment of protective legislation, in the factories during the early period of industrialization in the West. Child labour remains common in many developing nations today. Similarly, the age when people might be considered too old to work or, more graciously in contemporary modern societies, deserving of and eligible for a period of retirement, has also varied markedly over time and place. Currently, the age of retirement, after many decades of decline, is rising in some developed nations, such as the US, in response to increasing demands placed upon pension systems by increasing longevity.[16]

The distinction between those who are 'disabled' and those who are not provides another example of distinct categories that are often unquestioned but largely socially constructed and imposed upon people (Charlton 1998). The dominant medical model defines 'disabilities' on the basis of its identification of physical, sensory, behavioural, emotional, and cognitive limitations and 'incapacities' of individuals. However, many of these individuals do not view themselves as any less able than others. People in the deaf community, for example, effectively utilize non-verbal sign languages and have developed sophisticated lip-reading skills. Many of them choose not to 'correct' their hearing via operations, implants, or other aids. As in the case of age, we can more readily see the social construction of categories such as 'able-bodied' and 'disabled' when we employ a cross-national perspective. In some nations, including the Nordic lands, 'disabilities' are commonly viewed as largely a reflection of society's failure to furnish the kind of supports that people need to participate in their communities and more fully exercise their rights as citizens rather than as 'defects' of certain individuals, or groups of individuals, with personal issues and problems to overcome. The provision of glasses to people with poor eyesight, for example, can eliminate or reduce their astigmatism, and wheelchairs, ramps, and elevators can greatly facilitate mobility. The commitment of public resources and services to people who require them can begin to dissolve labels and attitudes that have marginalized or socially excluded them. In most nations today, however, gaining access to many forms of accommodations is often contingent upon peoples' ability to prove that they are deserving of support and upon their willingness to embrace labels, such as 'handicapped', that sharply set them apart from other people in society. Our wide range of abilities is more accurately understood as measurable along a series of continua, rather than through distinct binary categories. Everyone has certain abilities and strengths in some areas and others in which they are less able. And we all typically lose some of them, such as eyesight, hearing, mobility, and memory, as we age.

The creation of categories centred upon 'race' is often seen as more biologically based than socially constructed because there can be striking phenotypical differences (variation in complexion, facial features, hair texture, and so on) and other genotypical differences (variation in genetic make-up) among people.[17] But, again, these differences among people constitute a series of seamless continua—of darker and lighter hues of skin colour, or straight and curly hair, for example—rather than distinct and immutable racial categories. The creation of separate racial categories does more than purport to describe differences. It also inscribes inequalities, since the identification of separate races is virtually always accompanied by the notion that some races are inferior to others. The social construction of race is evident in the ever-changing number of racial groups that have been identified over the decades; while some schemes have identified as few as two races, others have suggested as many as 160 races. It is also evident in the fact that racial categories have been permeable and fluid, rather than immutable and stable, with some groups of people able to gradually obtain full admittance to the privileged 'white' or 'Caucasian' race.[18] In the United States, Jews, Mexicans, Italians, and people from various European nations, for example, were not always considered full members of this group (Jacobson 1998; Rattansi 2007). This was also true for the Irish in the UK, even though their skin colour was no different from that of the other British groups that excluded them.

Race has been both temporally and geographically contingent; the same person might change races on the basis of when they were born, or by simply moving from one region or nation to another. Although race is a social construct without empirical validity or scientific basis, the social creation of racial categories and identities—a process referred to as racialization—has, of course, had very real and pernicious consequences.[19] The classification of people into hierarchical categories based upon perceptions of biological differences or, in their absence, cultural markers, designating some groups as inferior, or even subhuman, has provided a rationale for colonialization, the institutionalization of slavery, the conquest and dispossession of Aboriginal peoples and First Nations, and even genocide. And, in virtually every nation today, those groups identified as outside the dominant racial or ethnic groups typically experience overt and covert discrimination and racism, resulting in lower incomes, higher rates of poverty, unemployment, poor health, various forms of social exclusion, and the denial of even some of the most basic human rights.[20]

Sexual orientation is another fault line or axis that has been used to construct allegedly discrete and stable binary categories of people (heterosexual/homosexual), resulting in unequal treatment. In many nations the rights of gays and lesbians have been gradually recognized and extended in recent years on the grounds that they are not abnormal or inferior to heterosexuals in any sense and, therefore, must be entitled to the same treatment, a welcome alternative to the persecution, suppression, and marginalization they have endured over the centuries. However, apart from marginalizing some people who do not fit easily into this dichotomy—such as those who identify themselves as bisexuals or transgendered—the lived experiences of most people have never reflected firm boundaries based upon sexual orientation. As sociologist Barry Adam (2007:79) has noted, 'studies of sexuality repeatedly reveal considerable behavioural bisexuality, experimentation, fluidity and change over the life course'. He urges us to consider why so much energy is put into labelling other people gay or lesbian and drawing boundaries that enforces a 'dictatorship of gender conformity'.

Dichotomies based upon sex are perhaps the most widely and confidently embraced as 'real', biologically based (rather than socially constructed) categories. But even they have been challenged. Most sociologists and many other social scientists typically distinguish binary *gender* categories (masculine and feminine roles), which are seen as socially constructed through social convention and socialization, from binary *sex* categories (male/female), which are viewed as biologically determined on the basis of anatomical, chromosomal, hormonal, and other secondary sex characteristics. But the notion that nature neatly differentiates all living creatures into two mutually exclusive and fixed categories does not really capture the complexity of reality; rather than clear opposites, nature often appears to offer shades of difference and similarity (Hird 2007:58). Members of several species, including homo sapiens, may be 'intersex', possessing varying arrays of some of the attributes (such as chromosomes, genitalia, or other sex characteristics) associated with both males and females.[21] Many are sequentially or simultaneously male and female. The designation of two reliably distinct and mutually exclusive categories representing two very different types of people that, by 'nature', have very different orientations and abilities, is another human invention. But, even if there were two biologically distinct sexes, and even if the biological differences between them necessarily led to different social roles for them, evidence from hunting and gathering and other societies suggests that high levels of inequality based upon sex/gender are not inevitable.

The identification of distinct groups along axes such as race, ethnicity, sexual orientation, sex, and ability is a social process; the groups would not exist or have meaning outside of human society. But once created, and ranked, the impact on group members can be all-embracing and absolute. As sociologist W.I. Thomas noted, when situations are defined as real, they become real in their consequences. In medieval times many women were believed to be witches whose very blood was thought to be different from everyone else's; the religious and political powers of the time sought to exterminate them.[22] In many parts of the world, gays and members of other ethnic and religious groups are openly persecuted today. Although there is greater 'toleration' of people who are seen as different across much of the developed world, social exclusion and the diminishment of rights, opportunities, and benefits are still very common. But there is marked variation between the approaches taken and the treatment of groups within and between the Anglo-Saxon and Nordic worlds of nations.

Power

At the heart of all systems of stratification is **power**, a fundamental concept that is indispensable to any serious discussion of social inequality. Power is a central social inequality metric. Like income, wealth, or status, it is a valued resource that is asymmetrically distributed across society. But it is typically attained through command over other resources. Moreover, those with power can wield it to gain, retain, and greatly increase their access to most other valued goods, rewards, assets, and positions, and to justify and legitimate grossly unequal dispersions across society, thereby further securing and increasing their power. Power is intimately related to other central dimensions of inequality; it lies behind and underpins most other asymmetrical distributions in society. Weber (1958:181) maintained that classes and status groups are 'phenomena of the distribution of power within a community'.[23] Marx also stressed the relationship between power and inequality, but he argued that it was the ownership of property that conferred power and shaped the distribution of material and non-material goods in society.[24]

Like social inequality, power is an exceedingly complex and particularly contentious concept that seems to defy a simple definition. Perhaps the most widely adopted and influential account of power is that provided by Weber.

He viewed power as 'the chance of a man or of a number of men to realize their own will in a communal action even against the resistance of others who are participating in the action' (Weber 1958:180). This approach has been adopted by many others, including the well-known and highly influential American political scientist and theorist Robert Dahl (1957:202–203): 'A has power over B to the extent that he can get B to do something that B would not otherwise do'.[25] Although widely embraced, the conceptualization of power they proffer has also been criticized because it narrowly highlights only some aspects of power while neglecting others. The Weberian approach is largely concerned with power that is: (1) *held by 'actors'* or agents, whether individuals or groups, (2) *intentionally exercised* by these actors in the pursuit of their goals, (3) necessarily *manifest in conflicts* in which some actors' interests prevail over the contrary interests, objections, and active resistance of other actors and, therefore, (4) *directly observable.*[26] However, this conceptualization of power is far too narrow, and the ontological, epistemological, and methodological assumptions that it is based upon do not necessarily hold up to careful scrutiny.

First, power is not only held and exercised by actors. It is also deeply embedded in social institutions, structures, and systems, including the prevailing ideologies and cultures in society. Second, the exercise of power by actors can sometimes have unintended effects that dramatically impact upon people and communities. The degradation and despoliation of the environment, the exhaustion of non-renewable natural resources, the upheavals of indigenous societies, and numerous other forms of 'collateral damage' occasioned by the single-minded pursuit of profits by large corporations provide obvious, and all too familiar, examples of actions that harm the long-term and short-term interests of people. But they are sometimes occasioned by unthinking, impulsive, and irresponsible power-wielding more than by conscious design.[27]

The third assumption in Weber's definition of power concerning conflict and resistance can also be challenged; while the exercise of power does often lead to conflict (the 'first face' of power), it does not necessarily do so.[28] Those with power are often able to shape political debates among actors, removing from the agenda entirely any issues that might threaten or undermine the status quo, and their own privileged positions (the 'second face' of power), thereby avoiding or greatly minimizing conflict. In North America, for example, the idea that people should have a *right* to a job is almost never seriously broached. Rather, discussions typically centre around the provision of public/social assistance or unemployment insurance to those who are unemployed. The central issues of debate typically centre around concerns about when benefit levels, conditions of access, and duration periods for these social programs become so generous that they undermine the work ethic and the proper functioning of the market. Instead of a right to work and a decent standard of living—goals to which the Anglo-Saxon nations claimed to be committed when they signed the United Nations Declaration of Human Rights over six decades ago—potential program recipients are routinely required to continually demonstrate that they are deserving of the often meagre, demeaning, and transitory benefits typically on tap.

Power may also be exercised without conflict when those at the top are able to convince others to embrace their narrow, sectional interests as general concerns that benefit everyone in society (the 'third face' of power). By consciously shaping the perceptions, cognitions, preferences, and goals of the subordinate the powerful can go beyond simply ensuring that any grievances that might threaten their position do not have a forum for expression (the 'second face' of power). They can inhibit the emergence of opposition to the existing social order and foster greater support for it, even though this may be contrary to the real objective interests of the subordinate.[29] Indeed, the durability of stratification systems from antiquity to modern times have been at least as much a product of 'cultural persuasion' as of blatant coercion or force, with those occupying the bottom rungs of the social order encouraged to endorse the legitimacy of existing hierarchies and even acknowledge their own inferiority. The institution of slavery that formed the foundation of ancient Greek and Roman societies, for example, was widely considered expedient, inevitable, and just. The slaves and servants that constituted the bottom stratum of these societies were viewed as inferiors, 'living tools' and 'possessions' marked for subjugation from the hour of their birth according to highly esteemed Greek philosophers and Roman statesmen such as Aristotle and Seneca.[30] In the American South in the eighteenth and nineteenth centuries, this idea of inferiority evolved into a full-scale race-based system of slave labour within a framework of agrarian capitalism. Biblical passages were commonly invoked to rationalize claims that slaves were entitled to few rights and deserving of the severe repression that was their lot.[31] The elaborate hierarchy of lords and nobles comprising the ruling classes of the feudal systems of western Europe that owned the land and exploited the labour of the large peasant and 'quasi-slave' serf populations during the medieval period rationalized their wealth, power, and status on the basis of their 'high birth', a notion underpinned by a powerful and widely accepted political and theological ideology known as the 'Divine Right of Kings'.[32] Since these 'high-born' elites did not look any different than their subjects, they often issued laws declaring that certain items of clothing, fabrics, and colours could only be worn by them so as to clearly distinguish themselves from others in society (Vincent 2003).

The caste system of India, arguably the most explicit, inflexible, thoroughgoing, and durable form of social stratification in human history, was premised upon the *idea* of ritual and spiritual purity.[33] The privilege and power of those in the higher, 'purer' castes, and the deprivations and severe hardships endured by those at the bottom, were ordained and ratified in powerful religious beliefs and quotidian practices. The only way to be reborn into a higher station was by embracing one's status and strictly, and unquestioningly, conforming to the myriad obligations, behavioural codes, and rules appropriate to the particular caste (or outcaste) to which one belonged.[34] Today the impact of the dominant ideologies and practices of the powerful is just as great. This is perhaps most readily observed in the US, where members of the lower classes are more likely to accept and internalize the anti-collectivist messages that they are continually bombarded with, castigating unions as 'big labour', and attacking social programs and other forms of government support as state interference. They are also more likely to believe that it is possible for those at the bottom to make it to the top if they just work hard enough—despite overwhelming evidence to the contrary, including their own personal experiences—and more likely to embrace the 'winner-take-all' free market ethos.

Fourthly, and finally, the Weberian account of power fails to acknowledge that power can sometimes assume a latent rather than a manifest form; it need not always be directly wielded or observable to have a significant impact.[35] For example, employees may endure sub-standard working conditions and very low wages, especially during periods of high unemployment, because they understand very well that their bosses and managers have the ability to discharge them, even if no one in the enterprise has been fired and no threats to that effect have ever been uttered. Similarly, women with violent partners and children with abusive parents do not have to be physically battered to experience fear or a sense of subordination and helplessness. In such cases power may not be overtly exercised, or observable in any visible conflict, but its effects may be dramatic and all-embracing. Power is, thus, best understood as a capacity. The role of the distribution or 'balance' of power in society is explored in chapter 6.

The Comparative Approach

Comparative research can play a central role in advancing our understanding of social inequality and other social and political phenomena and boasts a lineage almost as old as the study of human society itself. Written over two millennia ago, studies of the politics, government, and constitutions in over 150 city states in ancient Greece by Aristotle (384–322 BCE), one of the first great empiricists, and the juxtaposition of Greek and Egyptian societies provided by Herodotus (*c.*484–*c.*425 BCE) are among the earliest notable contributions to the comparative tradition. Other more recent comparative landmarks helped to lay the foundation for more current sociological and political analyses and profoundly shaped their character. These include the detailed accounts of the preconditions for political stability and prosperity in principalities and republics written by the Renaissance Florentine political theorist and diplomat Niccolò Machiavelli (1469–1527), the examination of the rise and fall of empires by the French nobleman, political philosopher, and novelist Charles-Louis de Secondat Montesquieu (1689–1755), and some of the central comparative works of the classical sociologists.

Neither of the two foremost comparativists in the history of sociology, Max Weber and Émile Durkheim (1858–1917), furnished clear, complete statements of their strikingly different strategies for comparative analysis. But both introduced ways of contrasting and classifying societies and established typologies in their efforts to impose order on complex social realities. Their work still exerts a powerful impact upon social researchers today.[36] Weber used comparisons to provide detailed accounts of the factors that condition the rise and spread of religious doctrines and to classify them, and he pointed to their implications for the development of the ethic and structures underlying modern, industrial capitalism. He set out, defined, and contrasted 'ideal-types' not only in his comparative examination of the world's great religions, but also in his studies of forms of economy, authority, and bureaucracy.[37] Focusing more broadly on 'social systems' and developmental 'laws', Durkheim's examination of the functional significance of social facts and social context allowed him to distinguish the forms of order found in simple and complex societies and identify and compare different types of suicide (egoistic, altruistic, anomic, and fatalistic) and their causes.

Like Durkheim, Marx also set out a kind of typology of societies that has been profoundly influential. Moreover, his classification of historical 'epochs', or modes of production (Asiatic, ancient, feudal, capitalist)—based upon a close comparative examination of key dimensions in each, such as the form of property relations and class structure, the nature of the social and technical division of labour, the relationship between state and society, and the purpose of production—was itself fostered through a comparative study of the development of European capitalist societies and, later, non-Western and pre-capitalist societies. While perhaps not as explicitly or widely comparative as these works, Alexis Comte de Tocqueville's (1805–1859) penetrating two-volume study of the United States, *Democracy in America*, is considered a comparative classic. This is largely because his observations about democracy and equality were filtered through the lens of his experience as a French aristocrat and because he used his earlier work on France, *The Old Régime and the French Revolution*, as a backdrop.[38] For Tocqueville, France's *ancien régime* provided a good example of an aristocratic, elitist, and highly unequal society while the US, where the traditional distinctions of hierarchy and status had been largely eradicated though universal suffrage, provided the best approximation of a society characterized by equality (Smelser 1973; Vallier 1973)—an observation that is difficult to defend today.[39]

Comparisons of groups, classes, cultures, practices, institutions, entire social systems, and other social and political phenomena, both across and within societies, have long been central to the sociological enterprise.[40] Indeed, as Durkheim (1982 [1895]:157) suggested in *The Rules of Sociological Method*, almost all sociological research involves an explicit comparison of cases or variables or the identification of typical, representative, or unique social phenomena that imply some sort of comparison: 'Comparative sociology is not a special branch of sociology; it is sociology itself in so far as it ceases to be purely descriptive and aspires to account for facts'. This is also true for the other social sciences; 'comparative politics', for example, has constituted a central sub-field of political science for several decades now. Today comparative research often focuses upon variation across nations or societies, and researchers fruitfully employ comparative methods, producing invaluable cross-national, intra-national, and cross-temporal studies of society. However, despite its time-honoured and pivotal standing, the cross-national perspective is still too infrequently employed in contemporary accounts of social inequality. Yet there are several good reasons, apart from simply satisfying academic curiosity, for adopting a comparative view.

First, cross-national comparison discourages ethnocentrism, helping to weaken the powerful embrace of the familiar and expose the often unquestioned assumptions of our own society.[41] The well-known cross-cultural field studies of anthropologists such as Margaret Mead in the first half of the twentieth century, for example, pointed to wide variability in gender roles and challenged many of the long-dominant and widely accepted beliefs in Western nations about what was 'natural' that had underpinned and legitimated many forms of gender inequality.[42] Similarly, the high levels of female participation in politics in the Nordic nations today suggest that the relatively low involvement of women in the politics of the other wealthy nations, such as Canada, the UK, and the US, is neither preordained nor inevitable.

A second benefit of cross-national analysis is that, by providing a broader backdrop, it can help to foster a closer understanding of our own society. Just as our ability to evaluate and provide an informed and useful review of a movie, a book, a concert, or a restaurant is greatly enhanced if we are 'experienced' reviewers, so too is our comprehension of our society. Without this comparative context it can be difficult for us to assess what it would really mean if we were to learn that a particular nation has a child poverty rate of just under 7%, a middle class that constitutes almost 60% of its population, or a life expectancy at birth among females of 78 years. Are these measures high, low, or average? Is that nation doing well or poorly? Cross-national comparisons provide perspective, allowing for much more meaningful interpretations of such data. The noted American sociologist Seymour Martin Lipset (1996:17) unequivocally insists that it may be impossible to truly understand any nation without knowing how it compares with others: 'those who know only one country know no country'.

Considering wider socio-economic and political contexts can also make us aware of unexpected or significant differences across broadly similar societies. The US, for example, has stood out even among other liberal, market-oriented, Anglo-Saxon societies as the only nation without a universal health care system; by 2010 the number of US residents without any health care coverage was approximately equal to the entire populations of Canada, Norway, and Sweden combined. Or it may bring to light surprising similarities, developments, and broad trends across rather different societies. For example, in the 1990s most advanced capitalist nations experienced periods of severe economic recession and high rates of unemployment and, whatever the political stripe of the incumbent governments, they responded by cutting back social programs and introducing other neo-liberal policies (although the character and magnitude of these developments differed markedly).

A third strength of cross-national research is that it allows us to assess, qualify, and rethink popular hypotheses, explanations, and theories about social inequality and generate new ones. For example, accounts suggesting that high levels of poverty and income inequality in Canada, the US, or the UK are a product of the negative impact of unions and expensive social programs on economic growth and job creation are not supported when these countries are contrasted with the Nordic nations, where poverty and income inequality rates are substantially lower but the labour movements and welfare states have long been much more vibrant and sturdy. Even a cursory historical comparison reminds us that modern welfare states and unions were a response to economic crises and attendant social ills, rather than their trigger. Similarly, theories that suggest that high levels of inequality are the natural outcome of biological or psychological differences, or view it as a functional and largely unavoidable necessity in modern, industrialized societies, are undermined by research demonstrating marked cross-national variation. Poverty rates, the distribution of income and wealth, the remuneration provided to those who head large corporations, and women's involvement in politics and the labour market, for example, can vary greatly across, and within, the Nordic and Anglo-Saxon groups of nations, as we will see in chapter 3.

Of course, no modern capitalist society has eradicated or even greatly reduced *all* forms of inequality: the power wielded by giant transnational corporations is everywhere unrivalled and increasing; a small fraction of the upper class invariably holds most of the wealth; and abject poverty, homelessness, gender inequality, violence against women and children, racism, and numerous other social ills are universally present. Much of this inequality is systemically determined or shaped, a product of long-standing capitalist, patriarchal, and racist structures and other institutionalized, systemic forms of discrimination. Despite this, as clearly indicated in Part II, some nations have made notable advances in greatly reducing at least some manifestations of social inequality—gains that are often ignored or dismissed by some Marxists, feminists, and others who focus entirely upon 'structural determinants'.

A fourth strength of comparative research is that it can provide instruction. How have other nations reduced inequalities? How are they addressing the social ills, problems, and challenges that we all face today? Have we fallen into traps circumvented elsewhere? Comparative research can provide perspective on our policies and strategies. It can show us which forms of social inequality have been attenuated, and how and where this has occurred. It can allow us to gain a deeper understanding of social institutions and processes and assess the significance of national cultures and ideologies, state structures (such as electoral and party systems, federalism, and so on), and social policies, as well as the role of key social actors and their impact upon the balance of power in society. A close examination of the policy approaches taken in other nations—their construction and content, their impact, and the socio-economic and socio-political contexts that fostered their emergence and implementation—can provide invaluable lessons and guidance in designing and shaping our policies and political strategies. It allows us to learn from the experience of others, to see what has and has not worked in other nations. Common trends, tendencies, and challenges, such as slow economic growth, rapidly aging populations, and an increase in the number of single-parent families, are often handled very differently across nations. The courses of action (or inaction) taken in other countries can provide positive and negative examples for us, allowing us to question increasingly familiar pronouncements that no alternatives exist to the neo-liberal agenda and Anglo-American capitalism.

Finally, with the growing interdependence among nations that is a hallmark of our times, it is becoming increasingly difficult to adequately comprehend and address inequality at a purely national level. Growing levels of inequality and poverty in one nation are often closely related to developments and choices made elsewhere. With more global integration—a widening, deepening, and accelerating of virtually all aspects of economic, social, and political life across the world—nations feel greater pressure to conform to the dictates of more powerful states and emulate their social and economic policy approaches. Cross-national studies can help us to identify these ongoing developments and trends, and identify global solutions. Our examination of inequality begins with an exploration of the various ways that equality has been understood and how this has shaped the nature of and approach to inequality in the Anglo-Saxon and Nordic nations.

Notes

1. The term 'Anglo-Saxon' has been widely employed in the literature on welfare states, social policy, and social inequality to refer to nations such as Canada, the US, Australia, and New Zealand that have strong historic colonial ties to the UK and that are predominantly English-speaking. Other similar terms, such as 'Anglo', 'Anglophone', and 'Anglo-American' have also been used to refer to these nations.
2. T.H. Marshall referred to these types of rights as 'civil' rights and 'political' rights, linking the former to developments in the 1700s and the latter to developments in the 1800s. However, as often noted, and discussed in greater detail in chapter 4, the civil and political rights attained during these periods were often incomplete, insecure, and restricted to certain groups, with significant cross-national variation in their dates of introduction and character (Bulmer and Rees 1996).
3. The terms **status**, **prestige**, and **honour** are sometimes used interchangeably because they all denote some aspect of social worth and can be closely related. **Status** usually refers to the standing or rank of an individual or group within a social hierarchy, and members of the same status groups typically display distinct styles of life and patterns of behaviour. **Prestige** can be detached from status or rank. It often connotes a more subjective and emotional dimension, signifying approval, appreciation, respect, esteem, or even reverence. An aristocrat has high social status, but may not be well-respected or admired. Similarly, famous and popular movie stars may have very high status that garner them top billing and top salaries but they may not have as much prestige as lesser-known actors who are considered artists and masters of their craft. **Honour**, in turn, refers to acknowledgement or recognition accorded to someone for deeds or accomplishments that often benefit society or some segment of it. Recipients of the Nobel Peace Prize, for example, may be so honoured. A useful discussion of these terms can be found in Sennett (2003).
4. Although often translated as 'happiness', Aristotle indicates in *The Nicomachean Ethics* that the term *eudemonia* refers to fulfilment and living a 'complete life' (Aristotle 2004 [350 BCE]).
5. Income deciles refer to ten equally sized income groups arranged in order of the magnitude of their income from lowest to highest. Those groups (individuals or families) in the bottom decile, or 10%, of income earners, have the lowest level of income. Those at the top, or tenth decile, have the highest level of income. The use of quintiles, or 'fifths', is also commonly employed in studies of the dispersion of income, wealth, health, and numerous other considerations. The use of quintiles hierarchically arranges the groups into units that each represent 20% of the population examined.
6. The idea of stratification is often, but not necessarily, associated with functionalist and other theoretical approaches that maintain, or imply, that the positions people occupy in hierarchies are largely determined on the basis of their natural abilities and/or choices made by individuals.
7. Members of status groups share a common lifestyle and typically have similar levels of privilege, prestige, and power. The castes in the caste system in India and the estates of the feudal period are sometimes referred to as status groups, rather than classes. However, the rigidity or more strictly fixed nature of the social orders and positions in these societies is, perhaps, better captured by the term 'stations'. Sociologists also use the term status groups in another markedly different way, referring to social positions or roles in society, such as those of child, parent, or teacher and their expected behaviours or roles.
8. Of course, people may also seek to identify and highlight their distinctiveness from others as a means of nurturing and promoting their collective interests and values, securing their well-being, and defending themselves. The identification of difference in these cases is an autochthonous means of empowerment that can foster greater solidarity.

9. Humans began living in foraging societies—small-scale, kin-based bands, tribes, and chiefdoms centred around hunting wild animals, fishing, and gathering wild plant foods, rather than on the domestication of animals and plants—around 150,000 to 200,000 years ago. About 10,000 years ago, during the Neolithic period (or 'new Stone Age'), the first agricultural revolution began, with the domestication of plants and animals. However, it is only in the last 4,000 to 5,000 years that hierarchical, highly inegalitarian human societies, such as the caste and slave-based systems rooted in antiquity, the feudal estates of the medieval period, and the class system associated with capitalism developed (Harman 1999; Lenski and Lenski 1982).

10. Writing over three centuries ago, the English philosopher and political theorist Thomas Hobbes (1588–1679) characterized early human society as a war 'of every man, against every man' in which life was 'solitary, poore, nasty, brutish and short' (Hobbes 1985 [1651]:185, 186). Over the next few centuries, numerous similar accounts of uncivilized, ignorant savages were steadily advanced by heads of state, explorers, and settlers seeking to justify their seizure of the land used by hunting and gathering tribes and the destruction of their civilizations around the globe. However, the great bulk of the archaeological, anthropological, and ethnographical research amassed over the past century provides little support for such speculation and claims. Indeed, early foraging societies most often reflect a dominant ethos of cooperation, reciprocity, exchange, and hospitality. Although there can be considerable variation in the nature and the level of social inequality across them, ranking or hierarchy was generally quite minimal, and privilege, prestige, and power were more symmetrically distributed than in later forms of social organization.

11. Advantages can be passed on directly through laws that allow people to inherit great wealth. However, the abolition or weakening of such legislation does not prevent wealthy and powerful individuals from using their dense webs of socio-economic advantages and social connections to promote the interests of their offspring and greatly increase their chances of filling positions that furnish the highest material and non-material rewards, including power itself.

12. For example, see Acker (2000); Collins (1993); Ferguson (1990); Glenn (2002); Ruddick (1996); Zawilski and Levine-Rasky (2005).

13. 'Objective' measures of class, which sort people into categories on the basis of some simple inequality metric related to standards of living and life chances (such as income, wealth, housing, or other possessions) or identify groups/strata according to some type of scale or scheme that considers occupation, education, status, and/or employment conditions, have been widely employed in the UK and the US. Prior to the 1970s studies employing these kinds of measures often explicitly or implicitly suggested that the class standing of individuals or groups largely reflected their level of achievement. Other more 'subjective' definitions of class have also been constructed through interviews or surveys that asked respondents to locate themselves and/or others in the social inequality configuration of the communities they reside within.

14. Weber's multi-dimensional stratification schema also stressed **status** (the distribution of honour and prestige) and **party** (an account of the distribution of political power) in addition to class.

15. Anthropologist Bruce Trigger (1990:131) indicates that 'both men and women appear to have had a stronger voice in those issues that affected their lives more closely. Thus, women had a preponderant role in deciding matters relating primarily to village life, while men had a stronger say in relations between communities'.

16. The legal voting age has also changed over time. While 21 years was the common age a few decades ago, it is now 18 years of age. A few states in Germany have lowered their voting age to 16 years of age and this change has been seriously discussed in many other nations over the past few years.

17. Inverted commas around the word 'race' are widely used in sociology texts to suggest that it is an essentially social construct used by dominant groups to classify people into mutually exclusive categories on the basis of arbitrary criteria and superficial differences among them.

18. 'Ethnic groups' are also somewhat ambiguous social constructs since it must be socially determined *which* cultural attributes and shared activities define a common ethnicity. Ethnic groups are typically constructed on the basis of cultural (non-biological) differences between groups such as ancestry, nativity, language, religion, or customs. Who determines which ones matter, or matter the most? What if two people share a common language but belong to different religious groups? Or what if they share the same religion but not the same language? The identification of ethnicity can also be situational. 'Hispanic' is a term that has been especially popular in the US to refer to people of Mexican, Cuban, Central American, South American, or Spanish origin. However, this 'ethnic group' can include people from over 25 different nations, and many of these countries house numerous sub-national or indigenous cultures and languages. Similarly, someone who is from Wales may be defined as Welsh within Britain, as British within Europe, or as European by people and groups outside of Europe. Moreover, as Ali Rattansi (2007:89) notes, 'ethnic identities are constantly subject to formation and re-formation and to contextual negotiation'.

19. There are numerous scientific critiques of the notion of race as a meaningful biological term, including Graves (2004).

20. **Racism** refers to the set of ideas and ideals that assert and attempt to justify the unequal treatment of different groups on the basis of racial categories, culminating in privilege and power for some 'races', and privation, exclusion, and subjugation for others. It involves both **prejudice**—irrational prejudgements, perception, and biases toward different 'races' and attitudes of antipathy and hostility against those deemed inferior—and **discrimination**—the unequal treatment of different groups—backed by power. Unlike race, ethnicity is widely understood as a cultural rather than a biological category, but it too is often used as a basis or axis to rank groups and justify their unequal treatment. For an excellent discussion of race and ethnicity with a focus upon the Canadian context see Fleras and Elliott (2000).

21. People with male and female reproductive organs, formerly referred to as hermaphrodites (after the Greek male and female Gods, Hermes and Aphrodite), were among the first people with intersex conditions to be identified.

22. They were often burned, hanged, or drowned.

23. For Weber, class, status, and authority reflected the economic, social, and political dimensions of power.

24. Working within the structural functionalist tradition, the American sociologist Talcott Parsons (1964), in stark contrast, viewed power as a collective resource, built upon a foundation of shared values and communal trust that is held by society and used to advance its goals.

25. Robert Dahl is a key exponent of the pluralist perspective in political theory. Pluralism suggests that power is widely dispersed in society across numerous lobby/interest/pressure groups, not concentrated in the hands of any one class, elite, or group. However, this research has been roundly criticized for its emphasis upon local issues and conflicts and observable decision-making rather than agenda-setting and other institutional and systemic aspects of power (see Olsen 2002, chapter 6).

26. Thomas Hobbes defined power as an actor's means 'to obtain some future apparent Good' (Hobbes 1983 [1651]:150). Similarly, the English political philosopher and writer Bertrand Russell (1938:25) defined power as 'the production of intended

effects'. These accounts also focus upon actors and the intentional use of power but, unlike those proposed by Weber and Dahl, they do not assume conflict and resistance.

27. Similarly, when hundreds of thousands of people are prompted to sell off the currency of some particular nation their actions may wreak unintended havoc, undermining economic and political stability in that nation. Of course the parties that encouraged this action may have fully intended to foster these developments too.

28. The notion of three different 'faces' or aspects of power is associated with the work of Steven Lukes (2005).

29. The idea of 'objective interests' sometimes devolves into arcane philosophical debates about how we determine what they are. But most of us would agree that when slaves accept their position as inferior servants, or women believe that they simply cannot do politics or anything else outside of domestic labour, or children believe it is acceptable if they are beaten, or the poor resign themselves to their earthly fate because their reward will come in the next world, an ideological imprint has undermined the objective interests of these groups.

30. However, the idea that slaves were intrinsically inferior could be more nuanced. Aristotle, for example, held that 'barbarian' (i.e., non-Greek) slaves were generally soulless 'lower sorts' with little ability to reason. But he also acknowledged that some people acquire their slave status as prisoners of war, rather than because of any innate inferiority, and may exhibit the virtues of patricians and nobles rather than the vices of the base-born. For him the only acceptable means of acquiring slaves was taking barbarian captives in war, and he opposed the practice of collective or communal slave-ownership as well as the employment of slaves on the land, in the mines and in other forms of production outside the household. He held that domestic servitude (employment in homes of the slave-owner) was the only legitimate form of enthralment.

31. Chapter 21 of Exodus in the Old Testament, for example, endorses the purchase of humans as servants, but states that in the seventh year of servitude the master should set the servant free (verse 2). It also indicates that it is permissible for a master to smite a servant with a rod, as long as this does not lead to death, because the servant 'is his money' (verses 20–21).

32. A similar type of feudal system of stratification could be found in Japan in the middle ages. However, between the early 1600s and the middle of the nineteenth century, it came to resemble the more rigidly hierarchical caste system of India, with an 'impure', 'sub-human' outcaste at the bottom, the Eta-Hinin (defiled or polluted non-persons).

33. Hindu India provides the best example of this form of stratification, but caste systems also have been established among Muslim and Christian communities within India as well as among Hindu diaspora settlements and communities in many other South Asian countries, including Bangladesh, Burma (Myanmar), Ceylon (Sri Lanka), Nepal, and Thailand. Other nations, such as Japan in the seventeenth and eighteenth centuries and, more recently, South Africa (1948–1992) also developed stratification systems that approximated at least some of the central traits of the traditional caste system. However, it is India, where the caste system has been in place for almost 3,000 years and affected the largest numbers of people, that provides the best illustration. Although there are several religious, biological, and socio-historical accounts of the origins of the caste system, it is closely associated with Hinduism—the majority religion of India—and the set of ideas and practices set out in ancient, sacred Hindu texts.

34. In the caste system, the Dalits ('Untouchables') were considered so impure that they were an 'outcaste', entirely outside the formal four-caste system. Although their situation might vary somewhat from one region to the next, they were typically denied freedom of speech, assembly, and political participation, barred from entering schools

and holy temples, prohibited from associating with higher caste members, and often forced to reside outside their own villages. Discrimination, degradation, repression, and humiliation were their lot, consigning them to lives of extreme poverty, deprivation, and disadvantage.

35. This is analogous to the discussion of energy in physics and the distinction made between its kinetic and potential forms. Kinetic energy is the energy of motion that is visible in, for example, the flight of an object propelled by a slingshot or the movement of a yo-yo. Potential energy is the energy that is 'stored' in an object by virtue of its position or structure; in the stretched elastic band of a slingshot before its shot is released or in a yo-yo just after it has climbed to the top of its path but before it begins to descend.

36. Widely employed in sociology today, **typologies** utilize dimensions that represent concepts rather than empirical cases. These concepts are usually based upon **ideal types**—mental or hypothetical constructs that deliberately accentuate certain traits. Ideal types are not necessarily, or typically, found in empirical reality. **Taxonomies**, in contrast, classify items on the basis of empirically observable and measurable characteristics (Smith 2002:381). In addition, typologies often classify social phenomena on the basis of two or more variables, sometimes highlighting an interaction among them while taxonomies typically classify cases, or taxa (e.g., nations), into lists on the basis of one or more variables that do not interact (e.g., rich, Anglo-Saxon nations).

37. A Weberian ideal type is a hypothetical construct or intellectual standard that can be used as a heuristic device to compare and classify empirically observable types. The use of the term 'ideal' here signifies an abstract representation that does not exist in the real world, not one that is thought to be perfect or normatively desirable. Weber's use of ideal types in his studies of legitimation and authority (charismatic, traditional, and rational-legal) and bureaucracy have been especially influential. Edward C. Page (1985) employs a Weberian ideal-type analysis in his contemporary comparative account of bureaucratic structures in Britain, France, Germany, and the US.

38. Aristotle identified six forms of government, three that ruled in the common interest (monarchy, aristocracy, constitutional democracy) and three that did not (tyranny, oligarchy, anarchy), without regard for whether they involved rule by one, few, or many people. Tocqueville contrasted democratic and aristocratic forms of government but, for him, the latter was viewed as a distinct historical form of rule that was giving way to democracy. Unlike Socrates, Tocqueville did not define aristocratic rule as rule by the wise, or the best suited to rule, but as rule by the wealthy, i.e, those with inherited property—a plutocracy.

39. Tocqueville's reference to the 'general equality of condition' in the US referred to a condition of political equality, rather than economic equality. He meant that Americans were equal before the law and thought to be equally deserving of respect and treatment. He expressed great concern about the rise of a new and ruthless 'industrial aristocracy' as well as the uniformity and conformity that could be imposed through a democratic system, which he called the 'tyranny of the majority'.

40. Intra-national studies focus on cities, states, provinces, and other regions, communities, or sub-cultures *within* a country while cross-temporal studies examine societies' structures over short or long periods of time.

41. Ethnocentrism refers to the tendency for people to see the world in terms of their own culture, sometimes uncritically assuming that it is superior. It should not necessarily be equated with ethnic or racial hatred, prejudice, and discrimination.

42. Mead's (1963 [1935]) studies of gender roles across three separate tribes in New Guinea demonstrated wide variability, stressing the importance of nurture over nature. Among the Arapesh there was little distinction between the roles of men and

women; both were passive, nurturing, non-aggressive, and emotionally responsive, exhibiting characteristics and behaviours traditionally associated in Western society with females. Among the Mundugumor there was little distinction between men and women as well, but both displayed characteristics and assumed the roles and behaviours that we tend to associate with males. And, most strikingly, among the Tchumbali tribe the roles of men and women were largely the reverse of those traditionally taken by men and women in Western societies.

2 Conceptualizing Equality: Four Ideals

In order to have a better understanding of inequality we need to closely examine what is meant by equality, perhaps the most controversial of the great social ideals. Several thinkers have strongly opposed equality on various grounds. The German philosopher Friedrich Nietzsche (1844–1900) contemptuously dismissed enlightenment ideals such as equality and democracy in favour of the aristocratic ideal of the *Übermensch*, or Superman. For him the goal of all human effort should be the enhancement of the power and personality of bright, talented individuals, not the happiness or elevation of the masses. The 'social Darwinist' Herbert Spencer (1820–1903) rejected the goal of equality for very different reasons. Spencer also enthusiastically endorsed the competitive order as the best means of identifying, cultivating, and rewarding the most superior people in society. But, unlike his German contemporary, he was ultimately concerned with the long-term good of the social collective. Spencer maintained that human society evolved through an intense struggle in which the most gifted, talented, and industrious individuals were rewarded and the most incompetent and indolent individuals were eliminated. For Spencer, social welfare, social planning, and other related social policies, programs, and measures only served to support and preserve society's inferior, deficient, and defective members, thereby interfering with this natural winnowing process and greatly impeding social progress.

Influenced by Nietzsche and Spencer, American (though Russian-born) philosopher and novelist Ayn Rand (1905–1982) vehemently argued that all attempts to foster greater equality perpetuate mediocrity. Unlike classical economists or contemporary 'trickle-down' theorists who advocate the free market on the grounds that everyone will benefit to some degree, at least in the long run, Rand sought to provide an explicitly moral defense of egoistic capitalism. She unabashedly extolled the 'virtues of selfishness'—the single-minded pursuit of self-interest and self-assertion that enables the most talented and creative to rise above the herd—and was hostile to any form of altruism, socialism, or state intervention and all efforts, public or private, to redistribute wealth. In turn, neo-liberal economists, such as Friedrich von Hayek (1899–1992) and Milton Friedman (1912–2006), whose ideas have so profoundly influenced governments in the West over the past few decades, view inequality as an acceptable price to pay for a dynamic capitalist economy. They contend that fiscal and social policies designed to reduce inequalities only hamper economic growth and restrict personal freedom. Moreover, they hold that such policies are simply an exercise in futility, since new inequalities will inevitably emerge to replace those that have been politically suppressed. Finally, in sociology functionalists have long argued that distinctly unequal rewards are an essential means of recruiting and motivating the most gifted and diligent members in society to attain the education, training, and skills required to fill its most critical positions. For them, social inequality is indispensable to a stable, efficient, and productive social order.

Anti-egalitarian arguments and theories such as these, which have long been employed to justify social inequality, and have enjoyed a resurgence over the past two decades, are addressed in chapter 5. Our concern here, however, is with the central ideas of **egalitarians**, those who *favour* equality. Equality is a complex, multi-faceted ideal and has been conceptualized in numerous ways and defended on varied grounds. Egalitarians all champion some form of equality, but they often disagree about what equality is and how it might be fostered. The debate over the character and value of equality, and the principles it is based upon, is our central focus.

What is Equality? Some Basic Considerations

One of the most prominent issues of contention among egalitarians concerns *what* it is that should be equal; that is, in what respects should people be equal or, at least, closer to equality? Egalitarians may emphasize basic rights, protections, and entitlements, more encompassing 'relational' issues involving status, prestige, honour, social exclusion, or power and influence and/or economic and distributional concerns, such as income, wealth, life chances, and so on. For others, it is primarily the provision of equal opportunities to fill the positions that confer these material and symbolic goods and advantages that is paramount. Of course, these different facets of equality can be quite closely related and interdependent. Inequality in one sphere is closely linked to inequality in other spheres. Poverty, for example, diminishes people's ability to fully participate in society by restricting their chances to access existing opportunities and rights and enjoy the benefits and provisions available in their society, furthering their marginalization and deprivation. And it garners little dignity, respect, or influence. Opulence, in contrast, typically furnishes a lavish lifestyle, a prominent stature, and widespread social approval. It also provides the affluent with significant political influence and power and can greatly enhance their basic rights.[1] Few would seriously contend that the poor and the wealthy are truly equal in a court of law, for example.

Closely related to this issue is how far we should go in the pursuit of equality across these different sites and spheres. Uniform or strict equality is generally embraced, at least formally, in the sphere of legal and political rights; there are few instances when it is considered entirely acceptable if the rights of an individual or a group only approximate those of others in society. But the ideal of strict equality or 'uniformity' in the economic or material sphere is sometimes almost as forcefully rejected by some egalitarians as by the staunchest opponents of equality. Strict economic egalitarianism is probably most closely and commonly associated with the ideal of equality today. Yet very few have ever advocated or sought to implement such an ideal or goal, including communist societies such as the former Soviet Union and its satellites.[2] Indeed, Joseph Stalin, the autocratic Soviet leader, dismissed the ideal of economic equality as 'petit-bourgeois'. Despite their vitriolic protest against poverty and the oppressive living and working conditions they examined in capitalist society, Marxists and socialists have typically focused much more upon the sphere of production rather than the sphere of consumption. Although critical of large disparities in income and wealth, their emphasis was on inequalities in the relations of production. Their calls for the abolition of classes and class society reflected their overriding concern with the largely unrestrained economic, political, and ideological power wielded by those who own and control the means of production. Great disparities in wealth or 'standards of living' were unacceptable symptoms or by-products of those unequal ownership and power relations. However, while few view economic equality, in the strictest sense, as either workable or desirable today, many call for significant reductions in economic disparities and much greater equality in living conditions and well-being as important components of their egalitarian vision. And the Nordic nations, as we will see in the following two chapters, have been considerably more successful in approximating this goal.[3]

A third issue that is debated among egalitarians concerns *who* it is that should be equal (or, equality among whom?). Should the focus be upon inequality among individuals, typically understood as the citizens or residents of a nation, or across groups? From a 'mainstream' liberal perspective, the emphasis is typically upon the unequal opportunities unfairly accorded to individuals, but most accounts of inequality in sociology today focus upon axes such as class, gender, race, and ethnicity and, increasingly, other bases such as age, ability, and sexual orientation. However, whether they emphasize equality among individuals or groups, most egalitarians focus upon equality *within* a given nation or society; that is, people's rights and well-being are understood in relation to those of others within their own society. Thus, while many egalitarians believe that we all have a responsibility to redress poverty and other forms of inequality across the globe, few would suggest that people who are not citizens or residents of a nation should have the right to vote in its elections or access its social programs and services on the same terms as nationals.[4]

Aristotle argued that only those who are equal in 'relevant respects' should be treated equally, that we should 'treat like cases alike'. While this idea has an egalitarian ring—all people should be treated equally—it has also been used to rationalize the unequal treatment of those deemed unequal in 'relevant respects', such as free men and slaves, men and women, or citizens and foreigners, as in ancient Greek and Roman societies. Today the idea that children are less competent than adults is often invoked to justify their denial of many rights and the nearly complete and often arbitrary regulation of their lives by adults, as well as the use of corporal punishment to discipline them. In the Anglo-Saxon nations, for example, this form of discipline is typically considered too harsh and demeaning for all adults, including criminals and prisoners because it constitutes a violation of a fundamental right to physical integrity, dignity, and protection. But it is considered entirely acceptable, and even beneficial, for children. In the Nordic nations, in stark contrast, children's legal rights to protection from such physical assault have been legislatively affirmed and childhood is viewed as more than simply a transitory period of incompetency, incapacities, and preparation for adulthood.

Finally, given the nature and number of points of contention briefly reviewed above, egalitarians, not surprisingly, also are in considerable disagreement over the most effective *means* of fostering equality. It is often argued that equality can only, or best, be achieved by treating everyone the same. For example, most egalitarians would agree that everyone should be entitled to an education, health care, the right to vote, and other basic civil and political rights, protections, and services. It would usually be viewed as unfair or unjust if such rights and benefits were only provided to some of society's members. Of course, simply treating everyone the same, without consideration of the nature of that treatment, will not necessarily do. An essential component or goal of the ideal of equality is the promotion, not the diminishment, of people's well-being. Egalitarian policies, programs, laws, and rights are only fair or just if they improve our lives. Eliminating the right to vote for all citizens, rendering everyone equally poor, making corporal punishment acceptable for adults again, or exploiting, oppressing, and mistreating everyone would obviously not be part of many egalitarians' conception of equality or their plan to achieve it.

Some egalitarians, however, suggest that, under certain circumstances, it may be advisable or necessary to treat people differently. On what grounds might people be treated unequally? Feminists, multiculturalists, and many other egalitarians sometimes advocate unequal treatment for particular groups in some instances as a means of promoting greater equality. For example, providing additional resources to some ethnic groups to prevent the erosion or loss of their culture and language, or to allow or encourage under-represented groups to achieve greater visibility in parliament or in some other central institution, can be essential to fostering these goals. In many instances, strictly equal treatment, or 'neutrality', might simply encourage the integration or assimilation of disadvantaged groups to pre-existing, unequal, and problematic structures and norms; differential treatment can sometimes help to reshape them.

More controversial here is the employment of affirmative action policies because they explicitly and actively advance the position of members of disadvantaged groups, rather than simply conforming to the principle of equality and encouraging it through the provision of supplementary resources and greater opportunities. Indeed, by definition and intent, affirmative action measures such as various forms of 'preferential treatment', 'positive discrimination', or quotas to promote and extend the well-being of certain long-disadvantaged groups—do explicitly 'privilege' them over others.[5] For many other egalitarians, however, it is never acceptable to discriminate against *any* individual or group on the basis of ascriptive characteristics such as sex, race, colour, ethnicity, ability, sexual orientation, or creed.[6] For them, affirmative action programs are self-contradictory; social policies should be providing a remedy for discrimination, not simply redeploying it. They argue that such practices are patronizing, degrading, and counter-productive, and contradict the principles that underpin the political institutions and legal framework on which modern, enlightened societies rest.[7]

Other egalitarians, in contrast, point out that these same institutions and laws have long allowed blatantly discriminatory practices and the gross violation of the rights of certain groups and their mistreatment and abuse. The enslavement and segregation of African Americans in the US, the extermination or near extermination of indigenous populations and their cultures in the Americas, the internment of Japanese citizens in Canada and the US during World War II, and the sterilization and eugenics programs in place in many developed nations in the twentieth century, including the Anglo-Saxon and Nordic nations, are only a few of the most prominent and egregious instances. At this juncture, it is maintained, policies cannot always be neutral or 'blind' ('sex-blind', 'colour-blind', and so on) because society is not yet neutral or 'blind'. Inequality is structurally embedded in society and people and institutions still treat different groups unequally. Preferential and unequal treatment, then, is advocated not just, or even primarily, as compensation for past injustices, but as a means of changing society, rendering it more egalitarian and fair. It typically involves re-examining, rethinking, and challenging the conventional goals and practices of the central institutions in society. Admission to universities and colleges, for example, should not be viewed only as a reward for those who perform best in high school and a means to further develop their talents. Institutions of higher learning that fail to educate a significant sector of society, no matter how justified on the basis of grades, default on their broader obligations to society. Similarly, preferential hiring can help break down stereotypes, inspire and create identity role models for children from disadvantaged groups, and create models of diversity for the rest of society (see Appiah and Gutman 1996). Moreover, the increased presence of under-represented, disadvantaged, and long-discriminated-against groups in parliament and other central institutions and organizations in society can allow them to articulate and help to resolve social issues and problems that have not been adequately addressed or even acknowledged before. In the Nordic nations, for example, the representation of women in parliament on a relatively wide scale has been crucial to the development and implementation of those countries' enviable family policies and social programs and allowed them to render other crucial components of their welfare states considerably more gender sensitive and 'woman-friendly'.[8]

Still other egalitarians are concerned that affirmative action policies and other similar measures may make society fairer, but they do not necessarily address social inequality head-on. This is because they focus upon *who* should be in the top positions and get the highest rewards, not whether such inequalities should exist at all, undermining a broader sense of social solidarity and community. Thus, inequality is still often accepted as reasonable, necessary, and inevitable, and hierarchy itself is not necessarily viewed as a problem. The differing perspectives and debates concerning the central aspects of equality discussed above have given rise to different conceptions or models of equality that have been embraced in the Anglo-Saxon and Nordic lands. Of course, these are closely related to attitudes toward inequality and have helped to shape social policy in these countries.

Four Models of Equality

It is conventional to identify four basic forms that equality may assume: (1) **intrinsic equality**, (2) **equal opportunity**, (3) **equality of condition**, and (4) **equality of outcome**.[9] They differ in the degree to which they focus upon description or prescription and in their emphasis upon relational or distributional concerns, as well as in their goals and the forms and extent of action they advocate to realize them. Given their different orientations and emphases, these four models or ideals of equality are typically presented as distinct, and even contradictory. Yet, while they may appear to conflict with one another in their most narrow or weakest interpretations, they may be viewed as largely complementary and even indispensable to each other in their stronger, more inclusive forms. However, the particular mix of ideas associated with these models varies considerably cross-nationally, with the Anglo-Saxon nations—especially the US—much more closely adhering to a more restricted interpretation of 'equal opportunity' while the Nordic nations have placed greater emphasis upon 'equality of condition', with at least some consideration of equality of outcome. It is crucial to recognize the different goals and ideals of equality across countries when examining and attempting to understand cross-national contours and patterns of inequality and the different ways inequalities have been addressed.

Intrinsic Equality

Although it is broadly inclusive, intrinsic equality is, in another sense, the most narrow or circumscribed expression of equality. At its most basic level it simply declares or describes an essential equality among human beings qua human beings—all people, as members of the species *Homo sapiens* are, ipso facto, equals—without requiring much by way of prescription. It is grounded in the universality of human nature and the human condition.

Also referred to as 'foundational' or 'ontological' equality, intrinsic equality is often closely associated with religious, ethical, and moral traditions. Humans are viewed as different or unique because they all possess a soul, a capacity for rationality or morality, or some other quality or attribute that other creatures are believed to lack. Almost all of the world's major religions suggest that all people are 'children of God', 'created in the image of God', and 'equal in the eyes of God'.[10] Most systems of ethical or moral reasoning explicitly or implicitly adhere to a similar notion. The English political theorist Thomas Hobbes (1588–1679) argued that it was the natural and basic equality among humans—roughly equal in their physical and mental capacities and appetites—that led to diffidence, competition, and war, and legitimated extensive, if not absolute, powers for the state to allow it to maintain order. By contrast, Hobbes's countryman, the philosopher John Locke (1632–1704), held a comparatively benign conception of human nature, and his notion of an essential human equality was one derived from the God-given rationality that was shared by all people.[11] Despite these differences, both asserted that people *are* equal by virtue of their divine origins and/or common humanity. This idea perhaps takes its most well-known political expression in the American Declaration of Independence of 1776:

> We hold these truths to be self-evident, that all men are created equal, that they are endowed by their Creator with certain inalienable Rights, that among these are Life, Liberty and the pursuit of happiness.

Many critics have suggested that such a conception of equality carries little weight, at least regarding the treatment of people in *this* world. However 'self-evident' their essential equality, many groups of people in the US (as elsewhere) have often been denied many very basic 'inalienable' rights. Religious institutions, for example, typically declare that men and women are all 'God's children' and 'equal in God's eyes', but often exclude women from positions of authority and power within their earthly organizations. Thus the Catholic Church proclaims that the doors to Heaven and eternal salvation are open but bars women from the priesthood.[12] Yet, while it is clearly very limited, intrinsic equality should not be facilely dismissed as trivial. The widespread acceptance of this ideal and its explicit, formal rejection of sexist, racist, and other doctrines and ideologies that identify some groups of people as superior, and thereby entitled to power and privilege, and others as inferior or sub-human, and legitimately eligible for discriminatory or inhumane and brutal treatment, is no minor achievement; such arguments have been employed for millennia to legitimate dictatorships and other hierarchical social systems based upon slavery, castes, and estates.

At the most basic level, intrinsic equality requires that everyone be subject to the same rules and punished in the same way if they break them. However, contemporary interpretations of this ideal typically recognize that divine decrees, official proclamations, and other assertions of our shared humanity and natural equality must surely obligate the state to provide and uphold some basic human rights and protections from certain forms of abuse as well as civil and political liberties for everyone. The latter have included freedom of thought, conscience, speech and assembly, universal suffrage, the right to hold public office, freedom from arbitrary arrest and seizure, and the right to equal treatment under the law, thereby transforming intrinsic equality into basic, formal equality.

Yet even when supported by such formal rights and liberties, intrinsic equality remains both incomplete and inadequate. It is incomplete because in most nations many groups have yet to be recognized and granted the same basic rights as others: gay couples may be denied the right to legally marry or adopt children; children may not benefit from the same protections as adults; immigrants and other groups may be denied social benefits, and so on. Moreover, even when groups are formally recognized as equal and have been granted the same rights and supports, substantial inequality often remains because society still values some groups over others: men over women, white people over people of colour, the able-bodied over those with disabilities, heterosexuals over gays, and adults over children. It is inadequate because it focuses almost exclusively on relational dimensions of inequality and has been largely concerned with securing the rights of individuals in the public sector. It has less often addressed social or economic issues, especially those that pertain to the private sector of the economy or the family and home. Homelessness, poverty and other privations, social hierarchies, unequal gender roles and norms, and racial discrimination have fallen largely outside the narrow interpretation of intrinsic equality and, hence, remained largely unaddressed. Nor does this ideal typically acknowledge how distributional inequalities can undermine the relational equalities it promotes in the political and civil spheres. Thus, while all (adult) citizens may have the right to vote in the developed capitalist nations, those with greater economic resources wield considerably more political influence. 'Equality before the law' is another formal right that is often subverted. De jure equality does not ensure de facto equality because state legislation and policies do not necessarily have the same impact on everyone, an observation succinctly captured in Anatole France's (1844–1924) wry quip: 'The law in France, in its majestic equality, forbids the rich as well as the poor to sleep under bridges, to beg in the streets, and to steal bread'.[13] Equality before the law also requires that two people who commit the same crime receive the same sentence. However, while this may seem egalitarian in one sense—treating everyone the same—it may not generate substantive equality. A $200 speeding ticket is much less of a hardship for a multi-millionaire than for a low-income motorist, and will do little to discourage future infractions among very affluent speeders. Several nations have attempted to redress such situations by, for example, introducing income-related traffic fines. Some of them, including Sweden and Germany, have introduced these fines with an upper limit on their level while others, such as Finland, have not employed such a ceiling. Clearly, the realization of intrinsic equality, in its fullest sense—the abolition of hierarchy and fair treatment for all—must be allied with other interventions that are more far-reaching than simply establishing and ensuring the same restricted civil and political liberties for everyone in society. These formal rights, rooted in the Enlightenment rejection of monarchical and feudal hierarchy and the recognition of intrinsic human equality, are a necessary but clearly insufficient first step toward establishing a more meaningful form of egalitarian society.[14]

Equality of Opportunity

Equal opportunity is the most common and widely accepted face of equality today, garnering a great deal of support across the political spectrum. It came into prominence with the spread of capitalism and the gradual displacement of conservatism by liberalism as the dominant political ideology. Along with freedom and reason, equal opportunity is a key component of liberalism—the official ideology of capitalism—and a legacy of the American and French Revolutions. The ideal of equal opportunity seeks to formalize and extend the rights that people have (or should have) on the basis of their intrinsic equality into other spheres. And it begins to address issues related to the privileges or disadvantages accorded to people at birth.

However, while staunchly opposed to any form of hierarchy fixed at birth, the ideal of equal opportunity does not reject hierarchy per se. Indeed, it is quite explicitly based upon an assumption of a hierarchy of social stations and roles in society that differ greatly in their importance and desirability, as well as in the material and symbolic rewards they furnish. It also accepts that idea that there are many more people who want the top positions than can attain them. The principal concern with this ideal of equality is simply that the *means* by which people are slotted into the positions and institutions that confer superior advantages are fair. In its most narrow formulation—**formal equal opportunity**—fairness is interpreted to mean that ascriptive factors, such as family background, social status, class, race, ethnicity, gender, creed, and other arbitrary factors beyond a person's control should not act as barriers that prevent access to valued and highly rewarding social positions.[15] Although the emphasis is usually placed upon the removal of discriminatory practices, policies, and other barriers that hinder a person's chances of applying for or obtaining these posts, it is also generally acknowledged that ascriptive factors should not improve them either. Thus, being poor should not hinder one's chances of gaining access to a good education, but neither should being rich increase them, an example that immediately brings the idea of equal opportunity as practiced in most modern capitalist nations into serious question.

In its somewhat broader and stronger formulation, **meritocratic equal opportunity**, greater emphasis is placed upon achievements and merit, rather than upon simply removing obstacles. This notion of fairness requires that the most highly rewarded and coveted careers and posts in society are open to talent, that they are filled through an open and even-handed competition.[16] The tests or criteria used to determine who is the most deserving or meritorious may be stiff, moderate, or virtually non-existent, depending upon the position or post under consideration, but they must be universally applied. From this perspective, the employment of ascriptive characteristics is to be avoided not only because they are arbitrary, but because they are also irrational. As such, they are harmful not only to those individuals who have been unfairly excluded or treated but also to society because the loss of their talents subverts innovation and efficiency. Discriminatory practices are even worse than merely whimsical or nepotistic hiring practices from this perspective because, in addition to unfairly depriving individuals of the positions they deserve, they also inflict long-term psychic damage on entire groups of people. So, too, are any forms of 'random procedure' in which all applicants have a statistically equal probability of filling key positions in society, since access should be entirely on the basis of merit, not chance.[17] Only *relevant* competencies should matter here; overt discrimination, serendipity, or selection on the basis of anything but demonstrated talent, initiative, and industry are entirely unacceptable. Consequently, considerable effort must be expended to monitor and regulate recruitment and promotion practices and procedures in the labour market as well as in educational and other institutions that are viewed as central means of advancement in society.

While the removal of arbitrary ascriptive barriers is obviously a positive and necessary measure, there are many serious limitations to the ideal of equality opportunity. First, true equal opportunity cannot be realized by simply eliminating discriminatory legislation and other official policies and practices because many informal cultural, institutional, structural, and economic barriers remain firmly in place. For example, the abolition decades ago of laws preventing women from holding public office has not greatly increased the numbers of women in politics in most nations because (at least outside the Nordic world) women's unequal responsibility for child care and other domestic commitments has been largely ignored. Moreover, many informal or undeclared sexist and patriarchal presumptions, attitudes, prejudices, and media images have not been acknowledged or adequately addressed, creating an oppressive socio-cultural environment that has served to occupationally segregate women and reinforce and legitimize traditional social roles. The labour markets in Sweden and the other Nordic nations are especially marked by segregation, with women dominating in the social service and caring occupations and other areas of the welfare state, and often working part-time.[18] However, viewed in terms of remuneration, benefits, and working conditions, they do not typically constitute the same kind of dead-end 'job ghetto' occupations that many women have been routinely consigned to in the Anglo-Saxon world. Similarly, universities and other institutions may formally open their doors to people from all classes and socio-economic backgrounds, but this does not ensure that the poor and those from less privileged families will be able to afford to attend them or have the cultural capital to successfully compete even if they do gain access.

Second, while the goal of equal opportunity is for the most talented and qualified people to achieve the top positions in society, there is little consideration of the central role that arbitrary factors such as social class and family background, native endowments, and 'brute luck' actually play in preparing, qualifying, and enabling those individuals to fill these positions. Few would dispute the idea that the numerous advantages afforded to children born to wealthy, highly educated, well-connected parents greatly increase their chances of being among those who are deemed to be the most 'meritorious', while the circumstances and backgrounds of less privileged individuals can greatly restrict their opportunities to get ahead. People born into lower income families face many more risks, disadvantages, and barriers. They are much more likely to have poor health, miss school due to illness, hold part-time jobs while in school, or have to quit school altogether to help support their families; they are much less likely to enjoy access to books in the home or to parents who have the time and energy to read to them and help them with their schoolwork; and they are unlikely to have powerful, high-level connections in educational institutions and the labour market. These disadvantages are cumulative and interactive, and often perpetuate themselves across generations.

Other competencies, such as intelligence, creativity, persistence, and many other innate abilities and attributes considered crucial for success in society, 'qualities of the mind or soul' in the words of the philosopher Jean-Jacques Rousseau (1984 [1755]:77), are talents that are distributed unequally by nature. They are the result of a genetic lottery that bestows a range of advantages (or disadvantages) upon people. These talents and attributes are 'accidents of birth', not earned through great effort and hard work, although they may be greatly accentuated by it. Few of us would suggest that someone who is born with a mental or physical impairment should bear the responsibility for it, but we commonly accredit, and highly reward, superior talents or abilities to those who were born with them. Finally, how well people make out is also dependent upon good or bad 'brute luck', the random fortuitous opportunities, circumstances, and lucky breaks—or, on the other hand, the unforeseeable and unavoidable accidents, misfortunes, and catastrophes—that befall us through no fault or responsibility of our own.[19] These difficulties inherent in the concept of equal opportunity have led many egalitarians to call for more far-reaching reforms that can foster a genuine or more substantive and meaningful equality of opportunity, sometimes referred to as equality of condition.

Equality of Condition

Discussions of equal opportunity commonly invoke the metaphor of a contest or foot race in which those who are the fastest (the most talented) win 'first prize' (get the best positions and rewards in society). Equality of opportunity is primarily concerned that everyone is allowed to enter the competition and that those who win do so entirely on the basis of merit. However, genetic make-up, socialization and training, and chance will—quite arbitrarily and unfairly—always play a significant role in determining who succeeds. To continue with the popular race metaphor, having good genes and the right physique, access to the best personal trainers, masseuses and equipment, not to mention the abilities of the competitors who happen to be entered in a given contest, will all greatly affect one's chances of winning. Equality of condition, or 'starting gate equality', seeks to ensure that such factors play a much more minimal or limited role, so that everyone who enters the race does so on reasonably similar terms. Although this conception of equality can take a variety of different forms it typically involves considerably greater political intervention than that required for strict equality of opportunity. Rather than simply ensuring that no one is excluded from participating in the race, the state must go much further to ensure that a person's background has as little impact as possible on their competitive prospects and that everyone has a genuine, substantive opportunity to become qualified to compete for the most rewarding positions in society.

There are several ways of construing and attempting to realize equality of condition. John Rawls (1921–2002) and Ronald Dworkin (b. 1931), two well-known and influential American philosophers and political theorists, have each offered distinct renderings of this ideal, setting out what it should entail and, through the use of hypothetical scenarios, suggesting the conditions that would be necessary to create it. In *A Theory of Justice* (1971), Rawls sought to reconcile the idea of liberal rights with a redistributive conception of social justice to create his version of equality of condition, or what he considered '*fair* equal opportunity'. People have an identity of interests, he argued, because they are better off living in society together than living apart. But they also have a conflict of interest because they prefer to have a larger rather than a smaller share of the social benefits that come from this social cooperation. Consequently, they typically support institutions and social and political measures that will provide the greatest benefit to themselves. The wealthy, for example, typically favour low taxes while those who are not as well-off advocate higher taxes on greater wealth and income to help pay for social programs and services. How can we create institutions and implement policies and programs that are fair and ensure genuine, substantive equal opportunity, when people's views are so strongly biased by their personal or particular situations? To answer this question Rawls suggests we begin with a 'thought experiment', a staple of classical political philosophy. He asks us to think about what principles we would choose to fairly distribute material and symbolic goods in society if we were behind a 'veil of ignorance', totally unaware of our personal characteristics and other conditions that prevent us from assuming an impartial stance. In this hypothetical 'original position' we are deprived of all knowledge of our personal talents, natural endowments, socio-economic position, and other characteristics such as our sex, race, ethnicity, age, and sexual orientation. The basic idea here, of course, is that ignorance fosters impartiality, and impartiality leads to a fairer distribution; we are more likely to cut a cake fairly if we do not know which piece we are going to get. Under such conditions we would not want to endorse weaker rights or fewer goods for anyone on the basis of social background or other ascriptive characteristics because we might well be a member of the group we are opting to disadvantage. Rawls also acknowledges that people are divided by more than their personal interests; they also have different beliefs, values, morals, ambitions, and goals, as well as different conceptions of the 'good life'. Thus, in the interest of impartiality, he suggests that these concerns be placed under the veil of ignorance as well. Only in this state of ignorance can we filter out all of our biases and establish a 'social contract' that would allow us to more fairly allocate goods in society.[20]

Under such conditions Rawls argues that we would choose three principles of justice to organize our society. First and foremost, we would decide that every person is equally entitled to the most extensive network of equal basic liberties compatible with a similar system of liberties for all. This first principle, the **liberty principle**, is the most fundamental and central for Rawls, the liberal core of his approach. These rights should protect everyone from discrimination, persecution, and other forms of oppression and cannot be overridden in the pursuit of equality. However, his second and third principles emphasize equality. The **fair equality of opportunity principle** acknowledges that for society to be just and distributions fair, the state must do more than simply eliminate barriers that prevent people from entering the competition to attain the positions at the top of the social and economic hierarchies. It must also ensure that people enjoy the same opportunities to develop their natural talents to the highest level possible so that no one competes with the handicaps sustained from a deprived background. It might achieve this goal by, for example, providing high-quality public education and numerous other social programs and interventions that improve life chances as rights of citizenship, and by developing institutional ways to prevent class, gender, race, and other ascriptive traits from interfering with the normal development of marketable skills and talents that genuinely qualify people to compete. However, while people should have the same initial expectations of positions and basic goods, this in no way precludes their ending up in different places in the hierarchy with different and unequal rewards. Finally, Rawls argues that marked inequalities should only be allowable if they tend to benefit those who are least advantaged in society. He calls this the **difference principle**. Thus, for example, it might be justified and beneficial to remunerate doctors with extraordinarily high salaries to entice them to move to a remote region of the country where they are desperately needed to attend to the medical and health-related needs of the residents there. Similarly, it might also be permissible to provide generous salaries and benefit packages to entrepreneurs who create good jobs with decent wages, benefits, and working conditions for all of their employees. Rawls does not indicate in any detail how much inequality he would allow or how much benefit the least advantaged would need to gain in order to justify the greater rewards for those whose actions warrant them. However, the commonplace contemporary practice of providing scandalously stratospheric bonuses and incentives to CEOs who increase the value of their companies for wealthy shareholders by callously slashing workforces, leaving higher unemployment levels, dislocated, impoverished families, and devastated communities in their wake, clearly would be entirely unacceptable.

Dworkin's (2000) approach is somewhat different. Like Rawls, he is concerned with the unfair advantages that some people have and, like Rawls, he develops a version of equality of condition that justifies considerable state intervention in the redistribution of resources. But his notion of a more 'level playing field' places somewhat greater emphasis upon equality over liberty. He is concerned that the distribution of goods in society is more sensitive to the *choices* people make, based upon their ambitions (including their preferences, goals, and convictions) and their character (including their energy, ability, and industry), and less sensitive to their *circumstances* (social background and other ascriptive characteristics, native endowments, and brute luck). His 'thought experiment', or imaginary society, depicts people arriving on an uninhabited island and immediately faced with the prospect of having to determine the fairest way to apportion the resources available to them. These new 'immigrants' are all given the same level of currency to purchase bundles of goods in an auction. The auction is not complete until everyone in the society is content with the bundle of goods they have purchased and no one in this society would prefer someone else's bundle to their own. He refers to this part as the 'envy test'. In addition to this market mechanism of distribution, he also proposes the use of a secondary market in insurance after the auction is completed. This would allow those who are less naturally talented and those who experience bad luck later on to secure their chosen positions and bundles.[21] However, unlike many other egalitarians, he argues that individuals should then be held responsible for the choices they have made; in short, everyone is given an equal chance to make their own bed, but then they must lie in it—one aspect that would be heartily endorsed by most neo-conservatives today.[22]

Neither Rawls nor Dworkin is a classical, laissez-faire liberal favouring a minimalist 'nightwatchman state'; both defend some version of social or welfare liberalism premised upon the recognition that equality of opportunity cannot be fully realized through simply establishing formal rights. Both of them call for substantial state intervention. Rawls's 'veil of ignorance' and Dworkin's 'auction' were explicitly conceived to minimize social exclusion and increase fairness. Consequently, they were critical of many neo-liberal developments in their American homeland over the past few decades. But neither was very interested in challenging capitalism, the market, or competition among autonomous individuals once starting points are roughly equalized and various social protections firmly in place.

Although it goes well beyond strict equal opportunity, equality of condition is still a species of it and bears many of its weaknesses and limitations. First, it must be acknowledged that, outside of hypothetical thought experiments, it is never possible to completely equalize 'starting points'; there are simply far too many conditions to take into consideration and no way to ensure that people are equally advantaged in all respects. But more importantly, while this ideal is concerned with how people become qualified to enter and win the 'race', it does not question the nature or rules of the game, or the very idea of a competitive contest itself. Thus, it largely accepts equality of opportunity's narrow concern with open access to key positions and posts in society as paramount. It also accepts the steep hierarchical ordering of these positions—and, under certain circumstances, their dramatically different levels of material and symbolic rewards—as natural and just, rather than viewing these conditions as social constructs that advantage and reinforce the position of the powerful and privileged. It is premised upon a conception of 'human nature' that views economic and other forms of incentives as necessary without seriously questioning whether this too is socially created, or contemplating what might be done about it. Like functionalist sociologists, Rawls accepts the widely held notion that people will not use their talents unless they are highly rewarded. Rather than call for a considerably more egalitarian distribution of goods in society to help the least advantaged, he renders their life chances—beyond the 'primary goods' and basic rights provided to all—largely dependent upon the rewards offered to the talented and their ability and willingness to comply. But perhaps most importantly, equality of condition does not fundamentally question inequality itself. Rather it is almost exclusively concerned with fairness, that is, with *how* inequalities are distributed in society. Inequalities and advantages that occur via inheritance, or on the basis of natural endowments or other ascriptive characteristics, or through the unfettered market may not be considered acceptable, but placing people in superior, advantaged, and highly rewarding positions by a fairer competition, or some form of affirmative action, would be acceptable. For Rawls and Dworkin the emphasis is upon *fair access* to these positions, rather than more level outcomes. Thus, equality of condition, like equality opportunity, is primarily about providing people with 'equal chances to become unequal'. Consequently, it undermines any sense of cooperation, community, and solidarity in society and largely ignores issues related to power and democratic control of the workplace and economy. In practice, advocates of equality of condition have called for, and in some places implemented, various forms of state intervention well beyond affirmative action measures, including generous income transfers and an extensive network of social services provided to all as a right of citizenship or residency. At least some of these types of generous and universal programs—most widely and closely embraced in the Nordic lands—begin to address issues more akin to equality of outcome.

Equality of Outcome

Equality of outcome, sometimes referred to as 'equality of result', is the most inclusive and far-reaching conception of equality, but it can be interpreted quite differently, variously requiring minor or more significant reforms to the capitalist system or its replacement with an entirely new socio-economic order.

Critics of the equality of outcome ideal often misrepresent its central concerns, setting up a 'straw man' version that is easily discredited but actually supported by few egalitarians in this camp. First, they sometimes suggest that it begins from an erroneous and romantic notion that people are equal, or at least roughly equal, in their natural capabilities and talents. Its advocates, however, typically harbour no such illusions; people are viewed as no more identical in their levels of intelligence, athletic or physical abilities, temperament, aspirations, or any other skills or characteristics that are said to matter for 'getting ahead' in capitalist society than they are in their weight, height, ethnicity, skin colour, sex, or age.[23] Indeed, like equality of condition, this ideal explicitly holds that people do not have equal opportunities or starting conditions partly *because of* marked differences in talent that are, to a significant degree, viewed as largely dependent upon innate endowments, who your parents are, the social environment you are raised in, brute luck, and so on, and thus arbitrarily allocated. Rather, proponents of equality of outcome simply hold that all people must be equally valued and protected and treated with dignity; no one should be oppressed, exploited, coerced, marginalized, excluded, demeaned, discriminated against, or harmed. However, this ideal does suggest that differences in ability need not culminate in the extraordinarily high levels of material inequality evident in societies today. Even *if* unequal rewards are deemed necessary to provide incentives, they can be limited in both kind and level. For example, it may be that, as in early and contemporary hunting and gathering communities, as well as in other more collectively oriented societies today, somewhat greater emphasis might be placed upon honour or status to reward those who excel at what they do instead of fostering great disparities in wealth and power.

Second, equality of outcome is often criticized for prescribing strict and monotonous uniformity across individuals and groups so that everyone in society ends up with the very same level and kind of resources or rewards irrespective of their abilities, efforts, or choices—a popular theme in many dystopian novels typically depicting failed attempts to create fairer, more egalitarian societies that invariably resemble the Soviet Union and Eastern bloc communism.[24] Using the popular metaphor of a competitive contest again, these critics portray egalitarian societies as perfectly handicapped races in which the more talented are proportionately weighted down so that everyone passes the finish line at the exact same time, garnering the exact same rewards for all competitors. This, too, is gross misrepresentation of what most proponents of the equality of outcome ideal envision. Of course, many basic rights, protections, benefits, and goods would have to be provided for all in any society premised upon equality of outcome. But those upholding this ideal do not necessarily, or typically, suggest that all goods in society have to be distributed equally, or that everyone should have the same level of income or wealth. (Nor, incidentally, have tax-and-transfer programs in any capitalist nation, contrary to the outcry of their neo-liberal and neo-conservative critics, ever even come remotely close to approximating such a goal.) Rather, it is recognized that there is a diversity of needs, preferences, and tastes across individuals and groups. For example, some people are more prone to illness; some would rather have more leisure time than a greater income. Moreover, many equality of outcome advocates largely accept the idea that individuals should be held accountable for choices they make. But they are more cognizant of the social factors that can affect or condition such choices. It is sometimes argued that if someone opts to smoke and, after decades of smoking, he or she contracts lung cancer or other smoking-related health problems, society should not be obligated to provide publicly financed medical care; after all, this person 'chose' to smoke. However, research demonstrates that the chances of someone making such a decision can be closely related to several factors such as social class, ethnicity, whether one's parents smoked, and one's neighbourhood and work environments, as well as a greater vulnerability or predisposition to nicotine addiction. Similarly, people's decisions concerning whether or not to pursue an education is greatly influenced by their social class, the education of their parents, the number of siblings they have, whether they were raised by a single parent, and so on.

Finally, critics of the equality of outcome ideal typically argue that equality and liberty are antithetical; from this perspective greater equality necessarily restricts freedom. However, the view of liberty they espouse is usually the classical, negative variety—'freedom *from*'—and is most often expressed in reference to freedom from the government or state.[25] This is reflected in familiar demands from the wealthiest members of society and powerful corporations for protection from state 'intrusion' or 'interference' in the marketplace—a demand most commonly and emphatically voiced in the Anglo-Saxon world, and especially in the US where, ironically, such intervention is patently least evident. Proponents of equality of outcome roundly reject this view. They too accept the need for freedom 'from'. But their broader interpretation of it acknowledges the need for protection not just from the state but from *all* individuals, groups, and institutions in society that wield great power in its various forms, whether economic, social, ideological, or political. Moreover, they insist that freedom can not be fostered by simply leaving people alone. Indeed, it may be advanced through positive actions taken by governments to support and protect the residents of their nations; this involves considerable freedom '*for*' the state, not just '*from*' it. From this perspective, publicly financed social programs, proportional taxation of income and wealth, protective legislation, and other forms of state intervention are essential to our liberty and our well-being. No one can be truly free or make meaningful choices if they are living in severe deprivation and formally, or more informally, barred from social and political participation in society. Freedom and democracy also necessitate strict limitations on those with great wealth and influence, especially the unrivaled and far-reaching power of large corporations, conglomerates, and other organizations.

Perhaps most importantly, the equality of outcome ideal categorically rejects the notion that society should be conceptualized or organized as a competitive race. Instead, it seeks to replace the 'survival of the fittest' and 'winner-take-all' ethic that underlies capitalism with a greater sense of community, solidarity, cooperation, and self-fulfillment beyond that of only individual gratification. Equality of outcome egalitarians are concerned that all people have a decent standard of living and are able to make meaningful choices; that they are all treated with dignity and all able to develop as autonomous beings and enjoy worthwhile and satisfying lives as full members of society.

How might these general and somewhat vague, if laudable, goals be realized? Equality of outcome would necessitate a broadening and deepening of social rights, opportunities, and entitlements, including an extensive range of resources and services associated with comprehensive welfare states. However, the security of these rights, opportunities, benefits, and entitlements would necessitate a major shift in the balance of power in society and a much more embracing form of democracy that includes economic democracy. The equal opportunity ideal, associated with classical liberalism, is most closely approximated in the US, where the state has made considerable effort to eliminate or weaken many long-standing formal barriers but has introduced very few measures to equalize starting points. Canada and the UK have done considerably better here. Their universal health care programs alone place them somewhat closer toward the equality of condition ideal, but the recent retrenchment of social programs and other measures have rendered them more similar to the US over the past two decades. The Nordic nations have gone farthest in developing a more encompassing form of equality, even if they still have a very long way to go before they can be considered egalitarian. They have generally gone much further than Canada or the UK to bring about greater equality of condition and, through the creation of universal, high quality social services and other measures—which are most developed in Sweden—they have at least begun to move a bit closer to the ideal of equality of outcome.[26]

Right-wing critics of the social democratic Nordic nations routinely denounce them as 'socialist' and imply that they resemble, or are somehow linked to, Eastern bloc communism. Their left-wing critics, in turn, routinely attack them for *not* being socialist, often suggesting that the programs and measures that they have introduced are only marginally different in their character and impact from those in more liberal nations, like the US. The first charge is entirely nonsensical; all of the Nordic lands are capitalist nations with nearly exclusively private ownership and control over the means

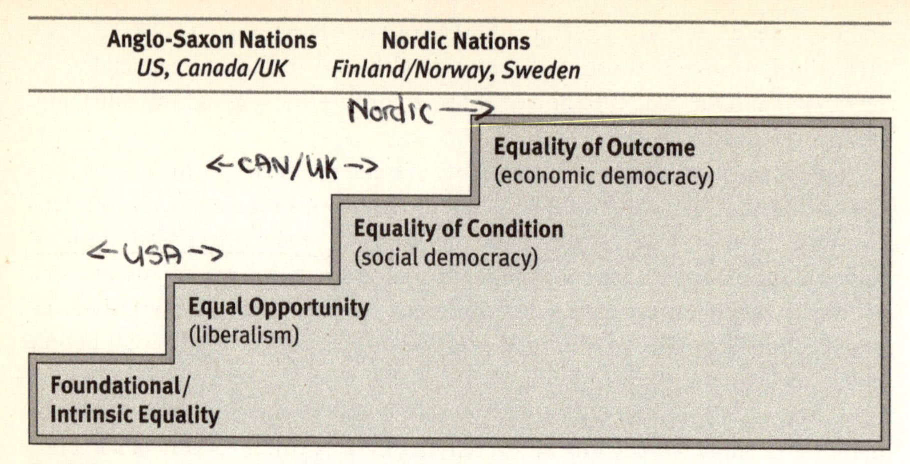

FIGURE 2.1 Cumulative Ideals of Equality in the Anglo and Nordic Nations

of production, and very wealthy and powerful capitalist classes at their apex. Despite their relatively small economies and populations, Sweden had ten billionaires in 2007 (including the seventh-wealthiest person in the world with a fortune valued at $31 billion) while Norway had four. The second charge, as we will see in the next two chapters, is somewhat misleading. The Nordic lands have done remarkably well, from a comparative perspective, in addressing several material and non-material forms of inequality. Their generous income benefits and services, often provided as a right of residency, should not be equated with the tight-fisted, means-tested, and often punitive and brutal programs that characterize the Anglo-Saxon/liberal welfare states, and especially that in the US. And the Nordic nations have typically been among the first to introduce and uphold rights for many groups, including children, women, gays, and people with disabilities, that are often marginalized or excluded. These accomplishments—which are key steps toward the realization of equality of outcome—are too often overlooked or cavalierly dismissed by left-wing critics of the Nordic lands, and of social democracy in general. But these critics are entirely correct to suggest that the achievements in place in the Nordic lands are all too insufficient and insecure.[27] However important and meaningful to the lives of the residents of these countries, they do not constitute fundamental ('non-reformist') reforms. They are designed to 'humanize' the capitalist system, not democratize and transform it. The full realization of equality of outcome would clearly need to address the imbalance in power, and the lack of meaningful participation and influence people have over their work and daily lives, that are inevitable features of systems in which a relatively small group of people own the means of production. It is also necessary to secure and improve the gains that have been made to date.

Notes

1. For example, while everyone may have a right to an education (at least at the primary and secondary levels), health care, and legal or political representation, the wealthy are able to purchase better services and have much greater influence on the political scene.

2. Gracchus Babeuf, who called for equal wages for everyone, is among the few more prominent thinkers that championed a simple, strict form of economic equality. He attacked the French Revolution for betraying its own egalitarian principles and was executed for his role in the Conspiracy of Equals. More recently, some have argued in favour of equality of income and challenged the notion that economic inequality is inevitable or necessary to motivate people in modern market societies. They suggest that it need not reduce economic efficiency nor restrict freedom (Carens 1981). Karl Marx, in contrast, adopted that idea that people should receive resources on the basis of their needs. This idea ('from each according to their ability, to each according to their need', mentioned in his *Critique of the Gotha Program*) was first advocated by the French Utopian Socialists and later embraced by the German Socialists (SPD) in their 1875 *Gotha Program*.

3. Perhaps the most successful examples of strongly, if not strictly, economically egalitarian societies are the kibbutz settlements in Israel and the Mondragón system of primary and secondary cooperatives in the Basque region of Spain. However, they were established as small communities in regions within nations, rather than at the national level.

4. It is often suggested that 'non-citizens', who have not paid into pension programs through taxes and/or contributions, should not be allowed to access benefits. Or, as in the case of post-secondary education, that they should pay higher tuition fees than nationals. Others, however, argue that everyone should have a right to a decent life in old age and that we have moral responsibility to provide for them. Moreover, we are often, directly or indirectly, responsible for the oppressive living conditions of people outside our nation. People living in the developing world, for example, work for sub-poverty wages and labour under some of the worst working conditions to provide cheap goods for people in the developed nations. Large tracts of their land are used by corporations to produce coffee, tobacco, and other products for consumption in the developed world rather than cheap food sources desperately required by the domestic populations there. On the basis of such considerations, and the complicity of states in the advanced capitalist world in fostering these conditions by championing the creation of free trade zones and other neo-liberal policies, it can be argued that many 'outsiders' *should be* entitled to at least some forms of social supports or programs.

5. Strictly speaking, the use of quotas is somewhat different from other forms of affirmative action because they require a particular outcome rather than a particular strategy or effort.

6. Although many people adopt the religious beliefs and outlook of the families they grow up within, creed, like class background, is not an ascribed characteristic like sex or race because it does not have a biological basis.

7. This position should not be equated with that of the opponents of what is commonly referred to as 'reverse discrimination'. Their use of the term 'reverse' (rather than 'positive') discrimination is highly loaded, often suggesting that too much has been done for minorities and other disadvantaged groups already while those that were previously privileged are now the ones who are routinely victimized or treated unfairly.

8. The high level of female representation in the Swedish parliament is largely due to the fact that the long-incumbent and widely supported Social Democratic Party (SAP) adopted the idea of alternating males and females on its list of candidates (the 'zipper system'). With the nation's proportional representation electoral system, this has meant that approximately half of the SAP's members of parliament are women. Other parties in Sweden have also sought to increase their representation of women.

9. Useful overviews and critical accounts of various ideals or forms of equality can be found in Arneson (2002), Clayton and Williams (2000), Mason (1998), and Tawney (1952 [1931]).

10. Hinduism, with its endorsement of the caste system, may be something of an exception to this ideal. However, even here all people have the opportunity to gradually move up through the hierarchy of castes to become part of Brahman (God) by faithfully and unquestioningly carrying out the behaviours appropriate to their station.

11. Of course, a humanistic justification for equality need not appeal to divine entities. Rationality—the ability to act for a reason—is often invoked as a characteristic that distinguishes humans from all other creatures and requires that they all be treated and respected equally. Although the soundness of such reasoning might vary, its universality is what matters. Similarly, Avishai Margalit (1996:71) suggests that equal respect can be justified on the basis that it is only humans who have the capacity to evaluate and re-evaluate their lives at any time and dramatically change them: 'Thus, respecting humans means never giving up on anyone, since all people are capable of living dramatically differently from the way they have lived so far'.

12. However, religious groups and movements are often strong advocates for equality, too, and have sometimes constructed egalitarian communities. Liberation theology is associated with a grass roots movement that emerged in rural Central and South America in the 1960s from within the Catholic Church. It challenged the Church's traditional role as defender of the status quo—and the exploitation and oppression of the poor by the rich—sometimes advocating revolution as the means of emancipation. And the Hutterites, an Anabaptist Christian sect founded by Jacob Hutter, migrated from Germany to Russia and then to Canada and the US, where they established egalitarian colonies based upon ideas of Christian community and equality.

13. Anatole France, the French author and Nobel laureate, is the pen name of Jacques Anatole François Thibault. This famous quote is from *Le Lys Rouge* (*The Red Lily*, 1894).

14. Many egalitarians have used Christian or other religious belief systems that stress intrinsic equality as a foundation for establishing a broader and much more extensive vision of equality.

15. Other characteristics, however, such as academic credentials or a criminal record are typically considered quite acceptable as bases for 'discrimination'.

16. This idea that someone who is talented may rise to the top from a low starting point or position of disadvantage was memorably illustrated in the famous maxim attributed to Napoleon Bonaparte: 'Every private in the army has a field marshall's baton in his knapsack'.

17. While placing the name of every applicant for a job into a barrel and randomly selecting one winner might, at least technically, qualify as a form of formal equal opportunity, it would clearly not suffice as a form of meritocratic equal opportunity.

18. Of course, it should be remembered that most caring work (e.g., child care, elderly care, care of the disabled, and so on) is performed by women as *paid* labour within the Swedish (and Nordic) labour market whereas in many other 'liberal' nations (such as Canada, the UK, and the US) and 'conservative' nations (such as Austria, Belgium, and Germany) this work is often performed as *unpaid* labour within the family or the voluntary sector, and hence excluded from official accounts of labour force participation rates and segregation (Nermo 1999). Women in Sweden also tend to work relatively long part-time hours, from a cross-national perspective. Sweden has also introduced policies to encourage women and men to enter non-gender-traditional

positions and occupations and encourage fathers to spend more time caring for their children—part of an attempt at 'gender reconstruction'.

19. 'Brute luck' is sometimes contrasted with 'option luck', which is more closely linked to deliberate choices people make. Being hit by a car when you are walking on the sidewalk is an example of bad brute luck; being hit when you are jay-walking or cross against a red light is an example of bad option luck because you chose to take a calculated gamble and lost. However, our luck oftentimes involves a mix of both; that is, it may be neither entirely imposed nor chosen voluntarily. People living near a fault line on the west coast of North America may be aware of the danger of doing so, but moving elsewhere may not be a viable or realistic option for them.

20. The idea of a 'social contract' has a long history dating back at least to Plato and is associated with the theories of many central political philosophers, including Hobbes, Locke, and Rousseau.

21. Unlike Rawls, Dworkin argues that people must be aware of their talents in his hypothetical scenario, or they give away too much of their personality to leave any basis for speculation about their ambitions. Some neo-liberal critics, such as Robert Nozick (1974), suggest that differences in natural talent are a central part of what most people commonly mean by 'dessert' and an entirely acceptable, even if ascriptive, basis for inequality. Rejecting our innate abilities as grounds for inequality, he suggests, would also negate our ability to take credit for our accomplishments and undermine our sense of who we are and our unique personalities.

22. Dworkin's notion of a neutral market (auction) does not take into account the long-standing feminist observation that choices made by certain groups of people, such as men and women, can be greatly influenced by their socialization and the construction of gender personalities that restricts or shapes their visions. Given their training and experience, women, for example, may 'choose' positions and goods related to caring and remain in the private, familial sphere.

23. Nor do they argue that there is some kind of overall fairness in the design of the universe that ensures that if someone has a deficit in one area, such as intelligence, it is made up for by greater skill in another, although this is sometimes attributed to them.

24. Such depictions have been provided by well-known authors from across the political spectrum including Aldous Huxley (*Brave New World*), George Orwell (*Animal Farm*; *1984*), Ayn Rand (*Anthem*; *Atlas Shrugged*), Kurt Vonnegut (*Player Piano*; *Harrison Bergeron*), and the Russian author who inspired them all, Yevgeny Zamyatin (*We*).

25. The distinction between 'negative' and 'positive' freedom is set out by Isaiah Berlin (1969).

26. Social democracy is commonly associated with the view that, through the introduction of a wide range of social programs and regulations, the capitalist system can be reformed and made more acceptable, and many forms of inequality can be eradicated or reduced. From a social democratic perspective, there is no real conflict between capitalism and these goals. For democratic socialism, in contrast, some form of economic democracy that places control over the means of production is also an important goal. Moreover, it is essential to protect and preserve the benefits achieved through social democratic measures that 'humanize' capitalism.

27. As their critics suggest, social democratic/labour parties have typically shown very little interest in proposals to democratize the capitalist system and, as in the case of the Swedish wage-earner fund program, have often vehemently opposed such measures. However radical social democratic parties might sound when they are not in office, once they assume power, they have typically become almost entirely preoccupied with administering the existing system and staying in office as long as possible.

Part II

Measuring Inequality: Non-Material and Material Indicators

3 Material Indicators of Inequality: Poverty, Income, Wealth, and Life Chances

When most people consider inequality they typically think about asymmetrical economic or material distributions in society. The dispersion of economic resources, such as income and wealth, and other closely related distributional patterns and concerns—including the levels of poverty and homelessness in society, the opportunities for social mobility, and health status among various segments of the population—are among the most central material indicators of social inequality in society. These dimensions of material inequality are almost always very tightly interlinked. People with very low levels of income, for example, often suffer from more health problems and have shorter life expectancies than people who are more affluent. They are more likely to have lower levels of education and endure various forms of social exclusion; they have far fewer opportunities for advancement; they are more likely to be incarcerated. Without an adequate level of material resources people are more easily marginalized, less able to take advantage of many of their formal rights and social protections, and unable to fully participate in society.

Over the past few decades material inequality has grown virtually everywhere and the gulf between the wealthy and the poor has become much wider. But inequality is significantly higher, and has risen much faster, in the US and the other Anglo-Saxon nations. Indeed, the income and wealth disparities and other related forms of inequality in the United States today closely resemble those of its infamous nineteenth-century 'Gilded Age'[1]. During that period great fortunes were amassed and great empires built by opportunistic industrialists, financiers, and rail magnates such as John P. Morgan, John D. Rockefeller, Andrew Carnegie, Cornelius Vanderbilt, and the other 'robber barons' who used their economic might to attain corporate subsidies, tax relief, land grants, access to the nation's natural resources, and permission to build national railways from federal and state governments, even while the workers they employed, and their families, struggled to survive. The police and the army (the coercive branches of the state) often largely operated as corporate subsidiaries—public-sector counterparts to private forces, such as the Pinkerton National Detective Agency—that capitalists routinely mobilized to counter strikes, uprisings, and other demonstrations of discontent by their severely underpaid and overworked workers. By the late 1800s even former American president Rutherford B. Hayes had acknowledged in his diary that the nation's real problem was the vast amount of wealth and power in the hands of the unscrupulous few who represented and controlled capital. Reworking a well-known phrase from Lincoln's 1863 Gettysburg address, Hayes aptly noted that government in the United States had become one 'of corporations, by corporations and for corporations' (quoted in Thelen 1970). During this period in American history, as today, government support was deemed beneficial only for corporations and wealthy elites. The best medicine for the poor and lower classes, contrarily, was to be constantly subjected to the harsh discipline of the market. Nineteenth-century poor relief measures were, from the outset and by conscious design, meagre and very difficult to access in order to ensure that the poor would accept the deplorable working conditions and starvation wages of the jobs the market provided for them. Spencer's 'social Darwinism', with its notion of natural hierarchies based upon inherent talents, was welcomed by many of the most prominent and powerful capitalists of the period; indeed, both Carnegie and Rockefeller soon became devoted disciples (Hofstadter 1955). For them, Spencer's work 'scientifically' sanctioned laissez-faire capitalism, widespread poverty, and the concentration of wealth and power, a view that has regained currency today.

Measuring Socio-economic Well-being Across Nations

GDP per Capita: A Popular but Misleading Measure of Well-being

Official and popular accounts of the prosperity, well-being, and progress of nations typically rely upon narrow economic or business measures. The size of the deficit, the rate of inflation, the balance of trade, accounts of consumer confidence, indices of the strength of stock markets (such as the Dow Jones Industrial Average or TSX Composite Index), and numerous other 'leading economic indicators' are routinely furnished by governments and the media as accurate and reliable portrayals of how well nations are faring. These measures greatly influence the way public policy is set today. The most revered and influential of such popular indicators is the Gross Domestic Product (GDP), a closely followed and widely quoted measure of total economic output. Put simply, the GDP tracks the size and growth of the overall economy. It tells us the monetary value of all of the goods and services provided within a nation (excluding transactions with other countries) during a specified time period, usually one year.[2]

GDP has long been widely employed as a proxy for economic progress and socio-economic well-being, but it not very well-suited to that task. Nor was it ever intended to be. Estimates of national wealth in the western world have a long history dating back to the seventeenth and eighteenth centuries in England and France, but contemporary measures of economic growth are closely based upon the work of British economist John Maynard Keynes (1883–1946) and, especially, that of Simon Kuznets (1901–1985), an American econometrician and winner of the Nobel Prize in economics in 1971. Keynes helped to devise policy mechanisms to boost economic growth during the Depression of the 1930s and smooth out the business cycle. He was also a driving force behind the creation of the modern welfare state. But it was Kuznets, the 'father of national income analysis', who developed the widely adopted measures of economic growth upon which the GDP is based today. Kuznets, however, expressed deep reservations about using such accounts of national income and economic expansion to gauge the welfare or well-being of nations because they did not distinguish between the *quantity* and *quality* of economic growth. Almost from the outset he called for better and more inclusive kinds of measures. Numerous other economists, including several other Nobel laureates, such as Amartya Sen and James Tobin, have also expressed deep reservations about the use of this measure. But their concerns and warnings have been largely ignored. Governments, politicians, the media, and others have found the prospect of reducing a very complex story to a single, all-purpose index far too irresistible. And powerful economic interests benefit greatly from the use of measures that treat all market activities—even those that result in significant social erosion and decay—as unquestionably positive (Cobb et al. 1995; Halstead and Cobb 1996).

Although it is the broadest of the popular economic indices, GDP is too restricted to even provide an accurate measure of a very narrowly *economic* account of national well-being and progress because it is based upon a pair of quite erroneous assumptions: (1) that growth is always good and (2) that everyone benefits from growth. The first assumption has two basic defects: what it includes in its calculations and what it excludes from consideration. GDP is the sum total of *all* of the goods and services provided in the market. But many of these commodities and activities are irrelevant to national well-being or may actually reflect a decline in the standard of living. A high GDP does not necessarily mean that life is getting better for people. Production that depletes non-renewable natural resources and degrades the environment, as well as the costs of cleaning up oil spills and repairing other forms of damage to the ecosystem, are all included in the GDP, but they are obviously not signs of progress and show little regard for the well-being of national populations or future generations. GDP also includes many contradictory goods and services, such as the production of cancer-causing cigarettes and several other forms of addictive consumption, as well as medical services and pharmaceuticals developed to address problems and illnesses related to such addictive products. The fast food industry, which makes people overweight and unhealthy, the advertising and gimmicks it uses to get them to consume more, and the growing medical bills for liposuction and other forms of treatment and products to restore health also greatly inflate the level of GDP. So, too, do greater expenditures related to auto accidents caused by overly crowded highways; the locks, alarms, protection devices, insurance, and other services associated with higher crime rates; and higher lawyers' fees in increasingly litigious societies. With the proliferation of automated teller machines, which were supposed to lower banking costs, we now often pay to access our own money, yet another innovation that increases the size of a nation's GDP. Other compulsory costs, such as that of bloated executive pay packages, passed on to consumers through the higher price of goods in the market, and numerous expenditures related to disasters and wars further inflate the GDP but clearly have little to do with national progress or our well-being. The use of GDP as a standard for our national welfare not only conceals an extensive array of forms of social breakdown, environmental destruction, and other socially toxic and costly developments—euphemistically referred to as 'collateral damage' or external 'dis-economies' when they are acknowledged—but also records and heralds them as gains.

GDP also excludes important dimensions of the quality or standard of living in a nation from consideration. It omits all non-market transactions from its purview; volunteer work and raising children, for example, are not counted. If someone produces a commodity for their own use, or provides a service for someone, it is not included in the calculation of the GDP. But if they sell that same product or service to someone, the GDP grows.[3] The loss of leisure time and the ruptures to family life when people are forced to take two jobs just to keep up with inflation do not factor into GDP either. Rather, this heightened level of activity, increasingly commonplace in the Anglo-Saxon nations, is blithely recorded as economic growth. Conversely, GDP does not register the higher living standards that derive, for example, from the longer vacations, extensive family leave programs, and shorter working weeks in Sweden and the other Nordic lands. Important social and economic issues such as poverty, hunger, homelessness, illiteracy, and crime rates, and a range of social inequalities and problems in societies can be largely sidestepped.

The second assumption underlying the use of the GDP is that everyone in society necessarily benefits when the GDP is high and climbing. This notion is especially deceptive when GDP is expressed on a per capita basis, which erroneously implies that the wealth that is created in a nation is widely shared among all individuals in society. US President John F. Kennedy's often-quoted adage—'a rising tide lifts all boats'—suggests that the best way to improve everyone's well-being, including those at the bottom end of socio-economic hierarchies, is by stimulating the economy. But in the absence of redistributive fiscal and social policies and other protective measures and organizations, economic growth often raises only the luxury liners and the yachts while swamping or sinking smaller craft, and leaving others bereft of boats altogether stranded on the shore. Indeed, economic and social inequality can actually increase dramatically when GDP is growing. The rates of poverty, homelessness, and inequality in the US, for example, are unprecedented in the modern era, despite sustained periods of high economic growth. The US is often celebrated as the wealthiest nation in the capitalist world. However, this notion is misleading; it suggests that all US residents benefit from its great wealth and periods of high and rapid growth. It is perhaps more accurate to note that great wealth is concentrated in the US and the nation has more of the world's wealthiest people than do other nations. While this group is not numerically large, it owns and controls a very large portion of the wealth and property in the US and across the globe. At the same time, the US has much higher rates of income and wealth inequality and poverty than most other nations in the advanced capitalist world. As Ted Halstead and Clifford Cobb (1996:199) note, the use of GDP as a measure of social progress and well-being 'reflects the desire of major forces in the economy to keep social and environmental destruction out of sight and therefore out of mind. It perpetuates illusions that progress and national well-being should be judged according to only one standard: the volume of production and consumption'.

Of course, many developments associated with economic expansion can and do greatly improve our well-being. But like the increases registered on our bathroom scales, economic growth is not necessarily a positive development. Critics of the widely employed GDP measure aptly liken it to a broken calculator that can only add; it is unable to process social stresses and strains, declining living standards, the need to work more hours to make ends meet, and myriad other social costs and forms of social decay. It also omits aspects of social life that people value most, including economic security, more family time, healthier lives and longer life spans, lower crime rates, and cleaner environments. And, contrary to the quotidian pronouncements of incumbent politicians and government officials seeking public accolades and re-election, it does not necessarily improve living standards for all.[4]

Mindful of the serious limitations of GDP as an indicator of national welfare, several researchers have developed more thoughtful and inclusive composite indices to more accurately gauge how well nations are doing. The Index of Social Health (ISH), for example, allows us to track trends across sixteen social indicators, including family income, child poverty, health care, infant mortality rates, education, the availability of affordable housing, crime trends, and drug use (Miringoff and Miringoff 1999). Another similar measure, the Genuine Progress Indicator (GPI), takes into account over twenty indicators, including estimates of the value of parenting, household and volunteer work, and the actual distribution of income in society, as well as several measures of social breakdown, such as crime rates, pollution, resource depletion, long-term environmental damage, and the loss of leisure time, that diminish social well-being (Talberth et al. 2006; Venetoulis and Cobb 2004). Research using such social barometers clearly indicates that the quality of life in the US has been declining over the past few decades in tandem with economic growth. While not without their problems or critics, these comprehensive indices provide much more reliable, valid, and useful accounts of national well-being than simple gross tallies of the monetary value of everything produced within a nation. Cross-national studies based upon similar broad, composite measures also indicate that the Nordic lands outperform the Anglo-Saxon nations. In a study of seventeen developed nations using a comprehensive Weighted Index of Social Progress (WISP) including measures of over forty social, economic, and political indicators across ten sub-categories (including education, health, the environment, demography, the status of women, social chaos, and welfare effort), the Nordic lands ranked first, the UK placed tenth, and the US was last (Estes 2004a, 2004b).[5] The next section closely examines a few key dimensions of material inequality in the Anglo-Saxon and Nordic nations.

The Distribution of Income and Wealth

The Distribution of Income

The distribution of **income** is one central dimension that is often employed to gauge the level of material inequality in society. This is understandable. First, income is a critical and highly valued resource in society because, as Aristotle (2004 [350 BCE]) noted more than two thousand years ago, it allows people to access and secure many of the goods and opportunities that they need and desire. Income is only one means to these ends, but it is a crucial one. And, second, while inequality is a very abstract concept that is difficult to quantify even when focused upon strictly material concerns, the distribution of income can be measured with a considerable degree of precision.

Income refers to the *flow* of money and goods to individuals, groups, households, or some other economic unit over a particular time period, usually a year. It includes earnings (salaries and wages) from employment and self-employment and other financial flows of money, such as dividends, interests, rent, and royalties, that accrue from savings or the ownership of property and other assets. It also includes public sector transfer payments (such as pensions and survivor's benefits; maternity, parental, paternity, and other family leave benefits; sickness benefits; social or public assistance; unemployment insurance and assistance payments; child allowances; veterans' benefits; educational grants and scholarships; and so on), various private sector social programs and benefits (such as occupational or workplace pensions), alimony, child support, and other 'in kind' monies, such as food stamps or the use of company cars.

Sociologists and economists employ several methods to measure, express, and track levels of income inequality in societies. The most standard or commonly employed measure of income inequality is the **Gini coefficient**. Devised by the Italian statistician and demographer Corrado Gini (1884–1965), the Gini coefficient provides a summary statistic of the relative size of income inequality in society. The value of the Gini coefficient ranges from 0 to 1. A Gini coefficient of 0 represents 'perfect equality'. It indicates that income in society is evenly dispersed across all of the income-earning units examined (individuals or households); each of them has exactly the same income. A Gini coefficient of 1 represents 'perfect inequality', indicating that all of the income in society is going to only one income-earning unit (individual or household), leaving all of the others without any income at all. In reality, of course, neither of these two extremes is ever obtained, but the Gini coefficient tells us how close the distribution in a given society is to 'perfect equality' or 'perfect inequality'; the higher the Gini coefficient, the higher the level of inequality.

The Gini coefficients listed in Tables 3.1 and 3.2 indicate something useful about the distribution of income across and within the Anglo-Saxon and Nordic worlds over time. Table 3.1 clearly shows that income inequality has increased in all three Anglo-Saxon nations since the 1970s. The US, the nation with the highest level of income inequality (0.372, the highest Gini coefficient) among them over the entire period examined here, has also experienced the largest increase in income inequality. Income inequality in the UK, which was the lowest (0.268) among the three Anglo-Saxon nations in the mid-1970s, has also increased dramatically. The level of income inequality in the UK surpassed that in Canada by the mid-1980s and has remained higher ever since.

TABLE 3.1 Income Inequality: Gini Coefficients and Percentile Ratios in Three Anglo Nations: Canada, the UK, and the US

	Canada			UK			US		
	1975	**1987**	**2004**	**1974**	**1986**	**2004**	**1974**	**1986**	**2004**
Gini Coefficient of Inequality	0.289	0.283	0.318	0.268	0.303	0.345	0.318	0.335	0.372
Percentile Ratios:									
P90/P10	4.3	3.9	4.4	3.4	3.8	4.5	4.9	5.7	5.7

Source: LIS (nd) Database: Key Figures.

TABLE 3.2 Income Inequality: Gini Coefficients and Percentile Ratios in Three Nordic Nations: Finland, Norway, Sweden

	Finland			Norway			Sweden		
	1974	1987	2004	1979	1986	2004	1975	1987	2005
Gini Coefficient of Inequality	n/a	0.209	0.252	0.223	0.233	0.256	0.215	0.218	0.237
Decile Ratios:									
P90/P10	n/a	2.6	3.0	2.8	2.9	2.9	2.7	2.7	2.8

Source: LIS (nd) Database: Key Figures.

Table 3.2 indicates an increase in income inequality across all three of the Nordic nations during this time period as well, with the greatest surge in Sweden. But income inequality has been, and remains, much lower in these three countries. Indeed, the highest level of income inequality across the three Nordic lands over this period was 0.252 in Finland in 2004. But this Gini coefficient was still lower than that achieved three decades earlier in the UK (0.268 in 1974), the lowest level achieved by any of the Anglo-Saxon nations, and that at time when inequality levels were relatively low in all of the nations. Moreover, income inequality began to decline again in Sweden between 2000 (0.252) and 2005 (0.237).

Another way to measure income inequality is through the use of **decile ratios**. To use this measure, all of the income earners (individuals or households) in society are ordered from the lowest income to the highest and are then divided into ten groups of equal size, called deciles (or tenths). Like the Gini coefficients, the decile ratios in Tables 3.1 and 3.2 indicate that inequality has been much higher in the Anglo-Saxon nations than in the Nordic lands, and that it has been rising since the mid-1970s. The highest level of inequality is seen in the US again, where the incomes of those at the 90th percentile were 5.7 times that of the incomes of those at the 10th percentile in 2004 (this is called 'P90/P10 inequality'). The UK had the second highest level of P90/P10 inequality, but the *increase* between the mid-1970s and 2004 was even greater here than in it was in the US. The level of P90/P10 inequality in Canada showed little change over this period. Income inequality was markedly lower over this period in the Nordic group, with the 90th percentile receiving less than three times the income of the 10th percentile in all countries.

We can also compare the levels of income inequality by examining the share of total income going to the lowest and highest deciles in each of the six nations. The share of the total income in society going to the top 10% of income earners in the UK (28.5%) and the US (30%) was higher than in Finland (23%), Norway (23%) and Sweden (22%). However, at 25%, the share of income going to the top 10% in Canada was closer to that in the Nordic lands. Correspondingly, the share of the total income going to the lowest deciles (between 3.6% and 4%) was higher in the three

Nordic lands than in the US (1.9%), the UK (2.1%) and Canada (2.6%) (United Nations 2009). While the discrepancies in the distribution of income between the two groups of nations are not great, they are substantial enough to make a difference to the lives of those at the bottom. The higher level of income going to the lower deciles of income earners in the Nordic lands, and the lower levels accruing to the top deciles, reflect the impact of social programs and fiscal policies. Social and fiscal measures in the Anglo-Saxon nations clearly have not been as redistributive. This does not mean, however, that they have not had any impact; without them, the distribution of income in these nations would be much more unequal.

Yet another way to compare income inequality across these nations is to examine the **distribution of income among households** in each nation to see what percentage of those households could be classified as (1) **poor** (households with incomes that are less than 50% of the nation's median income), (2) **near poor** (households with incomes that are between 50% and 62.5% of the nation's median income), (3) **middle class** (households with incomes that are between 62.5% and 150% of the nation's median income, and (4) **well-to-do** (households with incomes that are above 150% of the nation's median income. As Figures 3.1 and 3.2 indicate, the size of the middle class, circa 2004/2005, was much larger in the Nordic lands (between 69%

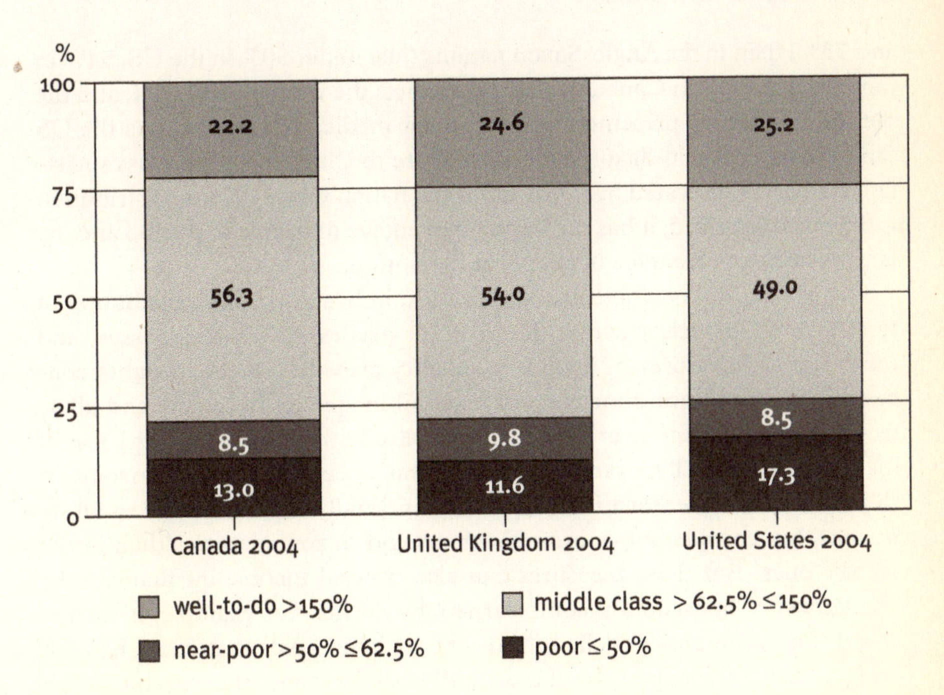

FIGURE 3.1 Distribution of Households by Income Categories Defined as a Percentage of Median Equivalent Disposable Household Income in the Anglo-Saxon Nations 2004

Source: LIS (calculations: Piotr Paradowski).

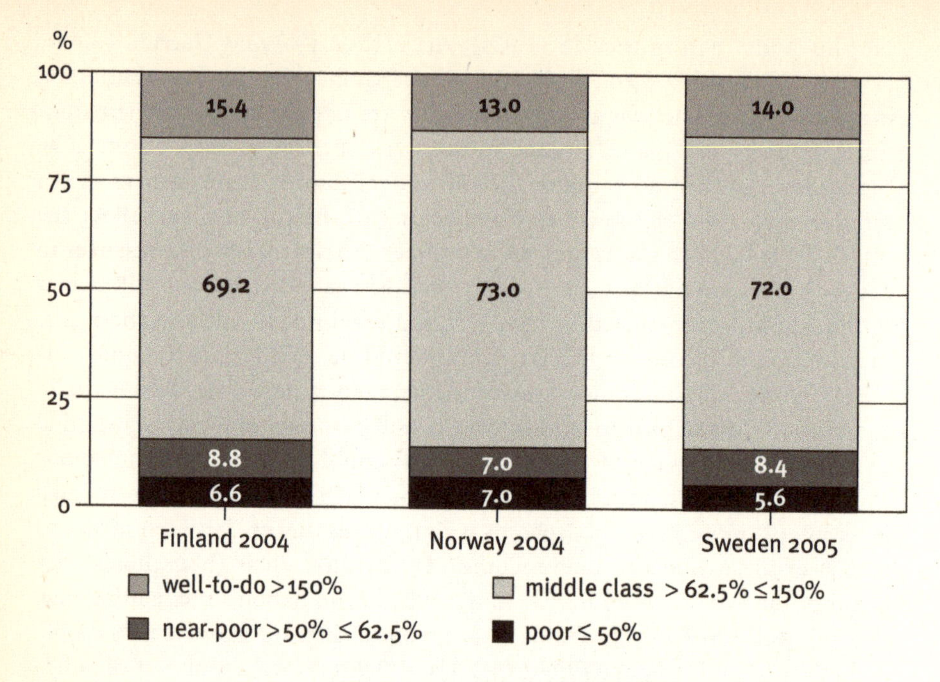

FIGURE 3.2 Distribution of Households by Income Categories Defined as a Percentage of Median Equivalent Disposable Household Income in the Nordic Nations 2004/2005

Source: LIS (calculations: Piotr Paradowski).

and 73%) than in the Anglo-Saxon nations (just under 50% in the US, 54% in the UK, and 56% in Canada). This contradicts the widespread belief, and the messages routinely presented in the popular media, that suggest it is the US (and the other Anglo-Saxon nations) that are the 'largely middle class societies'. Rather, as indicated here, the US is the nation where income distribution is the most polarized; it has the largest percentage of people at the top and, by far, the largest percentage of people at the bottom.

The use of Gini coefficients, decile ratios, indicators of the distribution of total income in society across quintiles (or deciles) or income-classes, and other similar measures of income inequality provide valuable insights concerning an important dimension of material inequality in society and allow us to observe change over time and compare nations. Through the use of income or deciles, for example, we can clearly see that the total income in the six nations under scrutiny here is very unequally distributed across all six nations, but considerably more so in the Anglo-Saxon countries than in the Nordic ones. But these measures can also conceal income inequality. The breakdown of household income earners by deciles, for example, is far too broad. First, the upper decile includes many households that could be considered part of the upper end of the middle class. Second, the extremely high percentage of total income going to the top 1%—the group that experienced soaring income increases over the past few decades—is hidden, buried within the upper decile. This increase reflects the higher salaries of those at the very top but, more importantly, it also reflects the increasing role of 'capital income' (income from interest, dividends, and capital gains) as a source of total income over this period. In the US in 2006 the top 20% (one-fifth) of households received 84% (over four-fifths) of all of the capital income; the top 1% of households received over one-half (55.3%) of all capital income; and the top 0.1% of households received over one-third (36.6%) of all capital income. Together, the bottom four-fifths (80%) of all households received only 15.2% of total capital income (Mishel et al. 2008). About 70% of the household income of this large group is derived from wages and salaries, and only 4% of it comes from capital income. In Canada the average earnings of the richest 10% of families was 82 times that earned by the poorest 10% of families in 2004, the highest income gap between the rich and the poor in the nation for three decades (Yalnizyan 2007). Wage restraint and other government policies fostering rapid growth in the financial markets were largely responsible for the surging income gap separating the wealthy and the great majority who largely rely upon wage and salary income to live; indeed, these measures helped to ensure that economic gains gushed upward, instead of 'trickling down'.

The exorbitant incomes of some of the highest paid entertainers, actors, authors, athletes, and models, such as Tiger Woods ($115 million), Shawn 'Jay-Z' Carter ($82 million in 2007), Beyoncé Knowles ($80 million), Will Smith ($80 million), Johnny Depp ($72 million), Howard Stern ($70 million), Eddie Murphy ($55 million), David Beckham ($50 million), Cameron Diaz ($50 million), Stephen King ($45 million), and Gisele Bündchen ($35 million), are often ebulliently endorsed in popular celebrity magazines.[6] But their incomes can be somewhat more unpredictable, vacillating markedly over the years with their popularity with a sometimes fickle and unpredictable public. And outside the US, where celebrity has sometimes helped facilitate the attainment of the highest political offices at the municipal level (e.g., actor/mayor of Carmel Clint Eastwood and entertainer/mayor of Palm Springs Sonny Bono), state level (e.g., actor/California Governor Arnold Schwarzenegger and professional wrestler/Minnesotan Governor Jesse Ventura), and the national level (actor/President Ronald Reagan), the high incomes of celebrities are not typically associated with significant economic power or political influence. The incomes received by those at the top of the corporate world are much less familiar, but they have climbed much more dramatically over the past two decades. Moreover, given their association with great wealth and managerial control over the largest corporations, their incomes *are* linked to great power.

In 1980 the average income of the top executives was 42 times that received by the average blue-collar worker in the US; by 2006 it was 364 times greater (Anderson et al. 2007).[7] The annual compensation packages of those at the very top are mind-boggling. For example, between 1998 and 2003, Michael Eisner of the Walt Disney Company received, on average, $121 million per year; Reuben Mark of Colgate-Palmolive received $141 million in 2003; and Lawrence Ellison of Oracle received $781.4 million between 2000 and 2002 (Burton and Weller 2005). The average annual income among the top 20 private equity and hedge fund managers in the US was $657.5 million, or 22,255 times the pay of the average worker. In Canada, Chief Executive Officers' (CEOs) salaries were considerably lower, but the 100 highest-paid CEOs still received 218 times as much as the average worker in 2006. This reflected an increase of 146% since 1998; average salaries and wages, by contrast, increased by only 18% during this same period. The top CEOs in Canada receive the average annual Canadian wage every 9 hours and 33 minutes (Mackenzie 2007).

Astronomical incomes in the corporate world are typically justified on grounds that those at the top are performing important leadership roles that must be highly compensated; it is often said that 'if you pay peanuts, you attract monkeys'. Apart from the fact that this same logic is rarely applied to other employees—who apparently must be motivated by desperation and the fear of losing their jobs instead—it cannot account for the fact that the incomes of the highest-paid leaders in other sectors in society are not comparable. In the US, for example, the heads of non-profit organizations, members of Congress and the executive branch of the federal government (the President, Vice-President, and members of the Cabinet), and military leaders receive much less than leaders in the corporate world. Of course, the compensation packages received by the CEOs in most other advanced capitalist nations are also far greater than those received by most other leaders in their nations. But their compensation does not even approximate that of their American counterparts. By the late 1990s, for example, the average total remuneration for the top CEOs in the US ($1,072,400) was much higher than that in the UK ($645,540), Canada ($498,118), or Sweden ($355,398) (Towers Perrin 1998). Another more recent study noted that the average CEO compensation package across thirteen advanced capitalist nations ($748,904) was only about one-third of that received in the US ($2,249,080).[8] Moreover, current CEO compensation packages increasingly feature a wide array of perquisites and other tax-free, or heavily tax-advantaged, forms of remuneration to take advantage of lower (and declining) tax rates on capital income (Burton and Weller 2005; Mishel et al. 2005).

The total compensation of the highest-paid executives has grown much more rapidly than corporate earnings and comes at the expense of both shareholders and workers. Rather than being a justifiable reward for leadership and performance, compensation of CEOs is (according to several studies) grossly excessive because CEOs enjoy very close ties to the directors who establish and shape their compensation packages (AFL–CIO 1998; Bebchuk and Grinstein 2005; Burton and Weller 2005). However important the distribution of income, the distribution of wealth is an even more crucial determinant of economic well-being, and much more closely linked to power. Wealth is often neglected in accounts of inequality, but it is much more unevenly distributed.

The Distribution of Wealth

Wealth refers to property, the stock of tangible and intangible possessions with a market value, held by individuals or households at a particular point in time. It is a much broader category than income and includes (1) **liquid financial assets**, such as cash, deposits, savings bonds, and guaranteed investment certificates (GICs) that are easily converted into money, as well as (2) **non-liquid assets**, such as stocks and shares, registered retirement savings plans, real estate, owner-occupied homes, cottages, the net value of unincorporated businesses, farms or professional practices, jewelry, antiques, works of art, vehicles, appliances, and other consumer durables. The wealth of an individual, household, or other economic unit is determined by totaling the value of the assets they hold and subtracting the value of their debts at a particular moment in time (Keister 2000).

The distribution of wealth in advanced capitalist nations varies much more widely than that of income, and for several reasons it is a much more consequential dimension of social inequality in society. First, as noted above, wealth can be used to generate income (via rent, royalties, interest, and dividends). But, because wealth typically appreciates over time, it also generates more wealth.[9] Furthermore, it can be used as collateral to secure large loans for further investment. Many of the wealthiest people in the world have leveraged their assets this way to significantly increase their riches. Like high income, great wealth can be used to access myriad luxuries and advantages, including safer environments, better health care, longer and more extravagant leisure time, and greater economic security. And, unlike income, wealth, in some forms, such as art or homes, can be enjoyed without being consumed. It also can be used to purchase greater freedom and autonomy by reducing or eliminating the need to work (Keister 2000; Spilerman 2000). While some approximation of 'equal opportunity', a central plank of liberalism, is widely accepted by most people as a reality in modern capitalist societies, very few people believe that the affluent do not enjoy infinitely greater opportunities to substantially improve their own socio-economic position and that of their children than those who are less well-off. Indeed, one of the central reasons that the rich accumulate wealth is to ensure—through inheritance, access to the best schools, and their carefully cultivated networks of social and political connections—significant advantages and opportunities for their progeny.

In addition to these socio-economic advantages, significant wealth can also furnish great political influence. The wealthy can use their economic resources to directly shape the political process by bankrolling political parties, candidates, and lobbyists; establishing research institutes, think tanks, and foundations that promote their interests and policy positions; and, through their ownership of the media or its heavy reliance upon their advertising dollars, shaping political discussions and debates. They can also reward compliant politicians with large monetary gifts and the promise of influential and highly paid positions within their enterprises when they leave political office. These kinds of influence over governments and state policy, in turn, enable the rich to foster a socio-economic environment that further increases their wealth and power. Directly and indirectly, the power of those who control large corporations and capital also greatly influences what governments—fearful of the impact of investment strikes and capital flight on their incumbency—will do. Although great wealth can confer great economic and political power on its holders, and is clearly a principal determinant of their life chances and living standards, it is commonly neglected in conventional mainstream studies of inequality and stratification because it does not easily fit with the dominant liberal ideology, or related theoretical traditions that are informed by it—political traditions that stress the role of 'natural ability', merit, and hard work over inheritance and privilege, which are viewed as characteristics of pre-capitalist societies.

Given its more inclusive and complex composition and the varied sources relied upon for data across nations, the distribution of wealth is much more difficult than income to examine comparatively. However, cross-national studies of wealth inequality have begun to appear in recent years (Davies et al. 2008; Sierminksa et al. 2006; Wolff 1996, 2002, 2006). This research generally suggests that (1) levels of wealth inequality far surpass those of income inequality in virtually every nation that has been studied, (2) the US has one of the highest levels of wealth inequality in the developed world, and (3) wealth inequality in the US has grown more rapidly over the past few decades than it has in most other advanced capitalist nations.

Almost by definition, capitalist societies are characterized by extremely high levels of wealth inequality. A very small percentage of the population in all capitalist nations owns a very significant level of capital. The wealth of most families is largely restricted to their homes, automobiles, consumer durables, and modest levels of savings. However, as we might expect, wealth inequality is lower in Norway and, especially, Finland than in the other nations; the top decile of households hold 50.5% and 42.3%, respectively, of the wealth in these two nations (see Table 3.3.). Table 3.3 also shows that the top decile in the US holds almost 70% of the wealth in the nation, a markedly higher level than in any of the other five countries examined here. What is perhaps more

TABLE 3.3 Wealth Inequality in Six Nations

Decile Ratios	Canada (1999)	UK (2000)	US (2001)	Finland (1998)	Norway (2000)	Sweden (2002)
Share of Wealth Held by Top 10%	53%	56%	69.8%	42.3%	50.5%	58.6%

Source: Davies et al. (2008).

surprising, however, is the high level of wealth inequality in Sweden. Although considerably lower than in the US, the top decile in Sweden had the second highest level of wealth inequality among the six countries. Long-term data on wealth inequality does not exist for many nations, but studies indicate that there was a reduction in wealth inequality in the US, Sweden, and the UK between 1920 and the mid to late 1970s. During the 1980s, however, both the US and Sweden experienced sharp increases in wealth inequality. Tax reform and an exceptionally dramatic surge in the stock market further increased the level of wealth inequality in Sweden in the 1990s. Wealth inequality also rose markedly in both Canada and Finland during the mid to late 1980s and early 1990s. However, the distribution of wealth in these nations is much lower than in the US, where the increase in wealth inequality has been most pronounced (Wolff, 2002, 2006).

As with income, the presentation of wealth inequality by deciles masks the tremendous riches of those at the very top. Moreover, many of the wealthiest people in society are often excluded from such accounts because they do not take part in surveys of wealth or income distribution. However, records of their vast riches can often be located elsewhere.

In 2007 there were 1,125 billionaires in the world; their combined wealth was $4.4 trillion. The combined wealth of the richest twenty was $661.4 billion. The US had 469 billionaires on the list of the world's wealthiest people, far more than any other nation.[10] These included investment banker Warren Buffet, whose net worth of $62 billion made him the richest person in the world in 2007, and, in third place, Microsoft co-founder Bill Gates—the wealthiest person in the world for the previous 13 years—with a net worth of $58 billion (Forbes 2008c). In 1996 the combined assets of the three wealthiest Americans had already exceeded that of the poorest 50 million Americans. But wealth inequality has surged since then. A special issue of *Forbes* magazine on 'Lives of the Very Rich' enthusiastically gushed that Bill Gates's wealth in 2006 was equivalent to the GDP of eleven African nations comprising 226 million people (Forbes 2008b). Tied for seventh place, the UK had 35 billionaires, while Canada had 25. The *Forbes* register of wealthiest people also listed 10 billionaires from Sweden, including IKEA founder, Ingvar Kamprad, whose $31 billion fortune made him the seventh wealthiest person in the world, and four from Norway, despite its status as one of the most egalitarian nations. The obscenely excessive levels of wealth and ultra-extravagant lifestyles of the 'super rich' are concealed by Gini coefficients, decile ratios, and other crude measures of distribution presented here.

Traditional measures of income and wealth inequality also conceal the maldistribution of wealth among various groups *within* societies. Unequal distribution of income and wealth by race, for example, is clearly evident when we examine the situation of Aboriginal people in Canada, or blacks in the US. The 2001 Census indicated that Aboriginal people in Canada (First Nations, Métis, and Inuit) had a markedly lower median income than non-Aboriginal people, and that the disparity between the two groups had widened between 1980 and 2000. In 2004 the median income for non-Aboriginal people was $23,000, while that for Aboriginal people (excluding those living on Reserves or in the Territories) was only $17,000 (National Council of Welfare 2007). The income of Status Indian males, the group with the lowest median income, was only 45% that of non-Aboriginal males. Moreover, the cost of living for some Aboriginal groups, such as the Inuit in the North and Aboriginal peoples living on remote reserves, can be significantly higher. It can also be much harder for them to access social programs and supports. (A somewhat similar situation is faced by the Sami population that lives across the northernmost parts of Finland, Norway, and Sweden, as well as Russia—a region known as Sápmi.) As a result of these conditions, the well-being of Aboriginal peoples, and their opportunities to improve their situation, are greatly diminished (Cooke et al. 2003).

In the US, average incomes have increased for white families and, to a lesser extent, black families, since the 1970s. Although some studies suggest that income disparity between the two groups has actually increased (Isaacs 2007), the size of the black middle class has certainly grown, as has the enrollment of blacks in post-secondary education, and their level of home ownership. But these middle-class gains have been accompanied by a severe degeneration in the living standards and well-being of millions of other blacks in the US, especially those concentrated in the urban ghettoes (Oliver and Shapiro 1989; Rivera et al. 2008). Moreover, several studies also indicate that the wealth gap between blacks and whites—an important material dimension of inequality that is often neglected—is far greater than income disparity, and it has grown. The significant presence of some very high-profile artists, entertainers, sports figures, and other personalities, including several who are among the highest paid people in their respective fields, such as the late Michael Jackson, Oprah Winfrey, Will Smith, and Tiger Woods, on lists of highly paid celebrities may convey the impression to some people that blacks and whites in the US have equal opportunities to 'reach the top'. But blacks are greatly under-represented on the much larger inventories of the wealthiest Americans, such as the Forbes 400.

The wealth gap between black and white middle-class families in the US is considerably more consequential, and much greater, than the income disparity between them. Moreover, while the most significant form of wealth for both black and white middle-class families is home equity, white families have a much greater share of their wealth in various income-producing financial assets such as stocks, mutual funds, pensions, and interest-bearing bank accounts. Home ownership represents a much larger share of black assets than of white assets (even though the value of the homes owned by white families is greater). This disparity in wealth between black and white middle class families clearly reveals the limits of equal opportunity and liberal reforms. While the civil rights revolution opened doors to post-secondary education and higher-paying jobs for many blacks, it did little to address social inequalities deeply rooted in historic injustices that have kept black families from acquiring wealth. Thus, a far greater proportion of middle-class white families have inherited wealth and been able to borrow money from their parents to buy homes and start businesses; for middle-class blacks such intergenerational wealth transmission was not a possibility. White middle-class families also had easier access to bank loans, and the homes that they bought appreciated in value much more than those prosperous blacks purchased in black neighbourhoods. These wealth inequalities, in turn, are perpetuated because families with higher levels of wealth—especially income-generating financial assets—can provide numerous opportunities and advantages for their children (Conley 1999; Oliver and Shapiro 2006; Orr 2003; Scholz and Levine 2004).

Poverty

Poverty is typically associated with a conglomerate of broad social and economic living conditions related to physical comfort, mental and physical health, security and safety, access to education, opportunities to participate and succeed in the wider community, lifestyle, and general welfare or well-being. Those living in poverty typically experience a wide range of deprivations since, compared to most others in their society, they lack adequate levels of goods, benefits, services, employment, income, wealth, or other resources required to meet their needs. Thus, the term 'poverty' both describes and helps to account for conditions of deprivation. Like inequality, poverty is a multi-dimensional concept that can be quite difficult to analyze and compare, not least because the data concerning most of its socio-economic aspects are not always readily available or adequately standardized and measured across nations. Consequently, cross-national, empirical studies of poverty generally restrict their purview to the *economic* well-being of individuals and families—one somewhat limited, albeit very central, aspect of overall living conditions—and then directly or indirectly evaluate the adequacy of available resources, examining levels of household consumption, or more commonly, simply focusing upon income levels (Ruggles 1990; Spricker 1993; Veit-Wilson 1987).[11]

Of course, studies that closely examine *both* household consumption and income levels can provide a much clearer picture of poverty.[12] Unfortunately, such studies can be prohibitively expensive and are not always practical or possible in many larger nations or when researchers are concerned with international comparisons. However, it is generally agreed that an inadequate level of income provides a useful approximation of poverty, and most industrialized nations have reliable records of income distribution, making cross-national analysis somewhat less difficult.

Defining and Measuring Poverty: Absolute and Relative Measures

Although intuitively clear, poverty can be difficult to precisely define and measure. All poverty measures are designed to include only those members of society whose level of resources is most limited, a feature that distinguishes them from broader inequality measures. However, unlike GDP, there is no common, internationally accepted definition of poverty. Poverty is typically conceptualized, defined, and measured ('operationally defined') in either absolute or relative terms. **Absolute poverty** is based upon the idea that people are poor if they cannot afford the goods and services considered necessary for subsistence. Drawing an absolute poverty line sounds simple, but it involves many decisions. Before someone can calculate a 'minimum income' required to purchase a basket of 'basic necessities', they must first determine which goods and services are essential, as well as the quantity and quality required for subsistence. **Relative poverty** is based upon the notion that people are poor if their means are very limited compared to most others in their society. This measure also requires some arbitrary judgments, evaluations, and choices.[13]

Absolute Poverty

The idea that people are poor if their income falls below some absolute minimum considered necessary for subsistence can be traced back to nineteenth-century England, where rigorous poverty research had its origins. It has served as a basis for more recent studies of poverty, as well as for proposals for the creation of welfare states, including the well-known and widely influential 'Beveridge Report' in Britain in 1942.[14] Because they are based upon putatively 'objective' physical needs, absolute definitions of poverty are sometimes thought to be fixed, both temporally and geographically, and thus independent of any given national social or political context. After all, minimum basic needs should be the same in all societies, past or present. In reality, however, unless one strictly equates subsistence with bare survival—an approach used in the most destitute, famine-stricken, and war-ravaged regions of the world but inappropriate for developed nations—the definition of 'subsistence' is always socially constructed and dependent upon specific temporal and spatial circumstances. Both the quality and quantity (minimal or optimal) of goods and services deemed necessary for survival is determined within particular economic, social, and political contexts. Even the most basic biological needs for food, clothing, and shelter cannot be prescribed in an entirely objective manner.[15] Attempts to determine what a shelter is, define 'overcrowding', or designate which amenities are indispensable (e.g., running water, flush toilets, washing machines), are always subject to social definitions and values that may change considerably over time. Placing male and female siblings in the same bedroom, for example, is typically considered unacceptable, at least beyond a certain (socially determined) age. Clothing, too, must be evaluated according to prevailing standards of decency and convenience, as well as by considerations of warmth and protection in a nation.

Decisions concerning which other resources or goods (apart from food, clothing, and shelter) to include or exclude in any list or 'basket' of essentials are also somewhat arbitrary and determined within particular socio-political contexts. Should education, books, newspapers, computers, telephones, good locks, safety and security, televisions, toys, leisure time, vacations and recreation, or reasonable access to some form of transportation be considered essential in modern societies? A strict absolute definition of poverty, strongly endorsed today by right-wing, conservative think tanks such as the Heritage Foundation in the US or the Fraser Institute in Canada, would consider many of these resources to be non-essential.[16] However, the earliest, classical attempts to establish a consistent standard of subsistence in Britain around the turn of the century by researchers such as Charles Booth (1897) and Seebohm Rowntree (1901) took some account of the 'social nature' of poverty.[17] And the Scottish political economist and philosopher Adam Smith (2003 [1776] :1102–1103) also noted, if somewhat ungraciously, the relative nature of poverty in his classic study, *An Inquiry into the Nature and Causes of the Wealth of Nations*: 'By necessaries I understand, not only the commodities which are indispensably necessary for the support of life, but whatever the custom of the country renders it indecent for creditable people, even of the lowest order, to be without'.

In addition, many researchers have suggested that, even if it were possible to objectively determine which goods are necessities, it would be difficult to put a precise monetary value on their cost. For example, it was pointed out several decades ago that the poor in the US often pay more than the non-poor pay for a variety of goods and services. This is partly because they lack the funds and storage facilities to allow them to buy food in bulk, and partly because merchants in low-income neighbourhoods often charge extortionate prices and provide credit at usurious rates of interest (Caplovitz 1963).

This situation was exacerbated in the US in the 1980s with deregulation and the subsequent proliferation of pawn shops, cheque-cashing outlets, rent-to-own stores, high-interest mortgage lenders, and other 'poverty industries' that prey upon the poor, developments that spread rapidly to the UK and Canada. Many of these enterprises are owned or bankrolled by huge corporations or financial institutions, such as American Express, Bank of America, Citibank, Ford, and Western Union. Cash America, the largest chain of pawn shops in the US, is traded on the New York Stock Exchange. By 1995 it already had 325 outlets in the US, 34 in the UK, and 10 in Sweden (Hudson 1996a, 1996b).

Relative Poverty

In reality, there are no purely objective, absolute definitions or measures of poverty. Poverty is an intrinsically normative concept that is defined within a specific social, ideological, and moral setting, and it has meaning only against that backdrop. Many poverty researchers today thus argue that so-called absolute poverty standards must be adjusted not only for inflation, but for changing consumption patterns. In other words, they should be rendered more relative.

Relative poverty is explicitly conceptualized in relation to the general standard of living in society, and its standard of need goes beyond basic material resources to include a variety of other amenities deemed crucial. The poor are defined in relation to the economic and social circumstances enjoyed by most other members in society. Echoing Adam Smith, Peter Townsend (1979:31), the well-known British poverty researcher, equates poverty with 'relative deprivation', i.e., deprivation in relation to the activities, living conditions, and other amenities that are 'customary' or 'widely encouraged or approved' in a particular society. Like absolute poverty, relative poverty may be operationally defined in a wide diversity of ways. Purely relative approaches typically utilize poverty lines that are statistically drawn. For example, poverty may be operationally defined to include all those individuals or families whose income is 50% or less of the average income level in a nation. Of course, decisions concerning which 'average' income level to use (e.g., median or mean), which cut-off line to use (e.g., 50%, 40%, or one-third of the median or mean national income), and what to include as income, are all somewhat arbitrary. However, relative poverty may require fewer individual, subjective judgments by researchers than do absolute poverty measures (Fellegi 1997).

This relative approach is not without its critics. They argue that attempts to employ relative measures universally, across time and space, often lead to illogical conclusions. Thus, in a society where a majority is living in desperate conditions, no one would be classified as poor because all are equally positioned. Second, they argue that poverty can never be eliminated if it is defined relatively. Nor can a nation's progress in reducing poverty be measured. From this view, some part of the population will always be defined as poor, irrespective of the level of economic growth and improvements in its level of income. As opposed to absolute definitions of poverty, which, at least in theory, allow everyone to exceed a certain basic poverty threshold, relative poverty is said to be a 'moving target' because, as the economy grows, average incomes grow, too. Thus the position of the poor, relative to others in society, is not altered. For example, relative poverty rates would remain unchanged in a society in which every household's income increased tenfold overnight; households considered poor a day earlier would still be considered poor, it is claimed, even though their purchasing power (and standard of living), in 'absolute' terms would have increased quite dramatically (Huston et al. 1994; Sarlo 1992).[18]

Such arguments, however, assume a strict reliance upon economic growth alone—the 'rising tide lifting all boats'—to address poverty and inequality. In fact, it *is* possible to significantly reduce, or even eradicate, relative poverty through the use of measures such as progressive taxation policies, generous income transfers, active labour market programs, and a commitment to full employment if, as in the Nordic lands, they are specifically designed to change the shape of income distribution. The dramatic reduction in the level of poverty among the elderly that resulted from the Canadian pension system is also illustrative (see Table 3.4 below). And, while a relative poverty measure would undoubtedly present major difficulties if used in cross-national research that focused upon both developed and developing nations, it is quite suitable, and extremely useful, for comparative examinations of poverty across wealthy industrialized nations.

The employment of an absolute or relative definition of poverty has been the subject of great political controversy among poverty researchers, policy

TABLE 3.4 Poverty Rates: Total Population, Children and the Elderly in Three Anglo-Saxon Nations: Canada, UK, US

	Canada			UK			US		
	1975	1987	2004	1974	1986	2004	1974	1986	2004
Poverty Rates (50% of Median)									
Total Population	13.9%	11.4%	13.0%	9.1%	9.0%	11.6%	15.9%	17.8%	17.3%
Children	14.4%	14.8%	16.8%	8.0%	12.5%	14.0%	19.3%	25.0%	21.2%
Children in Single Mother Families	56.4%	50.3%	48.3%	39.4%	21.1%	32.1%	60.1%	62.8%	48.5%
Elderly	34.7%	10.8%	6.3%	29.7%	7.0%	16.3%	27.5%	23.5%	24.6%

Source: LIS Database: Key Figures.

experts, politicians, and others. Those on the 'right' are often critical of relative poverty measures. They usually advocate an absolute approach because absolute measures tend to produce much smaller estimates of the incidence of poverty. Their accounts typically suggest that poverty is not a major social problem requiring more government intervention or greater public support; in fact, they argue, social programs should be further pared back. Relative measures, alternatively, tend to be advocated by policy analysts and social activists on the 'left' who want to draw attention to poverty as a significant social problem requiring the development or expansion of social programs for its amelioration.[19] Relative measures are also promoted by those who are concerned more generally with income inequality, marginalization, and social exclusion, not only with poverty. However, as one prominent Scandinavian researcher has noted, 'there are not two definitions of poverty between which we can choose according to taste, but instead two different aspects of poverty, which are both important in differing ways' (Korpi 1980).

Critics of proposals to create greater economic equality often argue that as long as those at the bottom have enough to get by, there is no need to worry about economic inequality. Some even suggest that people said to be living in poverty in rich nations are not truly poor because, compared to the poor in the developing world, they are well-off. But in many neighbourhoods and communities in the large metropolises of the wealthiest nations, and on many Aboriginal or First Nations reserves in North America, people often reside in conditions as desperate as those in some Third World or developing countries, and sometimes with greater levels of violence, higher incarceration rates, and lower life expectancies. Moreover, people living in poverty, or on low incomes, 'in the midst of plenty' in developed nations often experience greater social exclusion because they do not have certain widely held amenities. As Amartya Sen (2006:37) has noted: 'in order to take part in the life of the community, or for children to be able to communicate with others in the same school, the bundle of commodities needed may include a telephone, a television, a car, and so on, in New York, in a way that would not apply in Addis or in Dhaka (where an adult may be able to participate in social affairs and children can talk with each other without these implements)'.

Given the varied ways that information about poverty and income is collected in different countries, it is virtually impossible to completely 'standardize' national data sets for cross-national comparisons. Survey samples may be derived in varying ways, coverage of populations may vary, and data might be gathered through different channels (official tax registers or survey questionnaires, for example) across several nations. Standardization is, thus, always a matter of degree. However, the Luxembourg Income Study (LIS) project has created a 'harmonized' database that greatly improves cross-national comparability by adapting national household income micro-data sets to a clearly defined set of income variables and by translating and matching a wide range

TABLE 3.5 Poverty Rates: Total Population, Children and the Elderly in Three Nordic Nations: Finland, Norway, Sweden

	Finland			Norway			Sweden		
	1975	1987	2004	1979	1986	2004	1975	1987	2005
Poverty Rates (50% of Median)									
Total Population	n/a	5.4%	6.6%	4.9%	7.2%	7.0%	6.5%	7.5%	5.6%
Children	n/a	2.8%	3.7%	4.8%	4.3%	4.9%	2.4%	3.6%	4.7%
Children in Single Mother Families	n/a	6.9%	11.6%	15.7%	23.2%	13.9%	3.4%	5.5%	10.4%
Elderly	n/a	11.9%	10.1%	6.3%	21.7%	8.5%	13.9%	7.2%	6.6%

Source: LIS Database: Key Figures.

of other national social and demographic variables (such as the chronological definition of 'elderly' or 'children', for example). Consistent and high quality comparable data is readily available for the six Anglo-Saxon and Nordic lands included here, which were among the very first nations to be included in the LIS database.[20]

Tables 3.4 and 3.5 provide the most remarkable contrast between the Anglo-Saxon and Nordic countries. Poverty rates in the Anglo-Saxon world are clearly much higher, with the US rating notably higher within this group of nations again. By 2004, the level of poverty in the US, which has risen steadily since the 1970s, was 17.3%, about a third higher than in the other two Anglo-Saxon nations. At 21% the child poverty rate in the US was also markedly higher than in the UK (14%) and Canada (16.8%). Close to half of the children in families with a single mother were living in poverty in the US and Canada in 2004, notably higher than in the UK. However, it is the contrast with the Nordic nations that is the most striking. The total poverty rates in the Nordic countries are much lower than in the Anglo-Saxon nations. This is especially evident when the US, the nation with the highest rates of poverty, is contrasted with Sweden, the nation with the lowest poverty level. The US poverty rate is more than three times the Swedish rate; so, too, is the rate of poverty among the elderly. The child poverty rate and the rate of child poverty in families with a single mother in the US are almost five times as high as they are in Sweden. Perhaps the most surprising figure in Table 3.4 is the level of poverty among the elderly in Canada. At 6.3% Canada's level of poverty among the elderly in 2004 was at about the same level as that in Sweden, and lower than that in the two other Nordic nations. Three decades earlier the poverty rate among this group in Canada was more than six times higher than it was in 2004. The level of poverty among the elderly in the US was about four times as high as that in Canada. National data on poverty also suggests that poverty is much deeper in the US; the poor there are more destitute, living further below established poverty lines. The poverty figures in these tables clearly show that social policy (such as the introduction of the Canadian old-age security and pension programs) can make a meaningful difference.

Inequality Matters: The Impact and Consequences of Material Inequality

Two broad kinds of objections have been made to great economic inequality in society: **deontological objections** and **teleological objections**. In moral philosophy, **deontology** is an approach to ethics that stresses the inherent goodness or badness of something; from this perspective, inequality may be viewed as inherently bad. **Teleology** (or consequentialism), by contrast, suggests that things should be judged as good or bad, or right or wrong, on the basis of their impact or consequences.

Deontological objections to inequality focus upon social justice, moral issues, and the *direct* negative impact of inegalitarian distributions of material resources. Highly unequal material distributions generate a great deal of human suffering, both physical and psychological. Those at the bottom of class systems endure harsh living and working conditions and have poorer health, more stressful and shorter lives, and fewer opportunities for advancement. They are often marginalized and unable to exercise their formal rights or fully benefit from social services and supports available to others in society. Political and civil rights, such as the right to run for political office or the right to an education, for example, cannot be separated from economic status either. Rather, these rights interact with economic status, and they can be seriously diminished for people in lower socio-economic positions. Moreover, the disadvantages they face are typically passed on intergenerationally. Great material inequalities also allow those at the top to treat those who have less as inferior and to make them feel that they are inferior. From this perspective inequality is *intrinsically* unacceptable. This idea is especially central to the 'equality of outcome' ideal, but it is also critical to the other three equality ideals. Even equal opportunity, a very narrow and restricted form of equality, cannot be seriously approximated when material inequalities in society are great.

Teleological objections to material inequality highlight its numerous detrimental 'secondary' effects and consequences. This view focuses upon the *instrumental* value of equality; the rationalization of equality here appeals to concerns other than, or in addition to, equality itself. These concerns and issues may include everyone, not just those at the bottom of socio-economic hierarchies. Material inequality is unacceptable here because it prevents or obstructs the realization of these other important goals. For example, high levels of inequality can undermine democracy, make a sham of equal opportunity, encourage widespread resentment and social unrest, and lead to poor societal health. From this perspective, inequality causes great social harm. From the deontological point of view, inequality is unethical or unfair; we therefore have a moral obligation to address it regardless of whatever other benefits this may foster. Of course these two positions are not mutually exclusive and together make a very strong case for greater equality.

Political and Social Concerns: Democracy, Community, and Opportunity

As we have seen, highly unequal distributions of material resources bestow undue political influence upon those at the top of the class system. In class-ridden societies the wealthy and owners of the 'means of production' always dominate. They are able to use their great economic resources to promote their views, purchase political influence, and shape state policies in ways that serve their own interests over those of others, undermining the democratic process. Grossly unequal economic resources also allow for the distortion of the judicial process and the subversion of the notion of 'equality before the law'. The considerable costs of litigation and able counsel clearly prevent those from lower socio-economic classes from presenting their cases as effectively as wealthy people or large corporations. Moreover, even when (on relatively rare occasions) found guilty, wealthy and powerful interests almost never receive the same sentences or treatment as people from lower classes who have committed similar (or more minor) offenses. In short, great economic inequality begets power inequalities that further, and deepen, existing economic and political inequalities.

Material inequality can also fracture trust and undermine civic responsibility, social solidarity, and community, fostering elitism, resentment, social unrest, and instability in their place. This is reflected in much higher crime rates and rates of incarceration in less egalitarian nations, especially the US, 'far and away the most violent advanced industrial society on earth' (Currie 1998:1; Freeman 1995; İmrohoroğlu et al. 2001). Between 2002 and 2005, the incarceration rate per 100,000 of the national population was higher in Canada (116) and the UK (England and Wales, 142)—and strikingly higher in the world-leading US (714)—than it was in more egalitarian lands, such as Finland (71), Norway (65), and Sweden (75) (OECD 2007; Walmsley 2007; Western and Beckett 1999). The incarceration rate in the US has grown very rapidly over the past decade, mirroring the increase in social inequality, with disproportionate numbers of black and immigrant prisoners. The criminal justice system in the US exhibits the same preference for harsh and degrading forms of punishment over addressing root causes that is evident in its social policy approach (Pettit and Western 2004; Whitman 2003).

The more privileged classes—and the mainstream media—often dismiss the anger and resentment sometimes directed toward them as merely expressions of 'envy'. Of course, grossly unequal material distributions in status-conscious, consumerist capitalist societies may foster considerable envy among those who are less well-off. But what is much more striking, and typical, is the level of fascination with lives of the 'rich and famous' that the less well-off often exhibit, and their apparently insatiable appetite for books, magazines, and television programs that feature the elite. People only become truly incensed when material inequalities become grossly excessive and when they are convinced that these rewards have been unfairly acquired—and at their expense—rather than by the initiative, effort, and hard work of those at the top. The inheritance of great wealth and the exorbitant income hikes and bonuses that rich executives and CEOs award themselves regardless of the success of their enterprises, or as a reward for slashing hundreds or thousands of jobs, are common examples of this today. Moreover, the fact people may be envious does not discount their legitimate concerns; indeed, the American philosopher, John Rawls (1971) has suggested that envy can function as a canary in a coal mine, alerting us that inequality has reached intolerably unjust and highly indefensible and dysfunctional levels.

Of course, economic inequality is not simply a matter of envy. People recognize that large increases in the wealth of the upper classes, and their consumption patterns, can have a direct and very negative impact upon their standards of living. As wealth becomes increasingly concentrated at the top, many goods become scarcer and their prices rise (Frank 2000). As we have seen, greater wealth does not necessarily 'trickle down' to those at the lower end of the socio-economic hierarchy, but higher prices do. For example, a significant increase in prosperity at the upper end of the class system may induce developers to build more high-end houses and apartments, and gentrify old working class neighbourhoods, leaving fewer affordable homes for the less well-off and increasing the number of people living on the streets. When the wealthy purchase new houses, prices and rents at the lower end of the housing market often increase as well, forcing many people to move to cheaper suburbs and spend more of their time and money commuting to work. Greater wealth at the top may also lead to greater purchases of automobiles and private insurance and social services, undermining public transit systems and social programs. The increasing reliance of the affluent upon private health care draws doctors and other health care professionals away from the public sector. And their ability to hire private tutors and send their children to private elementary and secondary schools increases the chances of their progeny gaining access to preferred universities and positions over those of the less well-off. Increasingly reliant upon the private sector for these benefits and unwilling to support the public sector, the upper classes organize and fund unremitting lobbies to lower taxes, further eroding and endangering social programs and benefits.

Rapidly rising material inequalities today, and the ever-widening gulf between the rich and the poor, might be less of a concern if they were mitigated by a great deal of social mobility—if those at the bottom of the class system were able to rise to the top, and often did so. There is little evidence of this. Studies of social mobility examining income levels and occupations ranked according to prestige suggest that there is little social mobility within or across generations. However, most studies do indicate that social mobility is much greater in the more egalitarian Nordic nations than in the highly unequal Anglo-Saxon nations (Aaberge et al. 2002; Blanden et al. 2005; Bowles and Gintis 2002; Corak 2004; Erikson and Goldthorpe 1992; Gangl 2005; Jäntti et al. 2006; OECD 1996, 2007; Solon 2002). In the 1800s Tocqueville contrasted the distinct and rigid social status divisions in his native France with the seemingly boundless opportunities and great fluidity in the United States; the US, he maintained, was 'exceptional'. And during the first decades following World War II, the higher levels of inequality in the US, and the minimal level of security provided by its residual welfare state compared to those in Western Europe, were often justified on the grounds that 'circumstances of birth' could be largely undone by the greater occupational, geographical, and status mobility there. But these claims cannot hold up even within the Anglo-Saxon world today; social mobility rates are highest in Canada, followed by the UK, and *lowest* in the US. Ironically, the 'rags to riches' mythology and the widely held notion that anyone can make it to the top that underpin the 'American Dream' appear to fit the US scene least of all; its fiscal and social policies, minimum wage laws, and anti-union legislation were put in place, and fine-tuned over the past few decades, to actually forestall changes to its class system, apart from furthering the gap between the wealthiest and the rest. Today the US stands out as 'exceptional' because of these conditions and numerous barriers to social mobility.

Inequality and Health

Research has repeatedly shown that people living in poverty, or with very low incomes, tend to have considerably poorer health than those who are better off. This is reflected in significantly higher rates of a wide range of chronic health problems, disorders, and diseases; much higher mortality rates; and significantly shorter life expectancies. Epidemiological studies indicate that poor health among people in the lower economic strata is structurally and socially determined by living and working conditions marred by poor diets, inadequate housing, insecure jobs, high levels of unemployment, social exclusion, and neighbourhoods that have fewer amenities and greater environmental and social toxins, including higher levels of crime and violence, and numerous stresses, disadvantages, and deprivations (Kawachi and Kennedy 2002; Raphael 2004, 2008).

The deleterious consequences of poverty, and the range of vulnerabilities and difficulties that the poor have to endure, start very early in life. And their effects are cumulative. Higher infant and neonatal mortality rates are related to maternal health problems (prior to and during pregnancy) and to home environments that are closely associated with poverty. During the first few critical years of life, adequate nutrition and a stimulating environment are crucial for optimal brain development. The brains of children that are physically and socially malnourished may be sculpted or 'hard-wired' for a life of poverty. Poverty results in higher incidence of premature birth and low birth weights, which render infants much more susceptible to injuries and several illnesses. Childhood poverty is associated with many chronic conditions and infectious diseases, including anemia, measles, rheumatic fever, hemophilus influenza, meningitis, parasitic diseases, gastroenteritis, vision and hearing difficulties, mental problems, and learning and behavioural difficulties. Higher levels of illness ensure that poor children are absent from school more often. Higher levels of absenteeism, and the greater likelihood that they will not have books and other educational materials in their homes, or parents with the time, energy, and level of education to help them with their studies, mean that children from poor families are more likely to underachieve in school and to have lower aspirations. Poor teens, in turn, are much more likely to drop out of school and take on insecure, low-paying jobs, perpetuating the poverty cycle. This concatenation of indecent and distressing conditions and deprivations, and their direct impact upon the opportunities and chances of people in poor and low-income families, constitute compelling reasons to address material inequality (Bradbury et al. 2001; Huston 1994; Huston et al. 1994; Townson 1999; UNICEF 2007).

The effects of poverty on health have long been recognized and are rarely disputed. But it is sometimes suggested that the inferior health status of people in poor and low-income families largely reflects the choices, behaviours, and habits they undertake. Poorer people tend to smoke more, eat unhealthier foods, and exercise less. From this perspective they are largely responsible for their own poor health, and the best remedy for this situation is to strongly encourage them to adopt healthier lifestyles. But such accounts ignore the class-bound nature of these 'choices' and habits, and the socio-economic contexts they occur within; indeed, the very fact that they are more common among lower socio-economic groups calls into question the notion that they are entirely 'voluntary' (Evans et al. 1994). Smoking, for example, is closely linked to the stress associated with financial instability, job insecurity, and mind-numbing, routine work; people with low incomes are often unable to provide enough food for their families and may have to substitute cheaper, high-fat processed foods for more nutritional ones; they are also less likely to be able to afford memberships in health clubs and gyms, and their jobs often leave them with little time or energy for exercise. Historically, smoking, obesity, and sedentary lifestyles were once key indicators of conspicuous consumption and leisure; they were the 'choices' of the affluent, who were the only ones that could afford them. Yet, like their contemporary counterparts, they lived much longer and healthier lives than those at the bottom of the class system. Research that controls for such lifestyle factors indicates that they cannot account for most of the cross-class variation in health today. Efforts directed solely at changing people's lifestyles do not address their crucial social and structural determinants: the living and working conditions that led them to those choices and habits. Nor do they prevent or discourage others from adopting them.

Access to health care is another factor that is sometimes advanced to explain poor health among those with low incomes. Equal access to health care and other services is an important dimension and marker of equality. In the US, where health care is not provided as a universal right, those who cannot afford it are often not covered. There is no doubt that people who do not have health care are much worse off. Health care systems play a very important role in relieving suffering, restoring health and functioning, and limiting the effects of several risk factors. However, while they may provide several forms of 'primary' prevention, such as dental care, immunization, and pre-natal and post-natal care—especially in the Nordic lands—and many forms of 'secondary' prevention, such as screening, testing, and other interventions to head off further deterioration of health, the medical and hospital services that constitute the core of most health care systems are largely reactive, curative, and interventionist in nature. For the most part, they respond to illness and injury, rather than proactively promoting health or addressing root causes of health problems in the social environment. Access to health care and medical technology can restore health and save people's lives when they become seriously ill, but it cannot provide a very satisfactory explanation of why some people become sick in the first place and others tend to remain healthy (Evans et al. 1994; Kawachi and Kennedy 2002). Equal access to health care is important, but so is equal access to the conditions necessary for health.

Over the past decade a rapidly growing body of epidemiological research has suggested that the best way to improve societal health is through preventative measures that address social inequality itself at the outset, rather than by dealing with health problems as they emerge. But this is not simply a matter of eradicating poverty, or reducing the gap between the very rich and the very poor in society. Well over 100 studies have shown that health is graded by income or, more broadly, socio-economic status (SES). This research indicates that people at the upper end of the social ladder or hierarchy—those with higher incomes, higher levels of education, and better jobs—have far fewer health problems and live much longer lives, as we would expect. But, with each successive step down the social ladder, the frequency of a wide range of chronic health problems, disorders, and diseases (including cardiovascular, respiratory, digestive tract, and kidney diseases, several forms of cancer, diabetes, tuberculosis, high blood pressure, strokes, rheumatoid disorders, ulcers, degenerative eye diseases, hypertension, psychiatric problems, and suicide, among others) goes up while life expectancy declines. This 'social gradient' is continuous, so differences in health and life expectancy can be found even within the middle classes (Auerbach and Krimgold 2001; Kawachi and Kennedy 2002; Marmot 2004; Wilkinson 1996, 2005; Wilkinson and Pickett 2006).

Among the first studies to observe this 'social gradient' in health was the landmark Whitehall Study of British civil servants in the 1970s. This was a relatively homogeneous group of people; no one was poor or deprived or particularly wealthy; no one was unemployed; everyone had job security. And everyone had access to the same universal public health care system. But the civil service was a hierarchical and highly stratified bureaucracy, from the messengers and porters at the bottom to the clerical grades in the middle and the several levels of administrators and professionals at the top. The Whitehall Study found a clear and consistent relationship between the job status of civil servants and their health status throughout this public institution. Subsequent national and cross-national research observed the same pattern. These studies suggested that, once a certain level of wealth in a nation has been reached, the *distribution* of income becomes a central determinant of population health. When this 'standard of living threshold' has been attained, there are diminishing returns to the health of nations with increases in national wealth (GDP). But redistributing income in society *can* improve the health of the less well-off without affecting the health of those at the top. Populations in nations with more equal income distributions can be healthier than they are in wealthier but less egalitarian nations: 'for instance, countries such as the United States, and more recently Britain, have larger health differences than most of the social democratic European countries—particularly the Nordic countries' (Wilkinson 2005:16–17). Some research even tentatively suggests that the health of people in lower classes in the more egalitarian nations may be better, in some instances, than that of some higher classes in less egalitarian nations. One study, for example, indicated that 'the death rate for classes IV and V in Sweden is lower than that for classes I and II in England and Wales' (Vågerö and Lundberg 1989:35). Other studies have shown that infant mortality rates are also lower in nations with lower income inequality (Leon et al. 1992; Wennemo 1993). This relationship between inequality and health holds within the Anglo-Saxon world too; the Canadian population is healthier than that of its richer but less egalitarian American neighbour. The same social/health gradient was even observed intra-nationally, *across* the states in the US; the states with greater income inequality had higher rates of mortality (Kaplan et al. 1996; Kennedy et al. 1996).

The idea that the scale of income inequality is an important determinant of population health is contested by some studies (Beckfield 2004; Gravelle et al. 2002; Judge 1995; Mellor and Milyo 2003), although their conclusions represent a minority view (Wilkinson and Pickett 2006). The reasons for the relationship between income or socio-economic status and health are not yet entirely understood. However, a number of critical pathways and mechanisms have been identified. First, as suggested earlier, high levels of income inequality can undermine social programs. In highly unequal societies, people toward the top of the social ladder feel they have less to gain from tax-financed public expenditures on social programs that contribute to the health of the entire community. They prefer tax breaks that allow them to live in gated communities, hire chauffeurs, and support private schools, insurance, health care, and other services and amenities, undermining the fiscal and social support for redistributive social welfare states. Unlike the Anglo-Saxon nations, the Nordic lands provide universal high-quality public services and income programs to foster greater support for their welfare states and circumvent resistance to the considerably higher taxes needed to support those programs. And, as noted above, developed welfare states can greatly reduce income inequalities (Chung and Muntaner 2007; Coburn 2000; Korpi and Palme 1998; Navarro et al. 2006). Second, and related to this, high levels of income inequality can erode social cohesion and solidarity in society. In less egalitarian societies people feel more distant from one another, are more mistrustful, and have a weaker sense of community. This both harms their health and undermines support for common goals and programs. Third, people who are lower on the social ladder tend to have less autonomy, less control over their work, higher levels of stress, and lower self esteem. They are also more likely to be marginalized and to feel socially excluded.

This large and growing body of research suggests that decreases in income inequality lead to better health for everyone; conversely, higher levels of inequality lead to poorer health for all, not just those at the bottom, although they will likely be hit the hardest. These are disconcerting thoughts in a period marked by significant increases in income inequality and rising poverty rates almost everywhere. This research provides another powerful critique of the 'trickle down' theory of economic growth—the notion that the poor and others at the bottom should be content with the crumbs that fall from the sumptuous meals enjoyed by others being a particularly demeaning idea and approach from the start.[21] But even if it were true that economic growth benefited everyone, the minimal gains thought to accrue to the lowest groups would not affect health in societies that have passed the wealth threshold. Taken together, what this voluminous and ever-growing body of research on social inequality and health demonstrates is the urgent need to eliminate poverty, greatly reduce income inequalities, and provide a wide range of supportive social programs. The Nordic nations have been pursuing these strategies with a considerable degree of success for several decades. The rise in inequality along some dimensions there during the past 20 years is certainly disturbing, and is largely due to

TABLE 3.6 Health Commitment and Health Indicators in Six Nations

	Anglo-Saxon Nations			Nordic Nations		
	Canada	UK	US	Finland	Norway	Sweden
Health Expenditure (% of GDP, 2004)						
Public	6.8	7.0	6.9	5.7	8.1	7.7
Private	3.0	1.1	8.5	1.7	1.6	1.4
Physicians per 100,000 People (2000–2004)	214	230	256	316	313	328
Life Expectancy at Birth (2005)	79.8	78.5	77.4	78.4	79.3	80.1
Health-Adjusted Life Expectancy (2002)	72.0	70.6	67.2	71.1	72.0	73.3
Infant Mortality Rate (Deaths under One Year of Age per 1,000 Live Births, 2005)	5	5	6	3	3	3
Under-Five Mortality Rate (per 1000 Live Births, 2005)	6	6	7	4	4	4
Infants with Low Birthweight (%, 1998–2005)	6	8	8	4	5	4

Sources: UNDP (2007); OECD (2006, 2005).

their adoption of some more neo-liberal policies and approaches. But these nations have still managed to outperform their Anglo-Saxon counterparts. Table 3.6 indicates that, despite the higher total level of expenditure in the US—where there is much greater emphasis upon the private sector and, hence, much more unequal health care provision—the United States tends to do worst on most measures of health status, including measures of life expectancy, infant mortality, and low birth weight. The nations with lower levels of inequality and more accessible health care systems do better on most indicators of health.

Inequality and Economic Growth

Great material inequality also has economic effects. Studies concerned with the relationship between inequality and economic growth have long been a central concern. In the first decades after World War II, the focus was on the impact of economic growth upon inequality. During this period numerous studies suggested that economic growth would invariably lead to the eradication of poverty, greater income equality, the establishment of supportive welfare states, and higher standards of living for everyone in the wealthy, industrialized world (Cutright 1965, 1967; Galbraith 1971; Kuznets 1955, 1965; Rimlinger 1971; Wilensky 1975). However, by the late 1970s, it was becoming apparent that nations do not necessarily address inequality simply because they have the economic capacity to do so. Indeed, the US, the most developed and richest country in the world, was proving to be an inegalitarian social-policy laggard, with higher levels of poverty, greater income and wealth inequality, a much smaller middle class, and a much more underdeveloped welfare state than in most other industrialized nations, especially the Nordic lands. Tired metaphors about rising tides notwithstanding, inequality rose rapidly with economic growth in the US and in the other Anglo-Saxon countries because there were few mechanisms in place, such as fiscal policies, social programs, or a well-organized labour movement, to ensure that everyone could benefit from such growth (Björn 1979; Dryzek 1978; Esping-Andersen 1985a, 1985b; Hicks and Swank 1984; Korpi 1983; Stephens 1980).

Over the past two decades, studies of the developed nations have increasingly turned the research question around, investigating the impact of inequality on economic growth. The first studies suggested that inequality was beneficial for growth and that efforts to reduce poverty and inequality—through fiscal policy, government transfers, centralized wage bargaining, minimum wage legislation, and other measures—are counterproductive in the long term, reducing living standards for everyone in society (Arrow 1979; Browning and Johnson 1984; Okun 1975). This argument largely centred on the idea that redistributive measures employed to create greater equality diminish the incentives of both the wealthy and the less well-off. Enterprising behaviour is discouraged when earnings are taxed at a high rate. Increasing the incomes of the least well-off through social benefits only dampens their incentive to work longer and harder. Both these developments, it was suggested, retard economic growth. From this perspective the best way to motivate the wealthy is by lowering their taxes and other expenses and relaxing restrictions on their enterprises; the best way to motivate those at the bottom is to eliminate social programs or make them much less generous and harder to access, an approach best reflected in US 'workfare' programs and parroted in the UK and Canada.

A large and rapidly growing body of research has seriously challenged the idea that inequality fosters economic growth. Indeed, several recent studies suggest that inequality can actually hinder growth, although some of this research focuses more upon the detrimental impact of inequality in less-developed nations (Birdsall et al. 1995; Perotti 1996; Persson and Tabellini 1994). In the 1980s and 1990s, some very inegalitarian nations, such as the US, did experience periods of high growth, but other inegalitarian nations, such as Switzerland, did not; and several more egalitarian nations, including Denmark, Norway, Finland, the Netherlands, Austria, and Belgium, experienced levels of growth that matched or even exceeded that in the US. Sweden's growth rate was lower than that in the US during this period, but its productivity level was higher. Over the past decade the Nordic nations have had better records of growth and outperformed the Anglo-Saxon nations (Pontusson 2005, 2006). There is no unequivocal support for the prevailing idea that inequality is beneficial for growth. Recent reports by the OECD (Arjona et al. 2002:28, 2001) concluded that there is 'no evidence that the level of income inequality affects GDP one way or another', a position that has been reinforced by another recent study focused upon 15 advanced capitalist nations (Kenworthy 2004).

The problems with material inequality and the arguments that have been mounted against it are powerful; it is immoral, unethical, and unjust; it undermines democracy; it is socially corrosive and can lead to social and political instability; it results in poorer health; and, contrary to the most widely held view, it may even serve to obstruct economic growth. Fostering greater economic equality through some form of redistribution is justified because it is necessary to preserve democracy, ensure social stability, improve population health, and act as a spur on the economy. It might also be sought as a means to mitigate human suffering, secure other ideals, such as fairness and justice, and provide greater opportunities for people to achieve their goals. The brief review of several key dimensions of material inequality here suggests that the Nordic lands have done far better than their Anglo-Saxon counterparts, a pattern that is repeated for non-material inequality, as the next chapter will demonstrate.

Notes

1. The popular term 'Gilded Age' comes from *The Gilded Age: A Tale of Today* (2006 [1873]), a novel co-written by American satirist and literary icon Mark Twain (1835–1910) and Charles Dudley Warner. Though fictional, it provided an account of US plutocracy and rampant economic and political corruption in the latter part of the nineteenth century, a time of great economic prosperity. The liberal critique of the excesses of capitalism, pointing to striking parallels in the disparities of the original Gilded Age with that of the 'New Gilded Age' in the US today, has been the subject of several recent studies (Krugman 2007; Phillips 2002).

2. Gross domestic product (GDP) tells us the value of the production of all goods and services produced *within* a nation ('domestically') but excludes consideration of the investments that individuals or companies from that nation make abroad. Gross national product (GNP), in contrast, includes the value of all the goods and services produced by a country's residents whether domestic or international, but factors out the domestic production of goods or services that are owned by foreign companies. Nations that have a large portion of their domestic companies in the hands of foreign companies have smaller GNPs than GDPs. While GDP has become more commonplace over the past two decades, and is viewed as a better measure of a nation's economic activity, it can provide an especially misleading picture of struggling or developing nations with high levels of foreign investment because the profits of foreign multinationals often return home.

3. This is especially a problem when attempting to assess economic progress in developing nations, where a good deal of production takes place in the household economy.

4. Recognizing the inadequacy of narrow economic measures, the Nordic lands routinely conduct more inclusive national studies, using broad networks of social indicators to assess, track, and compare the well-being of their residents with those in the other Nordic lands. Other countries, including Canada, the UK, most of Europe,

and several developing nations around the globe, also issue annual or periodic reports that gauge national developments and trends.

5. Sweden ranked first, followed by Denmark, Norway, and Finland. Canada was not included in the report.
6. Some of them, such as Oprah Winfrey ($275 million), Jerry Bruckheimer ($145 million), and Steven Spielberg ($130 million), received considerably more when capital income and other income sources are included (Forbes 2008a).
7. According to Crystal (1992), the income of Steven Ross of Time Warner was already more than 9,000 times that of the average manufacturing worker by 1989.
8. The average CEO compensation level in Sweden ($700,290), however, had increased 217% between 1988 and 2003, nearing that in Canada ($889,898) and the UK ($830,223).
9. A few forms of wealth, however, including most automobiles and consumer durables, typically depreciate over time.
10. The nation with the second highest number of billionaires was Russia (with 87), followed by Germany (59), India (53), China (42), Turkey (35), the UK (35), Hong Kong (26), Canada (25), Japan (24), Brazil (18), Spain (18), Australia (14), France (14), Italy (13), Saudi Arabia (13), South Korea (12), Switzerland (11), Mexico (10) and Sweden (10) (Forbes 2008c).
11. As often pointed out, income level is an indirect and not an entirely satisfactory means of apprehending poverty. First, it can be difficult to measure. What should be counted as income? Because wealth is usually not taken into consideration, or only roughly approximated, some individuals or families whose money is invested in real estate, stocks and bonds, or other concerns may, through the use of tax loopholes, appear to be considerably less well-off. (Of course, it is exceedingly unlikely that such individuals could ever be classified as poor). Moreover, income data collected through interviews may be inaccurate because of underreporting or memory errors, while that obtained through official sources may be distorted by temporary changes in employment, income, and household composition during a year for which income information is collected and calculated (Halleröd 1996; Vogel 1997).
12. Sweden has conducted fairly exhaustive 'level of living' surveys since the late 1960s, which examine a much broader range of economic and social resources and conditions than those usually associated with more common 'standard of living' income studies (Erikson 1993; Erikson and Åberg 1987). Similar studies are conducted in the other Nordic nations as well.
13. Poverty lines might also be set more 'subjectively', through the use of surveys to determine who is poor.
14. William Henry Beveridge's (1879–1963) famous 1942 document, the *Report on Social Insurance and Allied Services*, set out a blueprint for the creation of the British welfare state.
15. For example, it may be somewhat more possible to scientifically specify requisite levels of nutrition, caloric intake, and protein today than it was many decades ago, but the determination of *which* foodstuffs will satisfy these human requirements and where they may be obtained is a social one. Some societies may accept, while others abhor, the eating of dogs, cats, horses, cows, pigs, or insects, although they all possess nutritional value.
16. People are sometimes quite upset to learn that someone with a poverty-level income owns a television set or VCR, but these are relatively inexpensive items that provide

a very cheap form of entertainment. Their attitudes suggest that a person or family does not 'qualify' as poor if they have access to any form of entertainment; it is not viewed as 'essential' for them.

17. Both Booth and Rowntree measured poverty indirectly, establishing poverty lines that estimated a range of income levels needed for subsistence. However, Rowntree also distinguished between those whose income was inadequate to meet minimum basic subsistence requirements (primary poverty) and those whose income was slightly higher, but still severely restrictive according to the conventions of the day.
18. Of course, this hypothetical scenario set up by the critics of the relative approach to measuring poverty does not take into account the fact that there would be much less real improvement in the lives of those at the bottom because, if everyone's income increased, prices would rise too.
19. There are some, however, such as Norwegian poverty researcher Stein Ringen (1988:362), who strongly support the welfare state, but are critical of relative measures of poverty because they seem to suggest that social policies and programs have been largely ineffective: 'Poverty research in Western Europe has for some time been producing estimates of the extent of poverty which show that this problem remains on a mass scale. If these estimates were accepted as valid, the unavoidable interpretation would be that of total failure in the redistributive efforts of the welfare state and serious imperfections in the mixed economy system'.
20. The LIS project was created in 1983, under the joint sponsorship of the government of Luxembourg and the Centre for Population, Poverty and Policy Studies (CEPS). It is now funded on a continuing basis by CEPS/INSTEAD (International Networks for Studies in Technology, Environment, Alternatives, Development) and by the national science and social science research foundations of its member countries (Atkinson, Rainwater, and Smeeding 1995). The LIS database includes a collection of over 100 household surveys in over 25 nations that covers a period of over two decades for several of them.
21. As seen in chapter 2, John Rawls's 'difference principle' provides a more compassionate version of 'trickle down' economics, suggesting that inequalities can be justified if they serve to improve the position of those at the bottom.

4 Non-Material Indicators of Inequality: Rights and Entitlements

Social inequality is typically associated with the kinds of economic or **material** indicators, such as poverty and the distribution of income and wealth, reviewed in the previous chapter. Although crucial to our understanding of social inequality, an exclusive focus on this dimension neglects other important **non-material** aspects of inequality. Recognition of the equal worth of all people also means treating them fairly, with equal respect and dignity, and ensuring that they are empowered and able to fully participate in society.[1] In decent societies institutions do not humiliate, marginalize, or exclude their members, especially their most vulnerable ones. Lamentably, outside of the world of hunting and gathering communities, this ideal has not often been approximated or very seriously embraced; few societies have treated all of their members decently, let alone equally or equitably. However, while enormous inequalities exist across the capitalist world today, some nations have gone notably further than others in recognizing and redressing them. Non-material aspects of inequality, most typically addressed through the installation of broad networks of rights, entitlements, and closely associated policies, protections, and provisions, are the focus of this chapter. After an introductory discussion of rights and entitlements, it highlights and contrasts some non-material aspects of inequality, including those linked to social policy and the welfare state, across and within the Nordic and Anglo-Saxon nations. The issues of primary concern in this chapter are human dignity, social inclusion, recognition, and other relational dimensions of inequality. As we will see, these issues are often closely linked to the material indicators of inequality examined in chapter 3.

Rights, Entitlements, and Social Policy

One of the central ways in which modern societies attempt to foster non-material forms of equality is through the recognition and provision of rights. The concepts of **rights** and **entitlements** refer to a potentially broad canopy of liberties, opportunities, claims, securities, and immunities from various forms of abuse, constraint, and compulsion. They are necessary for human beings to function and live a life of dignity and are central to the realization of equality. In capitalist societies liberal rights and protections focus upon the protection of the individual from the encroachment of others, including the state and other institutions and organizations. The assertion that *all* individuals have these rights has played a central role in promoting equality and in challenging long-standing hierarchical and discriminatory social structures, institutions, and ideologies. However, as products of bourgeois revolutions that developed with, and from within, capitalism, they are seriously limited by their character, orientation, and narrow purview. First, because they begin from assumptions that people are mutually hostile individuals, they can promote egoism and self-interest over broader societal interests. Marx referred to the right to hold property, for example, as the 'right of selfishness' because it allows people to utilize and dispose of their property independently from society, with little regard for the interests of others (Marx 1978:42). Unless they are protected by other countervailing rights that ground certain responsibilities and duties, the interests of other less powerful individuals, groups of people, and communities may be easily ignored or trampled upon by this right. Absent such protections and state intervention, there is little, for example, to prevent large corporations from clear-cutting on lands on which indigenous peoples reside or engaging in numerous other activities that could have a detrimental impact upon the environment and broader interests of larger communities. Second, liberal rights can also encourage people to view others primarily as barriers to their own freedom, rather than as allies and a potent means of securing and expanding their freedom through solidarity. These two aspects of liberal rights can foster the development of highly litigious communities and societies in which the rights of some individuals increasingly conflict with those of others, with little consideration of responsibilities to other individuals and larger communities. This is perhaps most clearly seen in the US, where the concept of individual rights is most dominant and well-entrenched.

The cloak of liberal rights stresses equality among citizens but also conceals fundamental inequalities. While people may be equal in their possession of certain rights, they are far from equal in their ability to exercise them or benefit from them. Liberal rights generally do not seriously address material or economic inequalities. Rather, they may obscure, minimize, or even endorse and promote them. The living conditions and interests of the poor and the homeless, for example, do not often receive serious consideration or support from these rights. Many basic rights, such as the rights to vote or receive an education, for example, are considerably less meaningful and serviceable to people who live in abject poverty. Most people have the formal right to run for office, but their chances of running a successful election campaign are highly dependent upon direct access to significant resources or close connections to well-heeled and powerful backers. Similarly, the 'freedom of the press' secured through the constitutions in many developed capitalist nations suggests that all people have an equal opportunity to express their views. However, as the American journalist and critic Abbot Joseph Leibling famously quipped half a century ago, this freedom is really guaranteed only to those who own a press—in other words, those who control the mass media, which remains the most important source of information and news for most people, however popular and democratic the Internet is believed to be today.

Simply eliminating formal barriers via liberal rights cannot bring about equality in a very full or entirely meaningful sense, as noted in the discussion of equal opportunity in chapter 2. But despite these serious limitations, liberal rights can be a central component of equality, a foundation to develop further and build upon as one part of a multi-faceted strategy to foster greater equality. Rights can reduce us to atomized, abstract individuals, but they also can be employed to acknowledge and defend our differences and alleviate some of the inherent inequalities and ill effects of capitalism. The effectiveness of rights as a means of generating greater equality depends upon several factors such as (1) their **latitude**—how inclusive they are and whether or not they acknowledge and promote the interests of various groups, (2) their **depth and scope**—the coordinated and coherent layering of interrelated rights to ensure that they can be effectively exercised, (3) their **weight**—how conscientiously they are respected and enforced, and (4) their **support**—the kinds and levels of resources that are made available to citizens and residents to enable them to actually utilize their rights, including legal and social policies and other entitlements. By way of illustration, the extension of the political right to hold elected positions to women must certainly be viewed as an important and genuine gain achieved nearly a century ago in most of the developed nations. But it is one that has been rarely exercised since then by women with lower levels of income and education, or burdened with double days of work. To render it practicable for many women, this right to hold office must be buttressed by other rights, entitlements, and forms of support that, for example, promote fair and decent salaries for women, subsidize the costs of political campaigns, ensure access to post-secondary education, and provide child care. These social services and other related provisions and entitlements must also be of a high quality, readily accessible, and free at point of use, or at least affordable for all. In nations where these conditions have been gradually built up, women's representation in parliament has gradually approached parity with that of men.[2]

Rights are not just sets of legal procedures and practices. They also are expressions of values and commitments, and they reflect power relations among political forces in nations. The demand for recognition of additional rights, or for a broader interpretation of existing ones, evolves over time in response to social and technological changes, changing values and ideas, and shifts in the balance of power in society. Consequently, the range of rights recognized in society can gain momentum, and the layering and enforcement of rights, as well as the type and availability of resources in place to support them, can vary greatly cross-nationally. For example, even within the group of Anglo-Saxon nations, the American approach to rights stands out as intransigently individualistic. The US has been generally very reluctant to recognize and provide group rights. Moreover, when it does provide rights to groups that have been historically disadvantaged and discriminated against, they have often been quickly challenged as forms of 'reverse discrimination'. The US has also been less enthusiastic about 'social' rights and much less willing to adopt or endorse social policies and programs to secure them. Other Anglo-Saxon nations, including Canada and the UK, have often been more amenable to the idea of at least some forms of group rights and, in these instances, have furnished a wider range of social benefits and services to secure them. However, the Nordic lands have often gone significantly further in their recognition of the rights of various groups, and they have typically provided denser layers of rights and far greater social supports and resources to uphold them in many instances. This chapter provides an account of natural, human, and constitutional/legal rights and a comparative examination of the rights to protection, provision, and participation in the Anglo-Saxon and Nordic lands, with a particular focus upon some groups that have been often denied them or inadequately supported.

Natural Rights, Human Rights, and Constitutional/Legal Rights

It is useful to begin by distinguishing among three broad forms or manifestations of rights—natural rights, constitutional/legal rights, and human rights—on the basis of their expression as primarily intangible moral doctrines or more concrete procedures and legal instruments that address specific problems and issues and secure a range of protections and entitlements.

Natural rights express ideal norms or standards that set out how people *should* be treated, but they have not been legally codified. Consequently, they are the most abstract form of rights and most readily conceptualized as universal, transhistorical, and inalienable; i.e., as applicable to all people for all times. But like the concept of intrinsic equality reviewed in chapter 2, they are also the most easily rendered rhetorical. Nevertheless, they have inspired and shaped attempts to cast them within more concrete legal instruments and frameworks. The onus for securing these rights in a more tangible form has typically fallen to states and to other international and intergovernmental bodies.

Rights find their most explicit formulation in constitutional and legal documents at the national level. **Constitutional/legal rights** are natural rights and norms 'in practice', as enacted in domestic constitutions and laws upheld by the state, rather than just abstract philosophical ideals. They presuppose the existence of particular practices and institutions, such as criminal trials and prisons, democratic elections, schools, social programs, and welfare states. Because their expression and enforcement is highly contingent upon national and local contexts, they can vary significantly from country to country.

Like natural rights, **human rights** also express and promote ideals and goals. The term 'human rights' is often used interchangeably with 'natural rights', and it originates from the concept and discussion of natural rights in the Enlightenment period. However, it has taken on a second and more widely employed meaning in the post-World War II period. Today it most commonly refers to a wide and progressively expanding range of rights that are embedded in international declarations, bills, conventions, laws, and other agreements among countries—or that seek such formal legal recognition. However, because these international agreements are not necessarily legally binding, and are typically much more difficult to monitor and enforce than those that are embedded in national legal frameworks and constitutions, human rights can be viewed as occupying a position somewhere between constitutional/legal rights introduced at the national level and abstract natural rights that transcend time and place.

Natural Rights

The concept of rights as an approach or means of establishing equal concern, respect, and dignity for everyone is most firmly rooted in the 'intrinsic equality' ideal—the foundational notion that people are innately or 'naturally' equal, and hence deserving of fair treatment and equal concern and respect—and closely linked to seventeenth- and eighteenth-century European thought. The British philosophers Hobbes and Locke were among the seminal figures who first proposed the concept of *natural* universal rights.[3] By contemporary standards, their discussion was vague, ambiguous, and severely restricted. Locke's discussion of rights in his *Two Treatises of Government* (1988 [1688]) identifies only three central 'natural' rights—the right to life, the right to liberty, and the right to estates (property).[4] But this idea of inalienable, imprescriptible moral imperatives and principles has been central to the modern conception of rights. The American and French Revolutions were inspired by it, and both the American Declaration of Independence (1776) and the Declaration of the Rights of Man (1789) established by the first French republic were profoundly shaped by it.[5] From this perspective, basic rights are pre-political; that is, they are not subject to human decisions. Nor are they derived from national or social origin, nationality, legal jurisdiction, citizenship, adherence to any belief system, or any other localizing or identifying factors or characteristics, such as class, sex, race, ethnicity, or religion that may be associated with any particular group.[6] Whether divinely endowed upon everyone by their Creator, or more metaphysically derived from our universal status as rational, purposive agents with the capacity to make choices in pursuit of goals and interests, all humans are born with the same rights, and inherently equally deserving of the same concern and respect.[7]

In stark contrast, Jeremy Bentham (1748–1832), another English legal theorist and political philosopher, ridiculed the notion of 'natural' rights as high-flown, sentimental drivel, which he famously referred to as 'nonsense upon stilts'. He argued that natural rights are merely figurative abstractions or fictions, unenforced aspirations at best. Bentham maintained that rights can only exist by convention and legal codification, through the enactment of national laws and their strict enforcement by the state. While natural rights may pre-exist society, and their legitimacy may precede contingent, historical circumstances, they must be interpreted, formulated, and secured via concrete, legal instruments to have real meaning and force. Moreover, they presuppose specific social structures and institutions and relations of power. Thus, rights have not been universal, transhistorical, inalienable, or transcultural 'on the ground'. For example, democratic nations all determine when people are old enough to vote in their elections, and they do so somewhat arbitrarily. The age for the acquisition of voting rights has varied widely cross-temporally, and continues to do so cross-nationally today. People convicted of serious crimes routinely forfeit their right to freedom of movement, whether temporarily or permanently, and have often lost their right to vote as well. And, in some nations, such as the US today, people convicted of capital offenses may even forfeit their right to life.

Bentham sought to provide a coherent and rational foundation for social and legal policy. Compared to Locke, he envisioned a somewhat larger role for the state, and he sought to reform almost every aspect of society, including the government, the legal system, the schools, and the churches. But he strongly maintained that rights must be firmly grounded in legislation. While his point is well taken, it should also be remembered that natural rights can serve as exemplars, higher standards to which societies may aspire. And they have often inspired people to resist and challenge dictatorial and corrupt governments that have sought to deny or restrict their freedoms.

Human Rights

Modern attempts to protect human rights through international agreements began in 1919 with the League of Nations. Today the expression of human rights and norms is most closely linked to the efforts of its successor, the United Nations, created in 1945 amidst international revulsion over the Holocaust. In 1948 the United Nations adopted and proclaimed a Universal

Declaration of Human Rights describing and enumerating a broad range of civil, political, and social protections, liberties, and entitlements. It was patterned on previous human rights documents, such as the US Bill of Rights and France's Declaration of the Rights of Man and of the Citizen. But, unlike them, it was meant to be applicable to *all* people in *all* nations, and it was much more extensive. However, the standards set out in its thirty articles were only recommendations and objectives, and not justiciable.

Subsequently, the UN created several international covenants and conventions that would transform many of the rights expressed in its Declaration into norms of international law that *would be* legally binding.[8] These treaties include the International Covenant on Civil and Political Rights (CCPR, 1966) and the International Covenant on Economic, Social and Cultural Rights (CESCR, 1966). A summary of the Articles set out in the Declaration of Human Rights and their reinforcement via the international treaties concerning civil and political rights (CCPR) or economic, social, and cultural rights (CESCR) is presented in Table 4.1.[9]

Other important and relevant international rights treaties include the International Convention on the Elimination of All Forms of Racial Discrimination (CERD, 1966), the International Convention on the Elimination of All Forms of Discrimination Against Women (CEDAW, 1979), and the International Convention on the Rights of the Child (CRC, 1989).

After more than two decades of work, the UN adopted a Declaration on the Rights of Indigenous Peoples in 2007. The UN has also adopted an International Convention on the Rights of People with Disabilities (2006), which entered into force in 2008.[10] The UN Declaration and these international treaties have been extremely valuable as a means of promoting rights, but they have not been as effective in actually protecting rights as had been originally anticipated by many of their advocates. Because the articles that comprise the Declaration are not legally enforceable, they really constitute an extension and elaboration of the natural rights identified and championed by the Enlightenment philosophers a few centuries ago, rather than legal guarantees. Embedding these and other human rights in international treaties has given them greater force but, for several reasons, this has not firmly established or secured them.

First, nations may become signatories to international treaties without ratifying them. A nation's signature is only a preliminary step, expressing an 'interest' in a treaty. It is only through the act of ratification that a nation indicates its definitive consent to be bound by the treaty.[11] Moreover, these treaties do not come into force until a critical number of nations have ratified them. The International Covenant on Economic, Social and Cultural Rights, for example, was adopted in 1966, but was not operable until a decade later. And it has never been ratified by some nations, such as the US. As noted in Table 4.2, the US has refrained from ratifying several of the principal UN

Table 4.1 Ten Rights Set Out in the Declaration of Human Rights & Secured in International Treaties

Declaration of Human Rights (1948)	International Covenant on Civil and Political Rights (1966)
Articles concerning civil and political rights	***Articles concerning civil and political rights***
Everyone has the right to life, liberty and security of person / Article 3	*Article 9; Article 6 (re: death penalty)*
No one shall be subject to torture or to cruel, inhuman or degrading treatment or punishment / Article 5	*Article 7*
All are equal before the law and are entitled without any discrimination to equal protection of the law . . . / Article 7	*Article 14; Article 26*
Everyone has the right to freedom of opinion and expression . . . / Article 19	*Article 19; Article 18*
Everyone has the right to freedom of peaceful assembly and association / Article 20	*Article 21; Article 22 (re: unions)*
Everyone has the right to take part in the governing of the country, directly or through freely chosen representatives / Article 21	*Article 25*

Declaration of Human Rights (1948)	International Covenant on Economic, Social and Cultural Rights (1966)
Articles concerning social rights	***Articles concerning social rights***
Everyone has the right to work, to free choice of employment, to just and favourable conditions of work and to protection against unemployment. Everyone, without any discrimination, has the right to equal pay for equal work . . . / Article 23	*Article 7*
Everyone has the right to a standard of living adequate for the health and well-being of himself and of his family, including food, clothing, housing, and medical care and necessary social services, and the right to security in the event of unemployment, sickness, disability, widowhood, old age, or other lack of livelihood in circumstances beyond his control . . . / Article 25	*Article 9; Article 11; Article 12*
Everyone has the right to education / Article 26	*Article 13*
Everyone has the right freely to participate in the cultural life of the community . . . / Article 27	*Article 15*

Sources: UN (nd) Office of the High Commissioner for Human Rights; UN (nd) The Universal Declaration of Human Rights.

conventions addressing various forms of inequality, or has done so belatedly. The International Covenant on Civil and Political Rights (1966), for example, was not ratified by the US until 1992, and then only with several restrictions placed on it.[12] Although it has less legal force, it is sometimes suggested that

TABLE 4.2 Ratification of Six Key UN Treaties in Six Nations

	Anglo-Saxon Nations			Nordic Nations		
	Canada	UK	US	Finland	Norway	Sweden
International Covenant on Civil & Political Rights (CCPR, 1966)	1976	1976	1992[a]	1975	1972	1971
International Covenant on Economic, Social & Cultural Rights (CESCR, 1966)	1976	1976	not ratified	1975	1972	1971
International Convention on the Elimination of All Forms of Racial Discrimination (CERD, 1966)	1970	1969	1994	1970	1970	1971
Convention on the Elimination of All Forms of Discrimination Against Women (CEDAW, 1979)	1981	1986	not ratified	1986	1981	1980
Convention on the Rights of the Child (CRC, 1989)	1991	1991	not ratified	1991	1991	1990
Convention on the Rights of Persons with Disabilities (2006)	2010	2008	not ratified	not ratified	not ratified	2008

[a] ratified with restrictions

Sources: UN (nd) Declarations and Conventions Contained in General Assembly Resolutions; UN (nd) United Nations Treaty Collection: Chapter IV: Human Rights.

the original Declaration of Human Rights carries more moral weight than any of the UN's subsequent treaties because it was adopted and openly embraced by the larger international community rather than a smaller subset of nations.

Second, UN treaties have few consequential enforcement provisions and rely primarily on the honour of national signatories to abide by their commitments. Compliance with international treaties is typically addressed via human rights committees comprised of independent experts, rather than through human rights courts. Nations are obliged to submit periodic reports to these committees indicating their compliance with those treaties that they have ratified. The UN Commission on Human Rights appoints special experts, or rapporteurs, to examine, monitor, and publicly report on states' conformity with the treaties and any measures taken to address domestic human rights issues and problems.[13] However, while these experts, committees, and other relevant bodies may express their views concerning whether or not certain national practices constitute violations of human rights instruments, they are not authorized to take legal actions or issue binding decisions against nations that are deemed to be in violation of any treaties that they ratified. In addition, some UN treaties, such as the International Covenant on Economic, Social and Cultural Rights, have few formal channels for individuals who wish to register complaints. This particular treaty, for example, simply obliges the nations that have ratified it to progressively work toward its fulfillment as their maximum available resources allow. Other treaties, such as the International Covenant on Civil and Political Rights, do have complaint mechanisms that allow individuals or representatives who have experienced human rights violations to appeal to the Human Rights Commission, but there is no effective mechanism for enforcement of its recommendations or compensation of those whose rights have been violated (Alston and Crawford 2000; Bayefsky 2001; Teeple 2005). Errant national signatories to the treaties may face censure from public opinion around the globe but, apart from moral suasion ('naming and shaming'), the UN has very few means at its disposal to foster compliance or impose its recommendations on them.[14] And, as the British political theorist Thomas Hobbes (1985 [1651]:223) forewarned several centuries ago, 'Covenants, without the Sword, are but Words, and of no strength to secure a man at all'.

Finally, in practice, nations have had considerable latitude in the ways that they *interpret* the rights set out in international declarations and treaties. The rights enumerated in the Covenant on Economic, Social and Cultural Rights, for example, look very different across the varied national contexts in which they have received ratification. The right of everyone to the enjoyment of just and favourable conditions of work has been interpreted and embraced in markedly different ways across the Nordic and Anglo-Saxon nations. This includes fair wages and equal remuneration for work of equal value without distinction of any kind (Article 7), the right of everyone to social security, including social insurance (Article 9), and, not least, the right of everyone to an adequate standard of living, including adequate food, clothing, and housing, and the fundamental right to be free from hunger (Article 11). The rights and protections set out in other international treaties addressing racial discrimination (CERD), discrimination against women (CEDAW), and the rights of children (CRC) also vary notably in the ways that they have been incorporated into national constitutional and legal frameworks and monitored, enforced, and supported across these two groups of nations.

Legal/Constitutional Rights

The establishment of national or societal-level social and political norms, rules, and laws that set out how people can or should be treated has a long history. Ancient societies of Mesopotamia, Persia, and the classical Greek and Roman worlds established legal statutes, codes of law, and other provisions to protect their citizens. The major religions around the globe have, for millennia, issued moral codes and injunctions exhorting rulers to govern their nations or empires justly and compassionately. But the approaches taken toward well-being and equality by virtually all of these pre-modern societies and political/religious traditions—Western and non-Western alike—have typically emphasized duties and privileges rather than the concept of rights as understood today. Moreover, while some of them made impermissible many acts that would be considered violations of basic rights today, and several even established certain benefits for their citizens, these prohibitions and endowments were most often derived from divine command or a ruler's personal sense of justice and bestowed 'from above', rather than viewed as natural or inherent (Donnelly 2003). Indeed, the bundles of duties and benefits prescribed and furnished in many of these societies and communities might be purposively truncated or entirely denied to some individuals or groups on the grounds that they were inferior or even subhuman, as in the social systems based upon slavery, castes, or feudal and other hierarchies.[15] Modern legal and constitutional rights, sometimes referred to as 'citizenship rights', are a relatively recent creation and distinct from earlier means of fostering and securing a measure of human dignity and equality. But the ways in which rights have been interpreted and institutionalized has varied greatly across nations, and this variation has become increasingly evident over past decades.

In his seminal work on citizenship, T.H. Marshall (1950, 1964) identified three broad categories of rights, civil, political, and social, introduced at the national level. Each of these three groupings, in turn, comprises several families and sub-families of rights that were cumulatively secured and expanded over the past 300 years, supported by the development of corresponding sets of laws and institutions. **Civil rights** emerged in the eighteenth century and were institutionalized in civil and criminal courts and the broader legal system. These rights included 'security rights' to protect people from violent crimes, such as murder, torture, rape, and other forms of cruelty, oppression, and maltreatment, as well as a range of prohibitions against arbitrary arrest, illegal detainment and imprisonment, excessive punishment, and other 'due process' rights.[16] The right to a trial (habeas corpus) is among the most familiar member of this family of rights.[17] Freedom of speech, thought, and faith; the freedoms to own property and enter into valid contracts; and freedom of movement are other important civil rights. **Political rights**, Marshall suggested, took shape next, in the nineteenth century, to provide and protect the liberties necessary for participation in the political process. These rights, including the rights to vote and to hold office and the rights to peaceful assembly, to protest, and to join unions, were supported by the creation of new political institutions, parties, and interest groups and built upon the idea of representative democracy and periodic elections. Finally, around the turn of the twentieth century, **social rights** began to establish roots and flourish. These have included protection against discrimination, the rights to fair pay and equal pay for equal work, the right to safe and healthy working conditions, the right to an education, and the right to social security through programs such as old age pensions, provisions for unemployment, health care, and a range of other benefits and services associated with the more or less comprehensive welfare states of the modern era.

Of course, the manifestations of these rights have often been quite dissimilar across the developed nations and they did not always emerge so linearly. Outside of the British Empire, as Marshall's critics have frequently noted, the three species of rights he identified were not necessarily secured during the same period or in the same sequence he set out.[18] Moreover, some of the specific rights listed above have not yet been enacted or enforced in some nations. And many of the rights achieved in nations of the capitalist world did not initially include all groups, or even a majority of their populations. Democratic political rights, for example, emerged only slowly and incrementally over an extended period of time.[19] Following the nobility's success in increasing its power by legally restraining that of the king, the ascendant capitalist classes gradually wrested control from the titled lords. However, the emergent political systems they established strictly, and quite deliberately, limited suffrage via property ownership or income qualifications, thereby excluding the great majority of the citizens and residents in their nations as effectively as the Greeks and Romans did in ancient times. It was not until well into the twentieth century that most developed nations would finally abolish most of these franchise restrictions, when their working classes were large and organized enough to challenge the political privilege and power of wealthy, propertied men.

Political rights also came much later for women, visible minorities, immigrants, and several other groups in virtually every Western capitalist nation and, again, only after significant power struggles. Women did not obtain the franchise or the right to stand for election until long after men in most of them, although unrestricted forms of female suffrage were generally in place earlier in the Nordic lands than in the Anglo-Saxon nations (Lovenduski and Hills 1981; Mackie and Rose 1982).[20] Other groups would not be enfranchised for several decades after that. In Canada, for example, the Inuit were not allowed to vote federally until 1950, while members of Canada's First Nations living on reservations were not enfranchised until 1960. In the US a wide variety of legal devices, such as literacy tests and poll taxes, were deliberately employed to effectively disenfranchise blacks, as well as many poor whites, in several Southern states until the mid-1960s.[21] Political equality—even very narrowly defined in relation to the electoral arena—has only relatively recently been universally secured in these nations.

These restrictions did not just apply to suffrage rights and issues. Numerous other civil, political, and social rights were also denied, restricted, and only belatedly and reluctantly handed over to many groups whose members were rendered second-class citizens and relegated to subaltern positions in their societies. Women's entry into the labour market, for example, has often been obstructed or limited to certain sectors of the economy deemed appropriate for them. Their right to remain employed after marriage or childbirth has been frequently restricted. In Canada women could not be appointed to the Senate until 1929, when the British Privy Council finally declared them to be 'persons', thereby reversing a contrary ruling by the Supreme Court of Canada the previous year. The Commonwealth Immigrants Act of 1962 rescinded the right of people from Commonwealth nations to freely enter Britain in an attempt restrict the influx of immigrants from the Caribbean and Indian sub-continent. Filipino men who immigrated to the US were not permitted to vote, own property, or marry 'Caucasian' women until 1946 (Harris 1995:95). And, like the First Nations and Aboriginal peoples in Canada and the US, the Sami—the only recognized indigenous people in the Nordic lands—have long been subject to paternalistic and segregationist policies and practices that have greatly restricted their civil and political rights.[22] In Sweden, for example,

> fifty years after the winning of citizen's rights by the Swedish working class, the Saami were still put under guardianship. The late nineteenth-century thesis that a Saami society could not administer its own assets was still alive as late as the 1970s (Kvist 1994:211).[23]

Indeed, the Swedish state did not officially recognize the Sami as an indigenous people until 1977. However, while the status of the Sami has differed across the three Nordic nations, its language, cultural, social, and political rights have been increasingly recognized and established in all of them over the past few decades, and Sami parliaments were created in Norway (1989), Sweden (1993), and Finland (1996) to enable them to more readily identify, promote, and defend their interests.[24] Sami rights are most developed and secure in Norway today, where approximately half of the Sami population lives. In 1990 the Sami language gained equal official status with Norwegian, and Norway became the first Nordic land to ratify the International Labour Organization (ILO) Convention on the Rights of Indigenous and Tribal Peoples of 1989.[25] While all three Nordic countries have recognized Sami rights to reindeer herding, a traditional Sami activity, and the land use this entails, only Norway has seriously considered broader arrangements that would provide greater legal rights to resources and land ownership (Hocking and Hocking 1999; Minde 2001). However, Sweden and Finland did join Norway, and 140 other nations, in endorsing the UN's non-binding Declaration on the Rights of Indigenous Peoples adopted in 2007; Canada and the US were two of only four nations to vote against it.[26]

Of course, the Nordic lands were not the only countries to expand rights during this period. Indeed, many nations have witnessed a 'rights revolution' since the 1960s. Numerous governments have tried to foster greater respect for human dignity, preserve the integrity and freedom of their populations, and encourage wider participation in society by amending their constitutions and/or introducing numerous other supplemental legal statutes, codes, legislation, and other policy interventions that provide further specification and detail about rights.[27] But greater social equality requires more than the existence of these measures. It is also dependent upon how committed governments are to respecting, supporting, and enforcing rights, and whether their efforts are coordinated within an overarching and coherent strategy. Social policies have played an important role in this capacity, especially in the Nordic nations where many social provisions are furnished as rights (or proto-rights) of residents or citizens, as we will see below.

The Nordic lands have generally come much closer than their Anglo-Saxon counterparts to approximating, defending, and in some cases, even expanding upon the rights set out in the UN Declaration of Human Rights and its subsequent conventions. While it would be impossible to provide an exhaustive account of rights and other non-material indicators of inequality, it is useful to highlight a few of them, focusing upon some of the groups that have most often experienced discrimination and great inequality, including women, children, gays, and people with disabilities. It is not suggested here that any of the Nordic lands have created equality across the board along any dimension or axis, or that there is not a long way to go in several areas in all of them. But significant achievements, often overlooked by those who suggest that social structures or biological essences ensure that there are no meaningful differences across nations, are fully in evidence.

Rights: Addressing Key Axes of Inequality in the Anglo-Saxon and Nordic Lands

The Nordic nations have a deserved and long-standing reputation as 'women-friendly'. It is perhaps in the area of gender equality that it is easiest to see how the constellation of rights, entitlements, and social programs and practices in these nations can be mutually reinforcing and promote further gains, establishing a 'virtuous circle'. The Nordic lands, and especially Sweden, have long provided a range of universal public social services, such as child care, care for the elderly, and several other programs that markedly reduce many forms of labour that have been traditionally relegated to women. This has provided Nordic women with considerably greater opportunities for higher education and involvement in pursuits outside of the home. For example, there are dramatic differences between the Anglo-Saxon and Nordic nations in the levels of female representation in politics. Sweden has long been a leader in this regard. Its unicameral parliament has the highest level of female representation in the developed world; by 2007 it had reached 47%, remarkably close to parity with men.[28] Finland (41.5%) and Norway (39%) also had comparatively high levels of female representation in their parliaments in that same year, while the percentage of seats held by women in the House of Commons in Canada (22%), and in the UK (19.5%), were much lower. With only 16.8% of its seats held by women, the House of Representatives in the US placed only 71st among the 189 nations surveyed, well behind many developing nations (Inter-Parliamentary Union 2009).[29] Three years later the percentages of women in parliament in these six nations, and their rank ordering, remained unchanged.

Few people would expect that a 'token' woman in power—even at the highest executive level, such as prime minister or president—would necessarily improve conditions for women or foster greater gender equality. Indeed, like Prime Minister Margaret Thatcher in the UK, they might reach such heights within mainstream or conservative parties and governments largely because they support traditional values, roles, and institutions, and a market unencumbered by social supports and other forms of state 'interference'. However, studies suggest that once a 'critical mass' is reached, the presence of women in power can make a significant difference (Lovenduski 2005; Phillips 1995; Wängnerud 2000). The presence of women in representative assemblies in numbers proportional to that in the population, and approximate to that of men, is in itself a significant and laudable achievement. And this more egalitarian, gender-balanced composition of representation in the state can help to counter long-standing stereotypes and encourage more girls and women to become involved in politics. But, apart from these substantial gains, higher levels of female representation also allow for the identification, articulation, and promotion of issues, interests, perspectives, and solutions to problems that are often neglected or sidelined by male biases, just as the views and concerns of the working class, the poor, and the homeless have been typically marginalized, misunderstood, and misrepresented by political representatives from very different class backgrounds and social origins. In the Nordic lands, women's greater presence in the political sphere has led to a much greater emphasis on child care, family policy, and many other 'women-friendly' and 'family-friendly' programs and issues. And these programs allow greater representation, further empowering women to bring about change.

The Anglo-Saxon nations have addressed gender equality primarily through an emphasis upon 'gender neutrality' or 'gender sameness' and, in many instances, they have not seen significant progress because of this limited orientation. Such approaches are typically restricted to largely legislative reforms that are designed to foster greater employment opportunities for women in the labour market, eliminate formal barriers to their success through anti-discrimination laws, and improve their levels of remuneration vis-à-vis their male counterparts.[30] Even here, however, the Nordic countries have often outperformed the Anglo-Saxon nations. In Sweden and Finland, women have been *encouraged* to enter the labour force through a conscious implementation of a web of fiscal and parental policies, child care, and legislation.[31] In the Anglo-Saxon nations, and especially the US, in contrast, women have more often been *forced* into the labour market by desperate straits, a dearth of alternatives, and the lack of public supports available to them. Nordic women do tend to work in more highly segregated sectors of the economy (the public sector/welfare state), compared to their Anglo-Saxon counterparts, and they do have very high rates of part-time participation in the labour force, two notable manifestations of gender inequality. However, it must also be remembered that most of this work is performed by women in these nations as *paid* labour. In the Anglo-Saxon countries this work is still carried out by women, but as *unpaid* labour in the family or voluntary sector (by relatives, friends, and neighbours), and often by working women themselves when they return home, as part of their double day of work. And, since it is unpaid, it is excluded from accounts of labour force participation and segregation in the economy (Nermo 1999).[32]

As suggested in chapter 2, liberal 'gender neutral' approaches based upon 'equal opportunity' do not generally acknowledge the additional informal tasks and difficulties that women face; they often just integrate them into pre-existing, unequal structures and norms. The provision of caring services and other programs in the Nordic nations, in contrast, reflects a stronger emphasis upon 'gender recognition'; there is a greater acknowledgment of some of the gender-specific barriers and responsibilities with which women are charged. More recently the Nordic lands have also begun to address 'gender reconstruction', consciously seeking to change some long-standing 'cultural' gender biases (Kjeldstad 2001). For example, Sweden was the first nation to expressly encourage men to take a more active role in child care by changing the accessibility rules for its generous family leave insurance. It had converted its maternity leave program into a parental leave program as long ago as 1974, allowing both parents the opportunity to share the benefit period as they saw fit.[33] But, not surprisingly given familiar and long-standing traditional gender roles and biases, relatively few men opted to take part in the program. In an explicit attempt to further encourage men to play a greater role in caring for their young children, Sweden changed its eligibility rules so that neither parent could claim the entire benefit period. In practice this meant that at least a portion of the leave would have to be taken by the father (currently two months, informally referred to as 'papa months') or that component would be lost. Finland and Norway have adopted a similar 'use it or lose it' approach (as did Denmark and Iceland).

In other areas, however, much less headway has been made. Thus, cross-national accounts of the division of domestic labour indicate that there are no significant differences in the sharing of domestic duties by men and women in the home across the Nordic and Anglo-Saxon nations. Rather, domestic labour is most egalitarian in families where women are paid well and not economically dependent upon their partners (Baxter 1997; Fuwa 2004; Geist 2005). Change in this area has not been nearly as rapid as hoped for. It is exceedingly difficult to undo long-entrenched gendered traditions and patriarchal practices and beliefs. And there is notable variation across the nations of the Nordic world.

Violence against women remains a significant problem in the Nordic nations (Elman 2001; Peter 2006). However, over the past decade, existing laws addressing violence against women have been strengthened, new legislation has been introduced, and extensive programs of preventive measures and supports have been adopted to combat this ongoing problem. The Swedish government, for example, approved a new bill on violence against women, introduced a new offence, 'gross violation of a woman's integrity' into its Penal Code in 1998, and has steadily worked to improve its systems for registering crimes and crime statistics since then. It also has strengthened its provisions regarding sexual harassment in the workplace in its Act Concerning Equality between Men and Women. And, on the grounds that prostitution is an aspect of male violence against women and children, Sweden became the first nation to make the *purchase* of sexual services a punishable offence (Ekberg 2004; Socialstyrelsen 2004).[34]

Children are increasingly featured in comparative studies that address poverty, health, and other economic concerns, but they are too often left out of cross-national research concerned with rights and other non-material dimensions of inequality. The Nordic nations have done very well in both areas. Having long abolished physical punishment in its schools, Sweden became the first nation in the world to introduce a ban to protect children from corporal punishment in the home in 1979, ten years before the United Nations Convention on the Rights of the Child (CRC).[35] The Swedish legislation states that children are entitled to care, security, and respect. It expressly forbids corporal punishment and other humiliating treatment, and suggests that children, like adults, learn best through arguments and persuasion, not violence (Durrant and Olsen 1997). Similar acts were passed in Finland in 1983 and in Norway in 1987. Norway's 1992 Child Welfare Act went even further, protecting children from all types of violence and abuse in the home and allowing for prosecution, under the Criminal Code, of those who assault, mistreat, or neglect their children. There the CRC has attained the status of law.

By 2009 twenty-five nations had followed Sweden's example, adopting legislation banning physical punishment in all forms and settings, an instructive example of how change in one nation can spread to others.[36] But Canada, the UK, and the US were not among this group.[37] Corporal punishment in the home is still legal throughout most of the Anglo-Saxon world, although its legality in the schools of these nations has typically been challenged, if somewhat belatedly.[38] Corporal punishment in schools was banned outright in the UK in 1986, but it has not yet been explicitly banned in two Canadian provinces, or in more than twenty states in the US (Global Initiative to End All Corporal Punishment of Children 2005a, 2005b, 2005c; Newell 2005).[39] The US is also one of only two countries among the 191 members of the United Nations that has not ratified the UN Convention on the Rights of the Child.[40]

The Nordic nations have established Children's Ombudsman offices to safeguard the rights of children and those under 18 years of age. Norway was the first to do so in 1981 but Finland established a Children's Ombudsman Office the same year within its Mannerheim League for Child Welfare, a domestic children's advocate that has been active since 1920. In 1993 Sweden followed their lead (as did Denmark and Iceland in 1994). These nations have also placed bans and a range of restrictions on television and other forms of advertising directed at children.

The Nordic nations have often led the way in the promotion of rights for gays as well. Sweden was among the first nations to take steps toward the recognition of gay marriages via its system of registered partnerships in 1987. In 1993 Norway provided virtually full rights and benefits to registered gay partnerships, and Sweden passed legislation acknowledging the right of gay couples to adopt children the same year. Since 1995, Sweden has provided the same rights and benefits for homosexual couples as for heterosexual couples, a position taken by Iceland (1996), Denmark (1999), and Finland (2002) shortly thereafter. Although gay marriages were not legalized until recently in Norway (2008) and Sweden (2009), they are still among the first nations to do so.[41]

In the Anglo-Saxon world the situation has been rather different, but Canada has clearly gone much further than the UK or the US. Indeed, at least formally, it even surpassed the Nordic nations in this important area, legalizing gay marriages before the Nordic lands did so. However, the recognition of gay marriages in Canada was 'through the back door' via court challenges declaring the banning of same-sex unions as unconstitutional, rather than through the promotion and introduction of new explicit legislation. It also came about incrementally, on a province by province basis. Between 2003 and 2005, nine of Canada's thirteen provinces and territories had declared same-sex marriage legal in this manner.[42] In 2005 same-sex marriage was legalized across the nation by the Civil Marriage Act, following a Supreme Court ruling that it was consistent with the Canadian Charter of Rights and Freedoms. Unlike in Sweden and the other Nordic lands, however, public opinion in Canada has been much more divided over the issue of gay rights and entitlements. In the UK, same-sex couples have been allowed to form civil unions and have been provided certain legal rights through the passage of its Civil Partnership Act in 2004, but this legislation does not provide the same recognition, status, and rights that heterosexual marriages enjoy there. Again, the US clearly stands apart even within the Anglo-Saxon world. Its 1996 federal Defense of Marriage Act (DOMA) explicitly defines marriage as 'a legal union of one man and one woman as husband and wife' and states that the term spouse 'refers only to a person who is the opposite sex of a husband or wife'. To date, Massachusetts is the only state to legalize same-sex marriages, although a few other states provide some rights to gay unions or, at least, do not outlaw them.[43] However, the 1996 DOMA allows US states to deny constitutional marital rights between persons of the same sex that have been recognized in other US states and in other nations. Moreover, the great majority of the states have expressly banned same-sex marriages via the enactment of state laws in recent years and, in many of them, through supplementary constitutional amendments.

The Nordic nations have also gone further in securing rights, benefits, and opportunities for people with disabilities. Although they have tended to address these issues earlier than most other nations, and typically assumed greater responsibility for the costs of reducing environmental barriers that restricted the involvement of people with disabilities in daily life, the Nordic nations initially accepted the same 'medical model' employed across the industrialized world that conceptualizes disabilities largely in terms of the perceived incapacities and limitations of individuals. Consequently, they too emphasized segregated provisions and institutional care to assist them and compensate them for their disadvantaged position. As in many other nations, this compensatory social policy approach gradually gave way to one geared more toward integration via deinstitutionalization, normalization of living and working conditions, and making public life more accessible. But the Nordic nations have provided a more extensive and generous range of cash benefits and social services, in line with their more developed and comprehensive welfare states. Sweden's wide-ranging package of programs for people with disabilities, for example, has long included several income benefits, including disability and assistance allowances to enable people to employ personal assistants and compensate them for the many extra costs they incur as a result of their disability. These include permanent and temporary disability pensions; housing modification grants and benefits; the provision of transportation benefits and services; access to lifts, wheelchairs, prostheses, computerized technology, and other technical aids; the production of literature and newspapers on tape and in Braille; grants for theatre performances for the hearing impaired; extensive medical and health care services; habilitation and rehabilitation services and therapy; education and training programs; pre-school and after school programs for children with disabilities; nursing facilities; and home-based personal care and domestic care (including help with shopping, cooking, and cleaning, and assistance with walks and visiting friends and other recreational and cultural sites).[44] These measures have gone a great distance in enabling people with disabilities to more fully participate in their communities and, since the 1990s, have increasingly reflected the steady displacement of the medical model by a 'social model'. Greater emphasis has been placed upon the inaccessible environments that many people face and upon citizenship and civil rights since the 1990s (Hvinden 2004; Lindqvist 2000). This has involved the introduction of laws prohibiting discrimination and new Acts, or new clauses within existing Acts, that apply specifically to people with functional impairments and legally entitle them to many benefits and opportunities. These new directions have come primarily in response to the demands of the large disabled people's movement in Sweden.[45] This new rights-based approach parallels the UN's 1993 Standard Rules on the Equalization of Opportunities for Persons with Disabilities, which Sweden initiated and which has been embraced in the other Nordic lands as well.

Although there is no specific law establishing the rights of all people with functional impairments, ombudsman offices that represent, defend, and promote the interests of people with disabilities, and many other groups, are common across the Nordic lands today. Sweden created the first ombudsman office in 1809, when its Justice Ombudsman (*Justitieombudsman*) was instituted to safeguard the rights of Swedish citizens. Since then it has established similar offices representing several other groups and issues, including the Ombudsman for Equal Opportunities (*JämO*), the Ombudsman for Children (*Barnombudsmannen*), the Ombudsman against Discrimination on Grounds of Sexual Orientation (*HomO*), the Ombudsman against Ethnic Discrimination *(Diskrimineringsombudsmannen)*, and the Disability Ombudsman (*Handikappombudsmannen*).

Entitlements: Welfare States and Equality in the Anglo-Saxon and Nordic Lands

Most developed nations have established welfare states comprising an array of social policies and programs to promote greater equality and the economic and social well-being of their citizens and residents. Welfare states can play key roles because they can directly confront and address both non-material and material aspects of social inequality. They may provide support for the elderly and those who have retired, or become ill, disabled, or unemployed, or face a wide range of other social contingencies and needs. They can also promote full employment, reduce poverty levels, create greater income equality, and foster more equal opportunities and life chances for disadvantaged individuals and groups. And they can expand the rights of individuals and groups, and secure and promote their existing rights. However, the ability of welfare states to reduce or eliminate many forms of inequality, and expand and reinforce rights, is greatly dependent upon their character: how they are constructed and how ardently they are promoted and sustained.

Welfare states generally comprise three broad forms of social supports: (1) income security measures, (2) social services, and (3) protective legislation (Olsen 2002). **Income supports** ('social transfers') transfer money to individuals and families. They take two primary forms, 'income *maintenance*' programs and 'income *security*' programs. **Income maintenance transfers**, such as unemployment insurance, sickness insurance, maternity leave, parental insurance, and old age pensions, provide monetary support to people who, for a variety of reasons, have left the paid workforce, thereby allowing them to maintain an income. **Income security transfers**, such as family allowances, child support, old age allowances, housing allowances, and social or public assistance, also provide monetary benefits, but their purpose is to provide individuals and families with a measure of social and economic security, not to replace lost market income.[46] **Social service programs,** in contrast, provide care and other non-monetary benefits. These programs may include a wide range of measures such as labour market training, health care, dental care, remedial and preventive counselling, and other forms of assistance for people with problems related to substance abuse, personal care services for the elderly and for people with physical and psychiatric needs, support programs to meet the safety, emotional, and physical needs of battered women and their children, transitional housing, assistance for new parents, child care, support for families in crisis, primary, secondary, and tuition-free or largely subsidized post-secondary education, subsidized housing programs, shelter and day programs for the homeless, language training and settlement programs and services for immigrants and refugees, legal aid, and numerous other 'in-kind' benefits, such as prescription drugs, eyeglasses, prosthetics, wheelchairs and other mobility aids, transportation passes, and hot meals at school. Such a list of services and related protections might appear almost utopian to many people in the Anglo-Saxon world, but most of them are currently in place in Sweden and the other Nordic nations, and many of them have been entrenched there for decades. Various forms of **protective legislation**—the third central component of welfare states—include workplace health and safety laws, equal pay for equal work laws, child protection laws, legislation making paid vacations and holidays mandatory, and other laws that entitle people to the social services and income programs listed above.

Of course, the particular constellation of income transfers, social services, and regulatory legislation, and the overall character, orientation, and impact of welfare states, can differ quite dramatically across the developed capitalist world. This is especially evident when the Anglo-Saxon and Nordic nations are contrasted. Indeed, as with most of the central material and non-material dimensions of inequality, these two groups of nations are usually at opposite ends along most continua tracking various aspects and dimensions of social policy and social welfare. Total public expenditure on social programs and benefits, for example, is generally much higher in the Nordic lands than in the Anglo-Saxon nations. This contrast is most marked when Sweden, the undisputed welfare expenditure leader, and the US, one of the most tightfisted social spenders in the developed world, are juxtaposed. Sweden's total public expenditure in 2001, as a percentage of its GDP, was twice as high as that of the US, and its spending on family benefits was almost ten times higher, as indicated in Table 4.3—a pattern that has held steady over the past few decades. While

TABLE 4.3 **Public Social Expenditure as a % of GDP in Six Nations in 2001**

	Anglo-Saxon Nations			Nordic Nations		
	Canada	UK	US	Finland	Norway	Sweden
Total Public Expenditure	**17.8**	**21.8**	**14.7**	**24.8**	**23.9**	**29.8**
(expenditure in 1990)	(18.6)	(19.5)	(13.4)	(24.8)	(24.7)	(30.8)
Family Benefits	0.90	2.20	0.40	3.00	3.20	3.80
Incapacity Related Benefits	0.80	2.50	1.10	3.90	4.80	5.20
Health	6.70	6.10	6.20	5.30	6.80	7.40
Unemployment Insurance	0.80	0.30	0.30	2.00	0.40	1.00
Active Labour Market Programs	0.40	0.30	0.20	0.90	0.80	1.40
Old Age	4.80	8.10	5.30	7.90	6.80	9.20

Source: OECD Social Expenditure Data Base (2004).

social spending as a percentage of GDP can be misleading—particularly when only one specific policy area, program, or time period is exclusively focused upon—it generally provides a good indication of a nation's commitment to supporting its population.[47] The Nordic nations have also generally introduced social programs much earlier than the Anglo-Saxon nations (Olsen 2002).

Welfare states typically allocate income transfers, in-kind goods, services, and other social benefits to people in three different ways. First, they may provide support on the basis of **need**. In such cases, potential recipients of income transfers (such as social or public assistance) or social services (such as Medicaid in the US), must first prove that they are poor enough to qualify for them through various forms of needs tests, means tests, income tests, or poverty tests. These programs are thus 'targeted' at a particular, and typically rather narrow, section of the population. Second, support may be furnished via social insurance programs, a central component of virtually all modern welfare states. In this case eligibility and the level and quality of support received are largely determined on the basis of **contributions** made by employers, employees, and the government.[48] Although social insurance programs include a far greater proportion of the population than targeted needs-based programs do, they can still leave many people without coverage because they are closely linked to employment status. Consequently, people with part-time, low-paid, or contingent employment in the secondary labour market—where women and immigrants have often been over-represented—and those who work in the unpaid domestic sphere (also largely women), do not often qualify for these benefits in some nations. Or, if they do, the level of support they can obtain is meagre. Insurance programs are thus said to rely upon 'work tests' rather than means tests. Finally, welfare states may provide support to everyone as a basic right or **entitlement**. These universal programs, such as health care, may literally include *all* of the citizens or long-term residents in a nation. Or they may be provided to everyone within certain categories or groups of people within a nation. Universal family allowances, for example, are provided to all families with children below a certain age; universal pensions go to all individuals who have reached a particular age, and so on. While most welfare states utilize all three forms of benefit allocation, they can differ markedly in the emphasis they place on each of them. The Anglo-Saxon nations, for example, stress the first two forms of provision, with a much stronger emphasis upon targeted needs-based programs than in most other welfare states in the developed capitalist world. They expect people to turn to private-sector social programs (employment-based social programs and commercial social programs purchased in the market) and/or the civil sector (community supports and informal support from friends and neighbours) rather than seek support from the state. The Nordic nations emphasize the second and third forms of public support, with a much stronger emphasis upon universal program entitlements than found in most other countries. And the private sector plays a much more minimal role there.

Comparative studies typically develop typologies classifying or grouping national welfare states according to their orientation and they almost invariably place the Nordic nations in a separate category of provision, designating them as 'welfare leaders', and characterizing them as 'institutional', 'social democratic', or 'encompassing'(Esping-Andersen 1990; Korpi 1983; Korpi and Palme 1998).[49] Full employment and the elimination of poverty, while never entirely realized, often have been among their most central goals, as has greater income equality. As we saw in the previous chapter, their efforts and accomplishments in these areas have been laudable. While there is some variation among the nations within this grouping, the Nordic welfare states generally have been much more comprehensive than most others, covering a wider range of social contingencies and needs. They typically have rendered the residents of their nations less dependent upon the marketplace, individual employers, or workplaces to meet basic needs. They furnish relatively generous income transfer programs and a dense network of social services, which arguably is the most definitive feature of their welfare states. Moreover, many of their programs are proactive and preventative rather than reactive. Active labour market training programs, child care, and the webs of income support measures, for example, are designed to anticipate needs and attempt to head off poverty, unemployment, and other social problems.

Most pertinent to this chapter's focus on rights, however, is the fact that the wide range of income benefits, social services, and protections that comprise the Nordic welfare states is largely provided universally, as entitlements to all long-term residents of their nations. In Sweden, for example, all parents who are employed or in school and have children under the age of seven are entitled to child care, which is of a high quality, centred upon learning ('educare'), and designed to meet the particular needs of local communities. Parents are also entitled to a 16-month paid parental leave (providing an income replacement rate of 80% of their pay for the first 13 months and a flat rate for the remaining three) plus an additional three months of statutory unpaid leave.[50] An additional paternity leave entitles fathers to ten more days of paid leave after the birth or adoption of a child to allow them to share in the care and welcoming of their new family members. Parents of functionally disabled children are also provided with 10 paid 'contact days' (per child and year) to allow them to take parental training courses, help their children adapt to their surroundings, and become more involved in their children's daycare and elementary school activities. Swedish residents also have a right to health care, including dental care for everyone under the age of 19. And Sweden's universal sickness insurance plan ensures that families are still financially secure when 'breadwinners' become too ill to work. Swedish parents can take up to 60 days per child, per year, of sickness benefits to allow them to stay home to care for sick children under the age of 12 (or 16 in special circumstances). Post-secondary education is also provided as a right, and everyone working full-time in the paid workforce, regardless of sector, is entitled to a 5-week paid vacation. The welfare states in the other Nordic nations are quite similar, if not quite as developed, although Norway has placed greater emphasis on supporting women in the home (Berven 2002; Hiilamo 2004; Olsen 2002, 2007; Sörensen and Bergqvist 2002). These are only a few of the numerous entitlements in place for families in the Nordic lands. The contrast here with the relatively few and meagre provisions of the Anglo-Saxon world, despite its prevailing 'family first' rhetoric, is quite stark. Several of the universal entitlements that the Nordic nations furnish are geared toward people in the paid workforce. But many others, including family allowances, housing allowances, flat-rate parental leaves, health/dental care, and tertiary education, for example, are not linked to participation in the labour force.

The welfare states in the Anglo-Saxon nations are, in many respects, mirror images of their Nordic counterparts. They too are typically grouped together in a single category designating them as 'welfare laggards', or characterizing them as 'residual', 'liberal', or 'basic' welfare states. They cover fewer social contingencies and needs, furnish relatively few social services, and provide comparatively low-benefit income programs. The social programs they do provide tend to be reactive and interventionist, designed to address social problems only *after* they emerge and take root. Thus, for example, they emphasize passive unemployment insurance measures to support people once they have become unemployed—and provide marginal levels of support for restricted periods at that—rather than active measures that would allow them to stay in the paid workforce and to secure and improve their socio-economic position. This is reflected in the expenditure data in Table 4.3; the Anglo-Saxon nations have always spent relatively little on training programs. In the US, which places the greatest emphasis upon the market and 'self-reliance', expenditure on training programs is lowest, and there are the fewest supports and programs to actually help people to become more independent. All six of the Nordic and Anglo-Saxon nations have placed greater stress upon 'work first' principles over the provision of income support in recent years. But in the Nordic lands this has been, at least partly, a reflection of some sense of a 'right to work' and a concern with social inclusion. In the US and the other Anglo-Saxon nations, in contrast, the increasing emphasis upon 'workfare' programs serves to push the poor and unemployed into the labour force under conditions that largely reinforce their subordination, marginalization, and social exclusion. Similarly, despite the priority assigned to 'equal opportunity' in the Anglo-Saxon nations, they opt to provide universal education only at the primary and secondary levels, even though the cost of post-secondary education has become increasingly out of reach for many families.[51] All nations, including the US, provide primary and secondary education through the public sector to ensure that everyone has the requisite literacy and numeracy skills and knowledge to function in society, and to foster equal opportunity. Yet, despite the stress upon equal opportunity in the US, public provision of tertiary education by the state, in stark contrast, would be viewed as 'socialist' and 'un-American', rather than as a vehicle to help people who are economically disadvantaged and a means of creating a more level playing field.

As noted above, many of the income benefits and services in the Anglo-Saxon nations are allocated on the basis of need, rather than as a right. Like the nineteenth-century British Poor Laws from which they have descended, these programs often require potential recipients to qualify for social support by demonstrating that they are poor enough. Moreover, living in poverty and desperate need are not necessarily enough to qualify some people for support if it is deemed that they are somehow responsible for their plight. Once identified, the poor are divided to separate the 'deserving poor' from the 'undeserving poor'. Premised upon the central notion that the market and the work ethic must never be undermined, those who have demonstrated that they merit public assistance are discouraged from becoming reliant upon it by long waiting periods, low benefit levels, and short benefit duration periods, and by the constant surveillance and supervision of recipients—program aspects expressly designed to ensure that the experience of being 'on welfare' is often distressing and demeaning. Like the Poor Laws of past centuries, these contemporary social programs often function as systems of temporary and limited relief within broader frameworks of repression. This depiction most closely fits the US welfare state, which stands out among the liberal, Anglo-Saxon nations as an especially threadbare 'social safety net'.

In the Anglo-Saxon lands, a great premium is placed upon self-reliance and autonomy. In reality, however, few if any individuals, groups, or institutions are truly self-sufficient. In fact, reliance upon family, friends, and neighbours for support is strongly encouraged. And, while not always so openly acknowledged, the 'independence' of male 'breadwinners' has almost always been premised upon female domestic work. In these nations the greatest animosity is directed at certain forms of 'public sector' dependence. While the dependence of large corporations upon the state to provide favourable fiscal policies ('corporate welfare'), underwrite the private risks of production, and provide the physical and technical infrastructure they require to expand and generate profit is rarely questioned, dependence of the poor upon the state for support is almost always viewed very harshly. In recent years, the Republican and Democratic parties in the US have often competed to demonstrate their greater commitment to 'self-reliance' by enthusiastically cutting back basic social supports for low-income families. Indeed, with the end of the long-standing Aid to Families with Dependent Children (AFDC) program in 1996 by the Democrats—which had at least entitled recipients to public assistance if they could demonstrate that they were poor enough—the US welfare state has become considerably less supportive in recent years.[52] Similar policy developments have taken place in Canada and in the UK over the past decade.

According to the constitution of the World Health Organization (WHO), 'the enjoyment of the highest attainable standard of health is one of the fundamental rights of every human being without distinction of race, religion, political belief, economic or social condition'. But it is well-known that, unlike all of the other nations across the wealthy, developed capitalist world, the US does not have a universal public health care system, nor does it ensure that all its citizens have access to private health care. At the Second National Convention of the Medical Committee for Human Rights in Chicago in 1966, the American civil rights leader and Nobel Peace Prize Laureate Martin Luther King stated that 'of all forms of inequality, injustice in health care is the most shocking and inhumane'. By 2010 nearly 47 million Americans had no health care coverage at all, and millions more have such inadequate coverage that they would be bankrupted by a serious injury or illness.[53]

As indicated in Table 4.4, truly universal social programs provided as an entitlement or right to everyone are not common in the Anglo-Saxon nations. Canada and the UK have done much more than the US has here, but their universal social provisions have typically been considerably less generous, supportive, and encompassing than those of their Nordic counterparts. And their universal programs have been in decline over the past two decades. Health care is the policy area where these two nations are most starkly different from the US and have more closely resembled the Nordic lands. But several studies indicate that their health care systems are not as comprehensive and/or have generally not performed as well as those in Sweden, Finland, and Norway in terms of outcomes and efficiency (Conference Board of Canada 2004; Nolte and McKee 2003; Swedish Association of

Table 4.4 Seven Public Universal Programs across Six Nations

	Anglo-Saxon Nations			Nordic Nations		
Program	Canada	UK	US	Finland	Norway	Sweden
Paid Leave:						
Maternity	15 weeks	39 weeks	—	18 weeks	9 weeks	—
Parental	35 weeks	13 weeks	—	26 weeks	4 weeks	64 weeks
Paternity	—	—	—	3 weeks	52 weeks	2 weeks
Family Allowances	— (abolished)	for all residents with children under 16	—	for all residents with children under 17	for all residents with children under 18	for all residents with children under 16
Child Care	— (Quebec only)	—	—	ages 1–7	ages 1–5	ages 0–6
Health Care	all residents	all residents	—	all residents	all residents	all residents
Post-Secondary Education	—	—	—	all residents	all residents	all residents
Statutory/Paid:						
Vacation	2 weeks	4 weeks	—	5 weeks	5 weeks	5 weeks
Holidays	8 days		—	9 days		
Old Age Pensions	Old Age Security (OAS)	basic pension	Old Age Insurance (OAI)[a]	basic *or* earnings-related pension[b]	basic pension	basic *or* earnings-related pension[b]

[a]'quasi-universal' (Some people qualify on the basis of their relationship to a spouse or partner who has coverage rather than independently, as residents or citizens).

[b]The restructured pension systems in Sweden and Finland now provide universal coverage through one of two complementary programs; Norway will follow their lead in 2010.

Sources: Columbia Clearinghouse on International Developments in Child, Youth and Family Policies, Columbia University (nd); OECD 2005; Olsen 2002; Ray and Schmitt 2007; Whitehouse 2007.

Local Authorities and Regions 2005; World Health Organization 2000). Universal family allowances, which have never existed in the US, have been less generous in the UK and in Canada, where they were abolished in 1992. Unlike the US, which provides no statutory paid maternity, parental, or paternity leaves—and only 12 weeks of unpaid family leave available to less than half of employed women through its Family and Medical Leave Act of 1993—Canada and the UK have maternity/parental leave programs ensuring a year of support to new parents. But their benefit levels have not been nearly as high as those furnished in the Nordic lands.

In the area of old age policy, the US, until recently, was the only country among the six nations examined here that did not provide a first-tier universal pension to all of its citizens as a right.[54] However, restructuring of the public pension systems in Sweden and Finland over the past decade culminated in the elimination of their universal pension programs. Everyone is still covered there, and receives some form of public support. But the old notion of universality—including all long-term residents in the same pension program as an entitlement—has been somewhat compromised in both Nordic lands, and a similar form of restructuring is currently under consideration in Norway.[55] Although they have not been as supportive as their Nordic counterparts, the Canadian and UK retirement systems still include a universal basic pension provided for all citizens.[56]

This very restricted role of universality in the welfare states of the Anglo-Saxon nations has meant that the rights, benefits, and treatment of various groups in their societies can differ greatly. The Anglo-Saxon welfare states have often been characterized as 'dual stream'. The first stream of programs, comprised of comparatively generous public *insurance* benefits, is accessed by people in the primary labour market. Since they have been earned through years of service and program contributions, these social benefits do not carry a stigma. Those who toil in the secondary labour market, in contrast, where employment is often part-time, insecure, contingent, poorly paid, and does not generally provide social supports or benefits, are forced to rely upon second-stream public *assistance* programs. The benefits they provide are typically meagre, mean-tested, hard to access, and highly stigmatized. This arrangement has made it easy to exclude many groups from accessing social supports, or to include them in ways that serve to maintain their disadvantaged, dependent, and subordinate positions. Consider the treatment of immigrants by the American welfare state, which most closely fits the 'dual-stream' welfare model. Socio-economic development and growth in the US has greatly depended upon immigrants, and the nation has actively promoted inclusive immigration policies. Citizenship is based upon birthplace (*jus soli*, the 'right of land'), rather than lineage or descent (*jus sanguinis*, the 'right of blood'). It has been relatively easy for immigrants to become naturalized; the children of immigrants are automatically US citizens if they are born in the US. However, their predominance in the secondary labour market has meant that immigrants have been much more likely to be either excluded from coverage altogether or included in second-stream social programs. Moreover, by instituting tighter eligibility rules and longer residency requirements and, echoing the distinction made between the deserving and non-deserving poor, distinguishing between 'qualified aliens' (such as refugees) and 'unqualified aliens', the US has made it considerably more difficult for many immigrants to even become eligible for its 'second-class' benefits (Sainsbury 2006). Indeed, from its beginnings to its most developed phase, the US welfare state has systematically and expressly excluded other populations, besides immigrants, from social programs, or consigned them to the second, inferior tier of benefits. Numerous studies have documented the ways in which black agricultural and domestic labourers were denied benefits or provided with much lower levels of relief, despite the promise of inclusion held by Roosevelt's New Deal social reforms in 1930s, although there is considerable debate concerning why this has occurred, and how it was made possible.[57] Their disproportional representation among the poor, the lowest-paid, and the unemployed is largely responsible for their disproportional representation in second-stream welfare programs today (Alston and Ferrie 1999; Brown 1999; Lieberman 1998; Quadagno 1994). Although it differs in details, the situation of indigenous peoples, and their treatment by the liberal welfare states in the US and Canada, has been broadly similar, characterized by higher rates of poverty and unemployment, poorer health, lower life expectancies, fewer life chances, weaker recognition of rights, and a disproportionately higher reliance upon second stream social assistance programs (Cooke et al. 2003; Kramer 1995; Moscovitch and Webster 1995; Shewell 2004; Stromwell et al. 1998).

By contrast to the Anglo-Saxon world, universality has been a crucial defining feature of the Nordic welfare states. It both reflects their greater commitment to equality and provides one crucial means to help realize this goal. When social programs are provided universally, as entitlements, there are no first- and second-class tiers, and all long-term residents receive the same or similar benefits, regardless of race, ethnicity, sex, sexual orientation, or other distinctions. Consider nativity, or place of birth, for example. In the Nordic lands, rights and benefits have been provided on the basis of residence (*jus domicili*, the right of domicile). Immigrants have been incorporated into their welfare systems after a short period of permanent residency on terms relatively equal with those enjoyed by other citizens. While immigrants have sometimes been hit harder by welfare retrenchment in these nations because they tend to have lower incomes than other citizens, they have not usually been a *target* of welfare reform, as they have in the Anglo-Saxon nations.[58] Similarly, the Sami population in the Nordic lands has also fared better than its indigenous counterparts in the Anglo-Saxon world. Indeed, in these lands, where the Sami have been entitled to the same benefits and on the same terms as other national residents, problems have sometimes occurred *because* they have been treated like everyone else (Olsson and Lewis 1995). As noted earlier, inequality cannot always be adequately addressed by simply treating everyone identically. It may *also* require the recognition of the particular situations and social policy needs of some groups.[59] However, the Nordic lands have often been considerably more successful than their Anglo-Saxon counterparts in recognizing the needs and rights of many marginalized groups.

As we have seen here, and in the previous chapters, the level, intensity, and forms of social inequality, and the ways in which they have been apprehended and addressed, have varied remarkably between the two groups of nations examined here. In the Nordic lands there has been greater acknowledgment that equality of opportunity is both insufficient and unattainable without an attendant appeal to some measure of equality of condition and equality of outcome. And a good deal more effort has been expended to address several forms of non-material and material inequality there. Residents in the Nordic lands have had a wider and more secure range of rights, including entitlements to many more social programs and benefits, than their counterparts in the Anglo-Saxon world. These nations also have larger middle classes and higher rates of social mobility, and they perform better on most indicators of health. Almost all forms of economic inequality are notably lower there, mollified by fiscal policy, social policy, and other measures. In the Anglo-Saxon nations, the ideals of equality of condition and outcome are eclipsed by a much stricter focus on intrinsic equality and equal opportunity that has been largely realized—and contained—through formal recognition in the legal and political spheres. This is particularly true in the US, where rising levels of inequality over the past few decades have been allied with an increasing toleration for it; inequality has been much more readily embraced and legitimated as essential for economic growth and prosperity for all.

Classical and contemporary theoretical accounts and explanations for social inequality have varied greatly. However, some of these approaches are better able to account for the cross-national variation seen here that is often ignored or downplayed by others. Theories of social inequality can be grouped into four broad schools of thought: (1) perspectives that focus upon 'human nature' and the biosocial characteristics of individuals (or particular groups of people) as the central source of inequality, (2) structural-functionalist approaches that treat societies as 'social systems' and view inequality as the largely inevitable and invaluable outcome of the increasing division of labour and role specialization that develops with modernization, (3) theories that stress the impact of cultures, values, and attitudes, and (4) theories that emphasize conflict and the imbalance in power among groups in society and how some gain at the expense of others.[60] The first three traditions have largely served to justify and legitimate social inequality, while the last approach has challenged these theories and the idea that extreme forms of inequality are inevitable. In Part III, these four theoretical schools are examined from the comparative vantage point. The dominant theoretical traditions that legitimate social inequality (examined in chapter 5) and those that challenge social inequality (chapter 6) are evaluated in light of the cross-national evidence presented earlier.

Notes

1. One of the few comparative studies to address this issue is the study of human dignity and social policy by Chan and Bowpitt (2005). However, their useful comparison of Hong Kong, China, the UK, and Sweden largely focuses upon the treatment of the unemployed in each nation. Avishai Margalit (1996) provides a thoughtful discussion of the idea of human dignity in *The Decent Society.*

2. The nature of the political, party, and electoral systems in place has also played an important role in fostering more gender equality. Electoral systems using proportional representation (as in the Nordic lands), rather than the 'first-past-the-post' plurality-win model (as in the Anglo-Saxon nations) and party lists, with alternating male and female candidates (a 'zippered party list'), foster greater female representation. Higher female representation is also encouraged by the presence of role models and media images portraying women in positions of power and non-traditional occupations.

3. This idea was further developed by others, such as the English political theorists John Stuart Mill (1806–1873) and Thomas Paine (1737–1809), and by the American writer Henry David Thoreau (1817–1862).

4. Following Locke, the American statesman and future President, Thomas Jefferson, referred to 'life, liberty, and the pursuit of happiness' when drafting the US Declaration of Independence.

5. The Magna Carta ('Great Charter') of 1215 in England, forced upon King John by the Pope and English lords, represents a much earlier attempt to legally limit the power of the Throne. In England, the 'Glorious Revolution' of 1688 and the English Bill of Rights of 1689 were designed to further restrict the power of the monarchy.

6. The Enlightenment notion of transhistorical 'natural' rights bears a strong similarity to the ancient Greek and Roman ideas concerning 'natural' justice. Aristotle and Roman Stoics, such as Cicero and Seneca, suggested that natural justice pre-exists specific political and social configurations. However, this natural law was divinely derived and was not based on the idea of equal rights or treatment for everyone. Indeed, the differential and unequal treatment of 'inferiors', such as women, immigrants, and slaves, could be considered just.

7. Of course, divine and secular justifications for rights need not be mutually exclusive, since human morality and rationality were commonly understood as derived from God. Locke was the quintessential exponent of this position. Other Enlightenment thinkers, however, such as the German philosopher Immanuel Kant (1724–1804), appeal to the authority of human reason rather than to a divine entity or authority. Similarly, the Dutch jurist and philosopher Hugo Grotius (1583-1645) held that 'natural law' was independent of the command of God.

8. In the 1950s the newly created Council of Europe created the European Convention for the Protection of Human Rights and Fundamental Freedoms. The legally enforceable rights set out in this document inspired the UN to establish legally binding treaties as well.

9. Together these three documents are sometimes referred to as the International Bill of Rights.

10. The 'adoption' of a treaty is a formal act that establishes the treaty's form and content and indicates that it is open for signature. States ratify treaties by agreeing to be formally bound by them. A treaty enters into force following its ratification by a fixed number of states.

11. The difference between signing and ratifying treaties is sometimes likened to the difference between dating and marriage.

12. For example, regardless of the restraints on capital punishment set out in Article 6 of the treaty (i.e., the CCPR), resolutions prohibiting the execution of pregnant women were only adopted at the federal level in the US after it signed the treaty, but not at the state level, where most executions take place. The use of capital punishment for offenders under 18 years of age has only been prohibited since 2005 via a Supreme Court ruling.

13. The UN Human Rights Commission was replaced by a new Human Rights Council in 2006.

14. Smaller organizations of independent states that are more closely economically, politically, socially, and culturally integrated may find it somewhat easier to promote, monitor, and secure their internal international treaties, such as the Charter of Fundamental Rights of the European Union.

15. During certain periods of the Roman Empire, Emperors provided free grain, bread, corn, and on occasion, wine and pork, as well as entertainment, to adult male citizens but excluded most women, children, slaves, foreigners, and other non-citizens.

16. Of course, in practice, such rights were always subject to interpretation and, in many nations, the use of the wheel, the rack, the stocks, and public beatings, whippings, and other unspeakable forms of torture and punishment, including execution, were deemed legal and fitting for many crimes. Capital punishment has been abolished in Norway (1905), Sweden (1921), and Finland (1949) for many decades and has more recently been banned in the UK (1973) and Canada (1976). Since 2002, Protocol 13 of the European Convention of Human Rights has made abolition of capital punishment, even during periods of war, a requirement for membership in the European Union. Although most developed nations have abolished capital punishment, the US has retained the death penalty for capital crimes and offenses at the federal level and in 35 states (although the specific crimes that carry the death penalty can vary across states). The District of Columbia and the following 15 states have abolished the death penalty: Alaska, Hawaii, Iowa, Maine, Massachusetts, Michigan, Minnesota, North Dakota, New Jersey, New Mexico (in 2009), New York, Rhode Island, Vermont, West Virginia, and Wisconsin.

17. The Latin term 'habeas corpus', which literally translates as 'you have the body', refers to a basic protection against arbitrary arrest and imprisonment. It is a writ or petition that entitles people held in custody to appear before a court to determine if they have received due process and been lawfully detained or confined.

18. In some nations, such as Germany, for example, social rights, in the form of the various social insurance programs that began to take roots in the late 1800s, were among the first to emerge and become institutionalized. Moreover, they were specifically designed to prevent or forestall the further advancement of political rights during a period when the socialist/labour movement was rapidly gaining strength.

19. Determination of the dates that nations introduced particular rights, such as the right to vote, can be difficult because nations may record when the relevant legislation was first drafted, enacted, made operable, or engaged. In the case of federal nations, rights have sometimes emerged at different times and been expressed or interpreted differently across sub-national jurisdictions (local, municipal, and provincial or state).

20. Women's rights to vote and hold office came early in Finland (1906), Norway (1913/1907), and Denmark (1915). In Sweden the right to vote in *local* elections was in place as early as 1862 but it was not until 1921 that women gained both the right to vote and the right to hold office at the *national* level without restrictions. Enfranchisement and the right to hold office occurred around the same time in Canada (1918/1920) and the United States (1920), but in the UK these two political rights were not in place until 1928. In 1893, New Zealand—an Anglo-Saxon nation that deviates from other members of the Anglo-Saxon world in a number of areas—became the first nation in the world to enfranchise women, but they did not gain the right to hold office there until 1921.

21. It is often suggested that the American Constitution originally contained a clause that designated blacks as 'three-fifths of a human being', reflecting the racist attitudes and demands of slave-holders in the Southern states. However, the 'three-fifths' clause—which, technically, distinguished between 'free persons' and 'other persons' (a euphemism for slaves), not whites and blacks—was created to determine the apportionment of representatives from the states to the House of Representatives and to set taxes.

The number of representatives in the House from each state is determined by the size of their populations. For the purposes of representation, the Southern, pro-slavery faction therefore actually *wanted* slaves to be counted on a one-to-one ratio with free people because this would inflate the size of their populations and significantly increase their representation and political clout in Congress, without any real change in the political or social status of their slaves. Northern abolitionists concerned with curtailing the power of the Southern states, in contrast, wanted each slave to count as less than one person in order to lower the number of Southern representatives in Congress. On the other hand, in matters of fiscal policy the Southern states would have preferred that the slaves did not count at all, because that would lower their levels of taxation. The 'three-fifths' clause was an attempt at a compromise between these contending interests and regional factions (see Fields 1990). The clause declaring that those unfree 'others' would each count as three-fifths of a person was later repealed by the Fourteenth Amendment in 1868.

22. Like the Inuit and Yupik peoples (formerly known as Eskimos) in the northern regions of North America and Greenland, the Sami (formerly known as Lapplanders or Lapps) are an Arctic people living in Sàpmi or Samiland (formerly called Lappland), an area encompassing the northern parts of four nations, Finland, Norway, Sweden, and Russia. The Sami population, now estimated to be somewhere between 80,000 and 100,000, once lived throughout most of Finland and across large parts of the other three nations but was pushed back with encroachment from the south. The majority of the Sami live in Norway today.

23. Like the indigenous peoples of North America, the rights of the Sami population living in the northern part of Sweden have been defined and restricted by the needs of the government and the politically dominant culture. In the late 1500s and early 1600s, the Swedish Crown attempted to extend its reach northward through aggressive territorial and fiscal policies. In the 1700s, the Crown began to recognize the importance of Sami trade to the northern economy and provided the Sami with settlement privileges, allowing them to buy, sell, and inherit land as long as they paid taxes. However, by the latter part of the same century, northern lands were again regarded as the property of the Crown, and the Sami's property rights limited to usufruct (land use)—an approach to which the government became increasingly committed with the growth of farming, forestry, and mining in the north in the 1800s. By the 1870s, the Swedish state had developed an economic interpretation of Sami ethnicity, declaring that only those people who still gained their livelihood through traditional means—hunting, fishing, and reindeer herding—would be regarded as Sami. Individual pasture rights were converted into exclusive communal lands rights for the Sami, but these were not to interfere with the competing claims of farming and forestry. Moreover, because these lands were no longer assessed as taxable property, the Sami lost some of their previous political rights and became subordinated to administration by the state. 'The low status of Sami civil rights', Kvist (1994:210; see also Korsmo 1993) notes, 'can be seen in the forcible removal of northern Sami to southern Sami villages during the 1910s and 1920s'.

24. Finland had established a 'Delegation for Sami Affairs' as early as 1973. Its Sami parliament is an office within this body.

25. Introduced by the UN's International Labor Organization (ILO), this treaty calls for the protection of natural resources in lands inhabited by indigenous peoples and their right to participate in their use, management, and conservation. It also upholds the rights of indigenous peoples to participate in the use, management, and conservation of these resources. Denmark has also ratified this Convention.

26. The Declaration on the Rights of Indigenous Peoples sets out individual and collective rights for the world's estimated 370 million native peoples, prohibits

discrimination against them, calls for the strengthening of their cultural identities, and promotes their participation in all matters that concern them. It also emphasizes their right to pursue economic development in keeping with their aspirations. This declaration was supported by 143 nations, including Finland, Norway, and Sweden, which have large Sami populations across their northern regions. The only countries to vote against its adoption were four Anglo nations with large indigenous populations—Australia, Canada, New Zealand, and the United States. However, Australia and New Zealand have since reversed their positions and now endorse the Declaration. Like the other UN declarations, the Declaration on the Rights of Indigenous Peoples is a reflection of concern and commitment but, unlike UN conventions and covenants, it is not legally binding. However, rights of indigenous peoples are recognized in other treaties including the International Convention concerning Indigenous People and Tribal Peoples in Independent Countries.

27. Constitutions are legal frameworks that describe the essential features of a country's government—identifying and regulating its powers and roles (and those of its various institutions and sub-central branches)—and establishing the rights and obligations of its population. They may be codified or uncodified (unwritten). Uncodified constitutions consist of customs reinforced by historical precedents. One of the most well-known examples of a largely unwritten constitution is the Constitution of Britain. The American Constitution of 1787, established after it gained independence from Britain, is the oldest written constitution. The Canadian Constitution has both written and unwritten components. The written part, called the British North America Act (BNA Act), was established through an Act of British parliament. In 1982 it was patriated and renamed the Canada Act and included a Charter of Rights and Freedoms. The Canadian constitution is supplemented by unwritten conventions. The Nordic nations all have written constitutions.

28. Sweden, the long-standing leader among all nations, was surpassed by Rwanda in 2003. By 2008 Rwanda became the first nation to have a higher percentage of women in parliament (56%) than men. However, unlike Sweden and the other Nordic nations, its impressive achievements in this area reflect the employment of formal gender quotas, rather than voluntary measures, and a new gender sensitive constitution put in place in the years following the 1994 genocide.

29. Female representation was notably higher in the Senate (or upper chamber) in Canada (34.4%) than in its House of Commons (or lower chamber). This was not true in the UK or the US. Female representation in the UK's House of Lords (19.7%) and the US Senate (15.3%) was about the same as that in their lower houses.

30. However, the Nordic nations have made considerable headway here as well since the 1970s. Sweden, for example, established a Commission for Research on Equality between Men and Women in 1972, appointed a Minister for Equality Affairs in 1976, and established a new division to deal with gender equality issues in 1982. Other important developments include the passage of the Equal Opportunity Act in 1980 and the establishment of a new national authority (the Office of the Equal Opportunity Ombudsman) to monitor compliance with the Act, resolve disputes, and call for sanctions against offenders (Fürst 1999).

31. Just as there can be notable variation in the levels of inequality, and in the ways they are addressed, within the group of Anglo-Saxon nations, variation may also be observed among the Nordic lands. In Norway, for example, there has been a surprisingly greater emphasis upon providing generous supports for women in the home.

32. Variation in levels of occupational segregation, pay equity, and other related matters among the Anglo nations (including Australia) is examined in O'Connor, Orloff, and Shaver (1999).

33. Sickness insurance, which allows either parent to take paid time off to care for their sick children, and several other programs are also 'gender neutral'.

34. This approach is markedly different from that of the Anglo-Saxon world, where the prostitutes are repeatedly charged, and from that of the Netherlands, where prostitution was legalized. From the Swedish perspective, legalization would only increase demand, endorse violence against women and children, and benefit pimps and traffickers.

35. Sweden banned corporal punishment in its grammar schools in 1926, and elementary schools in 1956, and throughout the entire school system via the Education Act of 1962.

36. Corporal punishment of children has been banned in the following twenty-six nations: Sweden (1979), Finland (1983), Norway (1987), Austria (1989), Cyprus (1994), Denmark (1997), Latvia (1998), Croatia (1999), Israel (2000), Germany (2000), Bulgaria (2000), Iceland (2003), Romania (2004), Ukraine (2004), Hungary (2005), Greece (2006), Netherlands (2007), New Zealand (2007), Spain (2007), Venezuela (2007), Uruguay (2007), Portugal (2007) Costa Rica (2008), Republic of Moldova (2009), Liechtenstein (2009), and Luxembourg (2009).

37. However, in 2007 New Zealand became the first Anglo-Saxon nation to ban corporal punishment of children.

38. Although legislation in Minnesota indicates that parents can use reasonable force to correct or restrain a child, some legal experts have concluded that corporal punishment in the home is not legal in this one state. However, the legality of the use of corporal punishment in this state is disputed.

39. The 1986 prohibition of corporal punishment in all state-supported schools in the UK (effective in 1987) was extended to cover private schools in 1998 in England and Wales, in 2000 for Scotland, and in 2003 for Northern Ireland. Section 43 of Canada's Criminal Code (federal law) states that teachers may use reasonable force 'by way of correction of a pupil'. However, Canada's Supreme Court ruled in 2004 that teachers may not use physical punishment. Therefore, it is unclear whether it is a criminal offence for teachers to use physical punishment in schools, as the law states that it is allowed while the Supreme Court's interpretation of that law states that it is not allowed. Moreover, each province and territory has its own Education Act regulating teachers' conduct. In 11 of these 13 jurisdictions, the Education Acts ban physical punishment by teachers. In the remaining two jurisdictions (Manitoba and Alberta), physical punishment by teachers is not explicitly banned in provincial legislation. The Canadian situation stands in contrast to those of more than 100 nations that have explicitly and unambiguously banned physical punishment in all of their schools.

40. The other nation that has not ratified the Convention is Somalia.

41. In 2001, the Netherlands, which did not introduce registered partnerships until 1998—eleven years after Sweden—became the first nation to explicitly recognize same-sex marriages without distinguishing them from heterosexual marriages. It was followed by Belgium (2003), Spain (2005), Canada (2005), South Africa (2006), Norway (2008), Sweden (2009), and Portugal (2010).

42. Two provinces (Alberta and Prince Edward Island) and two territories (the Northwest Territories and Nunavut) legalized same-sex marriage after the Civil Marriage Act was introduced (Bill C-38) in February 2005.

43. Massachusetts recognizes same-sex marriages via a court ruling that prevents them from being banned. The District of Columbia, New Jersey, and Vermont legally recognize same-sex civil unions but not marriages. California and Hawaii have also recognized same-sex unions but explicitly banned gay marriages. This ban was struck

down in California by its Supreme Court in May 2008. But voters in California passed a state ballot measure (Proposition 8) in November of the same year banning same-sex marriages again. Proposition 8 declared that only marriage between a man and a woman is recognized in California. In New York, same-sex marriages are not legal, but a 2008 ruling by the state's highest court declared that same-sex marriages from other jurisdictions must be recognized.

44. Some of the programs and measures for the disabled became less generous, or harder to access, in the 1990s, but others were increased and improved (see Lilja et al. 2003; Lindqvist 2000; Swedish Institute 2000).

45. Sweden has a long and deeply rooted tradition of popular movements. The Swedish Cooperative Body of Organizations of Disabled People (*Handikapppförbundenssamarbetsorgan*), an umbrella organization comprising 33 associations, is the most central national body, but there are more than 70 national organizations representing specific disability groups with some 2,000 local associations across the nation.

46. In addition to these two types of transfer payments governments may provide a range of fiscal measure including (1) **tax deductions or allowances**, such as those allowed for contributions to retirement or education savings plans, which lower an individual's or family's level of taxable income, (2) **tax credits and preferences**, such as child tax credits, which are subtracted from the tax bill, and (3) **tax exemptions or deferrals**, which eliminate or postpone tax liability under specified conditions. These kinds of measures, sometimes referred to as 'fiscal welfare', are much more common in the Anglo-Saxon nations—and especially in the US—than in the Nordic nations.

47. A high level of unemployment expenditures, for example, may simply indicate that a nation has allowed unemployment to get very high. Using expenditures as a percentage of GDP can also be problematic because if a nation's GDP declines but expenditures stay the same, it can appear that social spending is climbing. Despite these caveats, this is still a useful measure of a nation's welfare effort because it indicates how much of its available resources a nation is willing to commit to the social welfare of its population.

48. In some cases, such as the Employment Insurance (EI) program in Canada, the government no longer contributes to these public transfers.

49. The most widely employed and influential welfare state typology, based upon the work of T.H. Marshall and Richard Titmuss, is the 'welfare regime' approach developed by Gøsta Esping-Andersen. One of the strengths of this approach was that, instead placing national welfare states on a bipolar continuum identifying 'laggards' and 'leaders' in various quantitative and qualitative areas (expenditure levels, benefit generosity, coverage levels, and so on), it identified three distinct models of welfare provision. Later typologies, building upon this idea, identified four or five models. However, given this study's focus upon the Nordic and Anglo-Saxon nations, the linear, bipolar 'leader/laggard' typology remains useful and illustrative (Olsen 2002).

50. Most of the central income security programs in Sweden provide income replacement rates of 80%.

51. In the UK, student fees were paid by local education authorities after World War II. In 1997 the provision of universal post-secondary education by the government came to an end. (Scotland still pays student fees for Scottish and EU students, and in Wales tuition costs are highly subsidized.) As in Canada—but in marked contrast with the US—there are few private universities in the UK.

52. The Temporary Assistance to Needy Families (TANF) program that replaced AFDC is not provided to all people, as a right on the basis of their fundamental equality as humans, but only to temporarily compensate those who, through no fault of their own, have ended up in dire straits. Moreover, TANF recipients may only access this benefit for a maximum of five years over their lifetimes, regardless of the

level of unemployment or availability of jobs, and they may be required to enroll in 'workfare' programs to 'work off' their benefits.

53. In 2010, President Barack Obama signed historic legislation to overhaul the US health care system, but the impact and security of this legislation—which will be challenged from many quarters—remains to be seen.

54. Public *universal* pensions, provided to *all* citizens or residents of a nation, should not be confused with public old age insurance plans, such as the Q/CPP in Canada, which are contributory insurance programs provided for those in the paid labour force. Many nations also have income-tested, or pension-income-tested, supplements to top up low pensions.

55. Sweden's universal pension (*Folkpension)* was eliminated in the late 1990s when its old age security system was restructured. The principle that everyone is entitled to a public pension has been maintained, but not everyone is part of the *same* pension program now. Everyone in the paid workforce receives an earnings-related pension (*allmän tilläggspension* or ATP); those who do not get the ATP receive a 'Guarantee Pension' (Olsen 1999). While everyone is still covered by the new pension system, this change undermined the old principle of an entitlement for everyone on the same basis. In Finland a similar restructuring took place in 2005. Thus, as in Sweden, there is no longer a single pension program that provides benefits to everyone as a right, but coverage remains universal there (Kangas et al. 2006; OECD 2005).

56. However, as in Finland, Canada's first-tier, universal old age policy, Old Age Security (OAS), was undermined when the government began taxing back pension benefits for higher income seniors in the late 1980s.

57. Widespread racism, a federal decentralized political system, the design of particular political institutions and programs, and the power wielded by plantation and Southern Democrat elites are among the most common, and most persuasive, arguments put forth for this situation.

58. However, this does not mean that immigrants are as well off as people born in the Nordic lands. Although they are typically better off than their counterparts elsewhere, they still face higher levels of poverty, unemployment, and segregation, despite the efforts of Nordic states to assist them. Few nations, for example, have accepted as many refugees as Sweden has over the past few decades, reaching a peak in the 1990s, even though the nation was in the midst of a serious economic crisis and facing double-digit unemployment at this time. In an attempt accommodate this massive influx, refugees were placed in public housing apartments in many suburbs outside major industrial centres. Originally built in the 1960s, as part of the nation's ambitious 'Million Program'—when the government constructed one million apartments to ensure housing for everyone in Sweden—many of these residences had been vacated by Swedes who moved into their own houses. While the quality of the housing was good, the apartments were often in suburbs linked to industries that had collapsed or were in decline, and in other areas with high levels of unemployment. Ethnic segregation remains a problem in Sweden and other Nordic lands today (Andersson 2007).

59. This is sometimes referred to as 'equity'. As noted in chapter 2, creating equality in the end may require giving additional resources to individuals and groups with greater needs. People with disabilities, for example, may require resources and programs others do not require to ensure that they are not excluded or marginalized.

60. In sociology, theories of inequality are more commonly placed in one of two broad groups, those that emphasize consensus and those that stress conflict. The breakdown into four schools or traditions employed here is certainly not the only way to classify classical and contemporary theories of social inequality. Nor does this breakdown include every theoretical perspective.

Part III

Explaining Inequality: Theoretical Approaches

5 Legitimating Inequality: Sociobiological, Functionalist, and Culturalist Accounts

Early Statements

The idea that social inequality is natural and inevitable, and serves a largely positive function in society, has been a dominant tradition in sociology and the social sciences for many decades. But it has an ancestry that reaches at least as far back as ancient Greece, and was central to the work of both Plato and Aristotle, two of antiquity's most luminous intellects. Their influence on social and political thought in the West, and its traditions, practices, and institutions, has been momentous. And their ideas about social and political inequality are still passionately attacked or defended by many today, directly or indirectly informing and animating virtually all subsequent debates and discussions and profoundly shaping contemporary theoretical traditions.

Plato (429–347 BCE), an aristocrat and distinguished pupil of Socrates, was fiercely critical of Athenian democracy, the practice of giving all citizens a direct and equal voice in the political sphere ('political equality').[1] In *The Republic*, written in the form of a dialogue between Socrates and a group of his friends, Plato argued that since politics, like medicine, navigation, and other highly skilled crafts, requires good judgment, expertise, and dedication, society would be best served if only the most innately qualified were allowed to govern, and then only after completing lengthy and intense periods of education and apprenticeship. In his ideal regime all members of society would assume the positions to which they were best suited naturally, a notion that would feature prominently in the liberal-functionalist perspective over two thousand years later. He insisted that women, who were regarded as non-citizens and barred from participation in almost all aspects of social and political life in Ancient Athens, should be provided the same opportunities as men to become rulers or take on other positions and roles in society in line with their natural abilities and talents.[2] Plato believed that such a highly structured, ordered, and hierarchical society would promote interdependence and reciprocity among its members and foster harmony between rulers and the ruled. His vision has sometimes been characterized as closer to a blueprint for an oligarchy or dictatorship than for an egalitarian utopia. But he argued that such an organic socio-political order was necessary to forestall the emergence of great economic inequality, which he strongly believed would serve to undermine community and invariably culminate in social decay and breakdown. To prevent this, Plato advocated the introduction of several measures that were revolutionary for his time. He argued that those in power—the 'Philosopher Kings'—should intervene to prevent extremes of wealth or poverty in society, and even suggested that the income of the highest-paid to the lowest-paid workers in any organization should never exceed a certain limit (a ratio of 5:1), an idea adopted by many contemporary egalitarian cooperatives, enterprises, communities, and movements. He also proposed that the members of the governing class be denied private property beyond simple necessities in order to ensure that they would not be tempted to put their own interests and well-being ahead of the general welfare of society. Plato would certainly not countenance the kind or magnitude of material inequality associated with the 'winner-take-all' neo-liberalism embraced in the US and many other nations, or the great power wielded by economic elites in their own interest today.

Aristotle (384–322 BCE), Plato's most eminent student and eventual rival, also bequeathed a legacy that would vivify several competing contemporary schools of social and political thought. In *Politics,* and in other writings, he sought to justify some kinds of inequality, including at least one form of slavery, as 'natural'. But he also expressed deep concern about the highly unequal distribution of material wealth in Greek society. Like Plato, he was interested in ensuring social stability and he viewed the endemic conflict between the rich and poor, 'the most fundamental of all class divisions', as the main cause of social upheaval and revolution. The wealthy strive to impose an oligarchy or, more accurately, a plutocracy—rule by the rich—believing that their superiority in the economic sphere entitles them to greater rights and power in the political and social spheres. The poor, in turn, holding that all free-born citizens should be equal in all respects, demand democracy. Aristotle rejected both types of government as corrupt and perverted forms of rule in which the common good of society is displaced by narrow group interests. He was particularly critical of 'extreme democracy' with manhood suffrage ('in which all offices are open to all, and the will of the people overrides all law'), believing it would invariably lead to anarchy and mob rule. But, unlike his mentor, he maintained that ruling should not be entrusted to a few experts, however great their virtues or noble their intentions. Governing required practical knowledge and the wisdom of a collective. Thus the special talents and skills of the educated few must be supplemented by the consent of the many. For Aristotle the best form of government was a constitutional democracy in which free and equal male citizens take turns ruling, with executive power subject to the supreme rule of law. His preferred blend of oligarchy and democracy excluded most people from citizenship, including women, resident aliens, and the large slave populations upon which ancient society was primarily built, as well as artisans, manual labourers, and others whose occupation or limited wealth deprived them of the leisure required for political participation and the intellectual development it demanded. However, his concern with economic inequality led him to suggest that the best way to weaken class conflict and stabilize society was to foster the creation of a large middle class of property owners. This view has been advanced by many others, from the Greek philosopher Plutarch (46–120 CE) a few centuries later, who warned that an imbalance between rich and poor is the oldest and most fatal ailment of republics, to British Prime Minister Margaret Thatcher's facile proposals to foster 'people's capitalism' through individual share ownership.

The discourse of the ancient Greeks greatly influenced the discussions and debates of Enlightenment philosophers and scholars who adopted, modified, or challenged many of their ideas about economic and political equality. Fundamentally concerned with maintaining public order and preventing a return to the anarchy and brutality of the Civil War in his native land, the English political theorist Thomas Hobbes rejected democracy outright. His view of humans as naturally greedy, predatory, and cruel led him to conclude that civilized life was only possible through the supreme power of the state (or as he called it, 'Leviathan'), established through a social contract and the elimination of any rival political authorities. His well-known opponent and compatriot, the liberal philosopher John Locke, advocated a political system in which the state played a strictly limited role and was subject to control by the (propertied) citizenry. Locke's insistence on a separation of powers between the executive and legislative branches of government as a precaution against tyranny greatly influenced the shape of the US constitution and the architecture of the American state.[3] Other Enlightenment thinkers, however, such as the French philosopher Jean-Jacques Rousseau, fundamentally disagreed with this belief that the source of inequality and conflict in society could be traced to the self-regarding, avaricious, and insatiable qualities of human nature that remained largely unchecked until the advent of 'civil society'. Rather, as the familiar passage below from his *Discourse on the Origins and Foundations of Inequality Among Men* makes clear, Rousseau held that the roots of inequality and conflict were socio-economic. Social inequality arose with the creation of private property, the accumulation of wealth, and the consequent development of an unjust division of labour, resulting in intense competition, corruption, and violence.

> The first man who, having enclosed a piece of land, thought of saying 'This is mine' and found people simple enough to believe him, was the true founder of civil society. How many crimes, wars, murders; how much misery and horror the human race would have been spared if someone had pulled up the stakes and filled in the ditch and cried out to his fellow men: 'Beware of listening to this imposter. You are lost if you forget that the fruits of the earth belong to everyone and that the earth itself belongs to no one' (Rousseau 1984 [1755]:109).

With the emergence of civil society came the state and the proliferation of practices, obligations, rights, and laws explicitly fashioned to protect and institutionalize the interests and advantages of wealthy property holders and to coerce, control, and maintain the poor and the propertyless in their positions of disadvantage. Rousseau's vision of a more egalitarian society, like Plato's, is one in which people assume social positions and privilege on the basis of talent, ability, and merit, rather than through inheritance or property ownership. However, in his later work his incompatibility with Plato was more clearly evident, both in his call for direct democracy as the means to bring about greater equality and restore liberty, and in his suggestion, echoing Aristotle, that women be excluded from participatory citizenship and play a restricted role in public life, being more naturally inclined to the domestic sphere.

Adam Smith, the Scottish philosopher and political economist, famously put his faith in the unfettered, self-regulating capitalist market to increase productivity and societal wealth and thereby improve the lot of the masses. However, while celebrated today as the founder of the classical school of economics and patron saint of the discipline, he is often somewhat misrepresented as a doctrinaire advocate of economic liberalism. Although he believed that the natural self-regarding propensities and pursuits of humans interacting in the market would instil social order rather than chaos and improve society to the benefit of all, he also argued that human nature must be tempered by social justice. And, while greatly concerned about the encroachment of the state upon economic activity, he also prescribed a limited but indispensable number of functions for the state beyond defence, including the provision of certain public works and institutions, the financing of universal public education, and several forms of regulation. He acknowledged that the acquisition of valuable and extensive property necessitated the establishment of a civil government, but was concerned that it was 'in reality instituted for the defence of the rich against the poor, or of those who have some property against those who have none at all' (Smith 2003 [1776]:907). He cautioned that merchants, manufacturers, employers, and all those who live by profit—'whose interest is never exactly the same with that of the public, who have generally an interest to deceive and even oppress the public and who accordingly have, upon many occasions both deceived and oppressed it'—would always try to shape and orchestrate state policies to suit their own needs (2003 [1776]: 339). Smith was also more sympathetic than is commonly acknowledged today to the plight of the destitute and their right to a fair share of the wealth that they had helped to create:

> No society can surely be flourishing and happy, of which the far greater part of the members are poor and miserable. It is but equity, besides, that they who feed, cloath and lodge the whole body of the people, should have such a share of the produce of their own labour as to be themselves tolerably well-fed, cloathed and lodged (2003 [1776]:110-11).

Finally, contra Plato and many other more contemporary neo-liberal thinkers, Smith argued that the unequal distribution of 'inherent talents' among people in society 'seems to arise not so much from nature, as from habit, custom and education' (2003 [1776]: 25).

In sociology the study of social inequality has been a pivotal issue since the inception of the discipline in the nineteenth century. Most of its founders and formative figures engaged it, and for some it was a central concern. Some theorists, of whom Karl Marx is perhaps the best-known, sought to challenge ancient and Enlightenment ideas about the inevitability of inequality. But others, such as Herbert, Spencer, Émile Durkheim, and Alexis de Tocqueville, embraced and built upon these early statements, and their biosocial, functionalist, and culturalist accounts of social inequality and social change in society. These traditions have informed and shaped dominant contemporary accounts of the origins, nature, and persistence of inequality and possibilities for its eradication or attenuation.

Biosocial Explanations of Inequality

Most theories and accounts of social inequality make some appeal or reference, however faint, to 'human nature', inherent abilities, qualities and predispositions, instincts, or some other set of biological traits or characteristics that are said to vary across individuals or certain groups of them. Plato argued that people were innately suited to certain social roles and positions in society and warned that everyone must strictly keep to the work that nature fitted them for, or injustice and disorder would prevail. Human nature also figured prominently in the works of Locke and Smith, and in that of 'elite theorists' such as the Italian sociologist Vilfredo Pareto (1848–1923).[4] Pareto distinguished the elites in society—small groups that rise to the top in every sphere of social life—from the masses. The bases for their superior social positions could be found in outstanding inherent abilities, motivations, and characteristics that he referred to as 'sentiments' and 'residues'. These sentiments and residues were somewhat akin to instincts in animals but with much greater variation across individuals.[5] The most developed biological accounts of inequality, however, are rooted in (1) Social Darwinism, the ill-named approach associated with Herbert Spencer and his followers, and (2) the work of Charles Darwin, which gave rise to 'neo-Darwinian' sociobiology.

Social Darwinism

The explicit focus upon biology as an explanation in much of the contemporary work on social inequality can be traced back to the ideas of the British sociologist, Herbert Spencer (1820–1903). For Spencer, societal development closely parallelled that observed in the plant and animal worlds. He suggested that, like living organisms, societies respond and adapt to underlying and largely irresistible environmental forces that invariably produce progressive change. The highly competitive struggle for existence among individuals and groups in human society pertinaciously weeds out those who are the most 'unfit', including the poor, the idle, the weak, and those with mental or physical impairments, and allows those who are most 'fit' to assume the positions of greatest wealth and power. While this process appeared ruthless in its elimination of society's genetically and socially inferior elements, Spencer argued that the quality of the human race and human society would be greatly improved by it over the longer term.

> The poverty of the incapable, the distresses that come upon the imprudent, the starvation of the idle, and those shoulderings aside of the weak by the strong, which leave so many 'in shallows and in miseries,' are the decrees of a large, far-seeing benevolence. It seems hard that an unskilfulness which with all his efforts he cannot overcome, should entail hunger upon the artizan. It seems hard that a labourer incapacitated by sickness from competing with his stronger fellows, should have to bear the resulting privations. It seems hard that widows and orphans should be left to struggle for life or death. Nevertheless, when regarded not separately, but in connection with the interests of universal humanity, these harsh fatalities are seen to be full of the highest beneficence—the same beneficence which brings to early graves the children of diseased parents, and singles out the low-spirited, the intemperate, and the debilitated as the victims of an epidemic (Spencer 1969 [1851]:323).

For Spencer, attempts to help the people at the bottom of society via Poor Laws or other social programs and policies that artificially protect them and obstruct the adaptations necessary for human progress, however well-intentioned, are fundamentally misguided.

> There are many very amiable people—people over whom in so far as their feelings are concerned we may fitly rejoice—who have not the nerve to look this matter fairly in the face.... Blind to the fact, that under the natural order of things society is constantly excreting its unhealthy, imbecile, slow, vacillating, faithless members, these unthinking, though well-meaning, men advocate an interference which not only stops the purifying process, but even increases the vitiation—absolutely encourages the multiplication of the reckless and incompetent by offering them an unfailing provision, and *dis*courages the multiplication of the competent and provident by heightening the prospective difficulty of maintaining a family (1969 [1851]: 323–24).

> Fostering the good-for-nothing at the expense of the good, is an extreme cruelty. It is a deliberate storing-up of miseries for future generations. There is no greater curse to posterity than that of bequeathing them an increasing population of imbeciles and idlers and criminals. To aid the bad in multiplying is, in effect, the same as maliciously providing for our descendants a multitude of enemies. It may be doubted whether the maudlin philanthropy which, looking only at direct mitigations, persistently ignores indirect mischiefs, does not inflict a greater total of misery than the extremest selfishness inflicts (Spencer 1929 [1873]:314).

Spencer's ideas concerning social selection and societal evolution were never quite as prominent, or as fervently embraced, in his own country as in the US, where they were advanced by William Graham Sumner (1840–1910), an American disciple. Sumner's work, like that of his mentor, provided justification for the great fortunes and extravagant lifestyles of those at the top of his society, the grinding poverty and abysmal living and working conditions of those at the bottom, and the growing gulf between them. Wealth and power reflected natural talent and hard work; the impoverished and destitute simply lacked the intelligence and inner discipline necessary to succeed and, fittingly, were destined for oblivion. Sumner thus applauded the very inequality and social conditions that were becoming a source of great controversy and conflict and routinely decried by the social reformers of the period. And, while perhaps not as doctrinaire as Spencer in some ways, Sumner also vigorously opposed legislative meddling to ameliorate hardships suffered by the lower classes. Unlike Adam Smith, who defended laissez-faire capitalism on the grounds that everyone, including the poor, would benefit, Spencer and Sumner were primarily concerned that state interference would only sustain the shiftless, idle, negligent, and incompetent, preserving their unfavourable genetic and moral traits and subverting societal progress through the struggle for existence. For them, poverty would only be abolished when society was purged of its weakest members and populated by the industrious, prudent, and wise.

Spencer and Sumner, of course, were greatly influenced by the work of the British naturalist Charles Darwin.[6] However, while perhaps beholden to the general spirit of his evolutionary theory, their 'Social Darwinism', with its emphasis upon natural laws designed to ensure unilinear, developmental progress and the 'survival of the fittest'—a term coined by Spencer but often incorrectly attributed to Darwin—actually contradicted the general thrust of Darwin's account of evolution through blind, random mutation and natural selection, as well as his more cautious view of attempts to apply it to human society.[7] Nevertheless, Social Darwinism's emphasis upon economically acquisitive individualism and the free market, antipathy toward government intervention, and justification of the status quo garnered many supporters among the most powerful and wealthy in US society (Hofstadter 1955). Although Spencer and Sumner pointedly argued against any social policies and programs that would sustain society's weakest members, they did not advocate proactive measures to reduce their numbers or eliminate them. But their ideas soon became closely associated with the eugenics movement in the US and across the developed capitalist world in the late nineteenth and early twentieth centuries and anticipated Hitler's Final Solution and other instances of state sponsored genocide.[8] Not surprisingly, Social Darwinism fell out of favour for a few decades after WWII, discredited as pseudo-science. But the idea of the genetic superiority of some people and groups gradually began to gain ground in some circles again, and its compatibility with the neo-liberalism and social conservatism of the New Right helped to encourage a resurgence in the 1980s and 1990s.

The only 'scientific' trappings the work of the Social Darwinists exhibited were the prominent biological analogies they employed. Neither Spencer nor Sumner had made any real attempts to empirically demonstrate that there were superior or inferior people and groups, or to develop classificatory schemes or taxonomies of bio-psychological types. They offered simple tautologies; those at the top were superior because they were at the top, those at the bottom were clearly inferior or they would not be at the bottom. Contemporary incarnations of Social Darwinism, however, have tried to more rigorously demonstrate that the social stratum people occupy in society is, in large part, determined by genetics. For example, in their highly controversial study *The Bell Curve*, Richard Herrnstein and Charles Murray (1994) argued that those occupying the bottom rungs in American society are less intelligent, reflected in below-average IQ test scores. They argue that people with lower intelligence—the 'cognitive underclass'—are much more likely to drop out of school, become reliant on public assistance, engage in criminal activity, and exhibit other forms of social pathology.[9] In the most incendiary parts of their book, they suggested that the disproportionate number of blacks in the underclass in the US might be traced to lower, and largely genetically determined, IQs. High test scores, in turn, are a sign of greater intelligence, which correlates highly with success in school, high job status, and membership in the 'cognitive elite'. They also maintain that intelligence is a highly heritable trait. Consequently, attempts to help the dispossessed and disadvantaged to improve their situation through affirmative action or other social programs aimed at the school and workplace are destined to founder.

Societies with higher IQs, they argue, will have fewer social ills and brighter economic prospects but 'mounting evidence indicates that demographic trends are exerting downward pressures on the distribution of cognitive ability in the United States and that the pressures are strong enough to have social consequences' (Herrnstein and Murray 1994: 342). The 'most efficient way to raise the IQ of a society', they note, 'is for smarter women to have higher birth rates than duller women' but 'America is going in the opposite direction, and the implication is a future America with more social ills and gloomier economic prospects' (1994:548). Their policy prescriptions sound as distressingly familiar as their analysis:

> We can imagine no recommendation for using the government to manipulate fertility that does not have dangers. But this highlights the problem: The United States already has policies that inadvertently social-engineer who has babies, and it is encouraging the wrong women. *If the United States did as much to encourage high-IQ women to have babies as it now does to encourage low-IQ women, it would rightly be described as engaging in aggressive manipulation of fertility.* The technically precise description of America's fertility policy is that it subsidizes births among poor women, who are also disproportionately at the low end of the intelligence distribution. We urge generally that these policies, represented by the extensive network of cash and services for low-income women who have babies, be ended (Herrnstein and Murray 1994:548).[10]

In 1996, just two years after the publication of their book, their policy recommendations were largely realized when the Democratic Clinton government opted to 'end welfare as we know it' by slashing Aid to Families with Dependent Children (AFDC) and other programs for the poor.[11]

Deeply flawed, Herrnstein and Murray's research, and other similar studies, have been roundly criticized on numerous fronts (Arrow et al. 2000; Fischer et al. 1996; Fraser 1995). Some of their critics dispute the validity of the statistic ('g') commonly employed to represent and measure intelligence.[12] Others criticized both the narrow scope of IQ tests, which typically reduce intelligence—an encompassing and very complex attribute—to a few specific measures of logical reasoning, problem-solving, and other knowledge and skills taught in school, and the widely held notion that there is something that can be called 'general intelligence'. The noted psychologist Howard Gardner (1999), for example, suggests that there are many forms of intelligence. In addition to linguistic and mathematical intelligence—the ones traditionally focused upon by schools and emphasized on IQ tests—he identifies several additional types, including musical intelligence, bodily kinesthetic intelligence, spatial intelligence, interpersonal intelligence, and intrapersonal intelligence. Still other critics have pointed to further problems, such as cultural and class biases in IQ tests favouring some groups over others; the use of race as a legitimate concept; and questionable premises concerning genetics and heritability.[13] Perhaps most importantly, the authors fail to seriously address the range, depth, and impact of formal and informal social barriers, deprivations, and disadvantages faced by those in the lower strata or classes, especially those endured for centuries by blacks in the US. They suggest that low IQ scores correlate with poor performance in school and low job status. But the correlation is weak. And even if it were not, correlation does not equal causation. Moreover, as noted in chapter 3, all three tendencies reflect inferior socio-economic conditions, not inferior intellects.

It is strange that Herrnstein and Murray (1994; Murray 1984) point to social policy as a key source of the social problems that they identify in the US but fail to acknowledge that social programs in this nation have actually become more stringent during the period they focus upon. Nor do they acknowledge that the US is widely recognized as a social policy/welfare 'laggard' from a comparative perspective; it does considerably *less* than most other developed capitalist nations to support its citizens through educational, training, and other social programs. If social programs and welfare states are to blame for social ills in the US, the social problems that they are concerned about should be most pressing in the Nordic lands and other countries with much more developed networks of such measures. Their biological approach does not allow them to adequately explain change over time there either; the Nordic nations had rates of poverty and inequality similar to, or worse than, those in the Anglo-Saxon world in the first half of the twentieth century, but they declined markedly with the development of comprehensive welfare states and the consolidation of their powerful union movements over the ensuing decades. And these nations have seen increases in poverty and other forms of material inequality more recently when their governments deregulated, pared back social programs, and 'experimented' with other neo-liberal measures, and as their labour movements have been placed in more precarious positions as a result of increasing global integration. As in the Gilded Age, Social Darwinist views and theories appear to have been reactivated in recent decades largely to perpetuate and legitimate the numerous, and rapidly rising, forms of social inequalities associated with neo-liberalism that are in evidence virtually everywhere today.

Sociobiology

Few writers have had the impact of the British naturalist Charles Darwin (1809-1882). His most central work, *The Origin of Species* (1859), revolutionized biology and had a profound influence in philosophy, across the human sciences and throughout Western culture. Before Darwin most naturalists, and the general public, believed that species were immutable productions that had been separately, and divinely, created. Of course, the idea of evolution predated Darwin, and can even be traced back as far as ancient Greece, but he was the first to demonstrate how it worked.

Many of the classical social theorists writing in the nineteenth century were influenced by Darwin's thoughts about evolution, a concept he more commonly referred to as 'descent with modification'. Although their political perspectives could differ markedly, they posited broadly similar models of societal evolution from early, simple, 'primitive' communal or tribal social organizations toward more complex, industrial, and modern forms, typically indicating, or implying, a steady and inevitably progressive development, sometimes through a series of stages. Such an account, or at least some aspects of it, can be found in the work of several dominant figures in sociology and, most explicitly, in that of Spencer and Sumner. But the most central elements of Darwin's theory of evolution differ substantially from Social Darwinist approaches (Baldus 2004).[14] First, for Darwin there are no overarching grand designs or underlying natural laws of development guiding evolutionary development. Rather, it comes about entirely by chance, through *random* mutation—'blind mistakes' in reproduction. And, if they are better fit or adapted to their particular environments, the new modified variations of plants, insects, and animals could multiply and become dominant species, a process Darwin referred to as **natural selection**. Second, 'fitness' was not an absolute property for Darwin, but always stood in relation to the prevailing conditions in some specific milieu. New mutations were 'more fit' only in the restricted sense of being better adapted to the particular environments they emanated from within. Since evolutionary development occurred in this fashion, not according to a predetermined plan or specific direction, it could not be intrinsically geared toward progress or the creation of more complex, advanced, and superior species. Indeed, for Darwin evolution was not best characterized as a unilinear development. Rather, it might be better viewed as a branching tree with development occurring in many different directions over time, including some occasional U-turns. Finally, contrary to the violent imagery conjured by the Spencerian idea of a 'survival of the fittest', the emergence of new species with more adaptive traits did not always result in the elimination of existing species that did not possess them. As sociologist Bernd Baldus (2004:81) aptly notes, 'fish continued to swim the oceans of the world after some of their number had moved to a terrestrial life'.

As noted above, Social Darwinists, such as Spencer and Sumner, deviated considerably from all of these central aspects of Darwinian evolutionary theory. Other bio-social approaches, however, have more closely followed Darwin's approach, reorienting it to the study of human society. But while

Darwin focused upon random mutations in the physical traits of individual organisms that advantageously position them to flourish as a new species, writers working within the context of neo-Darwinian theory today, from a wide range of disciplines, employ the idea of natural selection to explain the social *behaviours* of animals including, most controversially, humans. Moreover, relying upon the science of genetics—knowledge about DNA and the biological mechanisms underlying inheritance (heredity) that were not understood in Darwin's time—they typically focus upon the role that genes themselves play in the 'struggle for survival', rather than upon the characteristics of individual organisms.[15] For them, 'genetically based behaviours' (like 'physical traits' for Darwin) that increase the chances of survival for humans will be 'selected for' by the environment and thrive. While some of this research attempts to identify *species-wide* social behaviours and activities (i.e., those that are characteristic of *all* humans) other studies highlight *sex-specific* orientations and behaviours.

The sociologist Pierre van den Berghe (1974) suggests that intense competition for scarce resources encouraged a strong biological predisposition toward aggression among humans. He argues that humans are among the most aggressive of all mammals because they compete for a much wider range of material and, especially, 'social' (non-material) resources that can never be satiated. In turn, humans developed strong tendencies toward territoriality and hierarchy as a way to suppress and regulate their intensely aggressive natures and establish social order. But, he notes, these means do not generally work well as a form of social control in the long run because the privilege, prestige, and power of those at the top must be constantly defended against continual, aggressive, and often violent challenges from those further down the social hierarchy who have fewer resources. Taking a different tack in his controversial book, metaphorically titled *The Selfish Gene*, zoologist Richard Dawkins (2006 [1976]:20-21) famously described humans as 'gigantic lumbering robots' and 'survival machines' blindly programmed to preserve the selfish molecules known as genes. But he also acknowledged the role of culture in shaping human behaviour and argued that, like genes, it could also be passed on via 'memes'—ideas, beliefs, behaviours, and other cultural phenomena that evolve by natural selection through the processes of mutation, variation, competition, and inheritance. Some of the most central, and more familiar, works in the neo-Darwinian tradition were written by Harvard entomologist and biologist Edward Osborne Wilson (1975, 2004 [1978]). E.O. Wilson popularized the term 'sociobiology' as well as the idea of applying evolutionary principles to human behaviour, highlighting the interplay between genes and the environment.

One of the most contentious ideas promulgated by some writers in this neo-Darwinian tradition is the notion that marked differences in the social behaviours, roles, and positions of men and women in society are largely determined through biology. Of course, anatomical, hormonal, and chromosomal differences in the biological make-up of males and females have long been touted as key determinants of sex-specific behaviours and roles. But anthropologists Lionel Tiger and Robin Fox (1972) were among the first to specifically emphasize the role of genes with their account of 'biogrammars'—genetically based programs similar to instincts but subject to socio-cultural modification—that predispose men and women to certain kinds of sex-specific behaviours. Sociobiologists maintain that genetically-based, sex-specific behaviours were selected for by the environment as the most adaptive. For most sociologists and feminists, **sex**—the biological division into two groups, male and female—is not the central concern. Rather, they focus upon the social creation of two **genders**, 'masculine' and 'feminine'. Differences in the character, behaviours, and roles of men and women, as well as the inferior positions and status of women across many social hierarchies and spheres, are viewed as social constructions, the product of socialization, dominant ideologies and cultural practices, social structures, and the distribution of power in patriarchal societies. Sociobiologists disagree. They do not deny that patriarchy, or male dominance, is a central, defining characteristic of human society. Indeed, like many sociologists and feminists, they view it as ubiquitous. But they argue that sociologists and feminists focus upon 'proximate', or more 'immediate', explanations for sex-specific behaviours and inequalities, while they are addressing its longer-term or 'ultimate' causes. Sociobiologists suggest that sex differences were not socially constructed over the past few centuries or even the past few millennia. Rather, they can be traced back millions of years. From their view, sex-specific predispositions and behaviours said to exist universally—for example, general tendencies for males to be more aggressive and competitive and for females to be more nurturing—are dominant only because they were 'selected for' by the environment as the most adaptive, promoting the reproductive success of particular gene pools. Following Darwin, they maintain that they are *not* saying that this social arrangement is necessarily good, desirable, just, or superior to an alternative arrangement in any other way.

> Traits with this effect have helped keep certain genes in the gene pool, not because it was good for the individual, good for the group, or good for the species as a whole, but because possession of these traits happened to be correlated with success in gene propagation (Alcock 2001:193–194).

Sociobiologists today are quick to refute charges of biological or genetic determinism on two grounds. First, they argue that they stress the role that the 'environment' plays in selecting the most adaptive genes. Other biological differences between males and females follow from this, including important crucial hormonal differences, sex-differentiated brain anatomies and wiring, and variation in sensation, cognition, emotion, and physical capabilities. Second, they argue that they do not maintain that present social arrangements are inevitable. E.O. Wilson, for example, states that, unlike mosquitoes, whose patterns of behaviour are genetically predestined,

> human genes prescribe the *capacity* to develop a certain array of traits. In some categories of behavior, the array is limited and the outcome can be altered only by strenuous training—if ever. In others, the array is vast and the outcome easily influenced (Wilson 2004 [1978]:56–57).

Of course, their notion of the 'environment' as a 'natural' agent that 'blindly' selects on the basis of adaptive fit is very different from the idea of 'social construction' that engages feminists and sociologists, and it largely precludes a significant role for conscious human agency and social power.

Sociobiological research has often been misused and misrepresented and twisted to support ends for which it was not intended. However, many of the central proponents of sociobiology have been forced to admit that there is limited room in their approach for the modification of human behaviours through socialization. Joseph Lopreato and Timothy Crippen (1999:154), for example, state that socialization 'can only intensify or conversely mitigate a behavioral predisposition'. John Alcock also indicates that the possibilities for altering our genetically evolved predispositions are restricted. He further counsels that we are much *more* likely to address social inequalities in society if we first acknowledge and understand the behavioural predispositions that they are based upon:

> [I]f it is sometimes possible for humans to overcome our evolved predispositions, and no sociobiologist would disagree, then wouldn't it be wise to understand just what effect past natural selection has had on us?... If the ability to engage in war has been shaped by natural selection, then humans are almost certainly more likely to initiate armed conflicts in some circumstances than others.... If we really understood the effects of past selection, perhaps we might better anticipate the circumstances likely to lead to warfare, the better to counteract them. In general, it should be easier to combat the negative consequences of natural selection if we knew what we were up against (Alcock 2001:195, 196).

Sociobiology is certainly not the only perspective that has been chastened for its strongly deterministic cast; indeed, some of its harshest critics, including adherents to some Marxist and feminist approaches, have been similarly castigated for placing greater emphasis upon the limits and constraints of capitalist and patriarchal structures than on the possibility of change and liberation through human agency. Moreover, however inherently disconsolate or unpalatable it may be, a tendency toward determinism does not ipso facto render a theory invalid. But there are several problems with the sociobiological approach that do bring it into serious question. First, most of the research that this perspective is based upon comes from observations of the worlds of insects and animals, rather than humans. There is still little convincing evidence that human behaviour is largely genetically based. Second, sociobiologists insist that certain universals exist, suggesting limited variability over time and place in levels of aggression and in the sex-specific behaviours and roles of men and women. Of course, even if this were true, such universals could be socio-culturally generated and maintained over time. But many sociological, ethnographic, and anthropological studies strongly dispute this idea. Rather, they suggest that there is strong evidence of significant cross-temporal and cross-national variation in levels of aggression and aggressive behaviour, in levels and forms of social inequality, and in sex/gender roles themselves and in how they are evaluated and rewarded (Draper 1975; Endicott 2006; Mead 1963 [1935]). For example, with some attention to socialization, education, and the provision of greater structural supports (e.g., child care and several forms of parental leave), the Nordic nations, as we have observed, have been able to involve many more women in their political arenas, a sphere that has been widely accepted as the 'natural' preserve of males until recently. Although not necessarily intended for this purpose, sociobiological accounts, like those from within the Social Darwinist tradition, have often been employed to rationalize existing patterns and trends toward greater social inequality.

Functionalist Explanations of Social Inequality

The functionalist approach to social inequality in sociology can be traced back to the work of the French sociologist Émile Durkheim. Durkheim was not centrally occupied with the issue of social inequality. Rather, his overriding concern was with social order: how it is established and how it is maintained. Following Spencer, he adopted an organic conception of society and argued that sociology should focus upon the interrelationships and interactions among society's central 'organs' or components. But he rejected Spencer's contention, shared by Adam Smith and Utilitarian philosophers such as John Stuart Mill, among others, that social order could be spontaneously generated by self-regarding individuals, each in pursuit of their own particular interests in the market.[16] For Durkheim, the very existence of a market based upon contractual relations presupposed the prior existence of a common moral framework. Instead, he emphasized social structures and 'social facts'—objective social phenomena that are external to individuals but constrain their actions—as the key to understanding social order, cohesion, and stability.

Durkheim most directly addresses social inequality in *The Division of Labour in Society* (1964 [1893]), his classic early study of social solidarity and social order. Social order in pre-modern societies, he argued, was a product of homogeneity. In addition to having very similar socio-economic roles, lifestyles, and (minimal) levels of material wealth, the members of these simple, small-scale societies had a 'common consciousness' (a shared awareness and understanding of the world), and a 'common conscience' (a shared set of morals and values). This extensive and extreme homogeneity engendered a strong sense of community and solidarity across society's members. Conveying an image of people that are as similar as cogs in a machine, Durkheim used the term '*mechanical* solidarity' to describe the source and nature of social cohesion and stability in these pre-modern societies.[17] With economic development, industrialization, and modernization, however, this homogeneity gradually gave way to greater social differentiation, reflected in a much wider range of beliefs, values, and morals, an increasingly elaborate social and occupational division of labour, and greater specialization in the workplace. Under normal conditions, he maintained, this growing heterogeneity fosters a good measure of interdependence among the members and components of modern society, giving rise to a new form of solidarity he called, conjuring imagery from biology, '*organic* solidarity'.[18] However, under abnormal conditions, when there was a lack of adjustment among the various parts and functions of the social organism, the division of labour might assume pathological forms that can seriously threaten or undermine social solidarity and cohesion. This is where Durkheim addresses social inequality.

Durkheim identified two central pathological forms of the division of labour. The first he referred to as an **anomic division of labour**. It occurs when there is a lag between the decline of the old moral order of pre-modern society and the creation of a new one in modern society—especially in the economy and at the workplace. In simple societies, and even in the early stages of modernization, when industry is still relatively small-scale and a detailed division of labour has not yet emerged, members of society have a clear sense of their role. With modernization and the further development of the division of labour, however, people increasingly work through routines, repeating 'the same movements with monotonous regularity, but without being interested in them, and without understanding them' (Durkheim 1964 [1893]:371). Under these conditions people are degraded and debased; the individual is no longer 'a cell of a living organism' and experiences anomie, a loss of a sense of significance and larger purpose. Durkheim believed this problem could be readily remedied through a kind of 'moral re-regulation' of the organs of society. Social solidarity could be re-established when the 'moral individualism' that accompanied social differentiation was replaced by a new form of 'moral consensus'. Neither the creation and enforcement of new rules, nor the provision of a general education for all members of society, would create the integration and cohesiveness necessary for social order. And while the state could play some role in helping to create a new moral framework at the broad level of the economy, the increasingly large-scale, impersonal, and alienating workplaces that characterize modern society would need to re-establish occupational groups and organizations, similar to the guilds of medieval times, to integrate and reconcile the interests, activities, and sentiments among, and between, workers and employers. Durkheim envisioned these corporate groups as more like contemporary professional associations than the trade unions of his day, which he viewed as primarily conflict-oriented pressure groups agitating for the narrow and specific interests of their memberships, rather than as moral communities with a larger purpose (Giddens 1978).

For Durkheim, the elimination of the anomic division of labour through the establishment of corporate organizations would not be possible if the second abnormal form of the division of labour, which he called the **forced division of labour**, was not adequately redressed as well. Here he more explicitly deals with social inequality, pointing to the unequal distribution of aptitude, talents, and interests among the members of society, which he viewed as both natural and ineradicable. Following Plato, he argued that social and occupational roles are best filled 'spontaneously', on the basis of these natural, inherent inequalities; the social division of labour cannot be imposed upon people without regard for their 'hereditary dispositions'. People can spontaneously fill their proper social roles and occupations only when 'no obstacle of whatever nature, prevents them from occupying the place in the social framework which is compatible with their faculties' (1964 [1893]:377). Under abnormal circumstances, however, people may assume roles and occupations through custom, inheritance, and ascribed characteristics, resulting in the creation of 'external inequalities'.

Durkheim observed that, while some of the causes of external inequalities, such as the transmission of social position and status through birth, were being steadily eroded with modernization and the gradual dissolution of the aristocracy, others, such as the hereditary transmission of private property and wealth, continued to give advantages to people that were 'not necessarily in keeping with their personal worth' (1964 [1893]:378). Under such conditions the division of labour cannot properly interconnect and integrate the members and components of society, and organic solidarity, which presupposes social justice and equal opportunity, is not possible. However, Durkheim believed that organic solidarity could be fostered through legislative and social reforms, such as the abolition of the transmission of wealth through inheritance, to ensure that people assumed the positions that were more commensurate with their natural abilities and merit and that 'social inequalities' in society always express 'natural inequalities'. Durkheim's work has been highly influential, providing fertile ground for later contemporary neo-functionalist accounts of social inequality that dominated the field for several decades in the post–World War II period—especially in the US—emphasizing consensus and social equilibrium. These include the work of Talcott Parsons and that of Kingsley Davis and Wilbert E. Moore, the most central proponents of the neo-functionalist perspective in sociology.

Neo-functionalism

The contemporary functionalist tradition in sociology builds upon the work of the American sociologist Talcott Parsons (1902–1979), a major theoretical figure in the US in the first few decades of the post-war period, who attempted to integrate aspects of the theories of Durkheim and Weber.[19] Employing an organic analogy—a definitive mainstay of the functionalist tradition—Parsons viewed modern societies as social systems comprised of four major subsystems that each play essential roles in maintaining the whole. These four interrelated subsystems are designed to address four central concerns or problems that all modern societies must resolve if they are to survive, maintain equilibrium, develop, and thrive. First, they must adapt to the environment, producing essential goods and services for the members of society. This is largely accomplished through the creation of the network of institutions that constitute the economy; the central medium of exchange here is money. Second, they must set short-term and long-term goals for society and establish the political institutions that allow for their realization. The medium of exchange here is power; people give power to elected officials who exercise authority on behalf of society. Third, they must ensure that people are well integrated in society. This is done through the creation of elaborate stratification systems that typically endow greater levels of prestige, status, and influence upon those who use their special talents and skills to promote the central goals that have been identified. Finally, they must foster and maintain stability, solving potentially disruptive conflicts that sometimes emerge when the self-interest of individuals collides with those of the larger collective. This need is met through an array of cultural and educational institutions, including schools, churches, and the media, as well as through a range of recreational institutions that help to restore and reinvigorate people (Parsons 1964). Parsons's **'AGIL' model** (an acronym using the first letter of each of the four 'functional prerequisites' that he identified [*a*daptation, *g*oal attainment, *i*ntegration, and *l*atent pattern maintenance]) sets out a 'basic institutional division of labour' in society, highlighting social inequality/stratification as an elementary precondition for society (Baldus 2004). A key aspect of Parsonian functionalism is its emphasis upon culture and shared values in society. He maintains that people in society largely agree that certain positions are more important than others and should be more highly rewarded. Of course, Parsons's functionalist view does not address power imbalances among groups in society or consider that shared values—even if they were found to exist in a society—might be cultivated 'from above', an idea more fully explored in the discussion of theories that emphasize power and conflict in the next chapter.

While Parsons laid the foundation for contemporary functionalist thinking about social inequality, two of his students, Kingsley Davis (1908–1997) and Wilbert E. Moore (1914–1987), furnished its most familiar and widely embraced contemporary formulation. Although only seven pages in length, their original contribution to debates about social inequality, published in 1945, is one of the most widely cited articles in American sociology, generating a storm of critiques, replies, rebuttals, rejoinders, and revisions (Hauhart 2003; Tumin 1970). Davis and Moore's (1945) neo-functionalist perspective is less abstract than the work of their mentor, centering around their idea of effective role allocation and performance. From their perspective social inequality is 'an unconsciously evolved device by which societies insure that the most important positions are conscientiously filled by the most qualified persons' (Davis 1948: 367).

Davis and Moore's general approach can be readily summarized as a series of interrelated propositions. First, they argue that social roles and positions in complex societies vary greatly in their functional importance. The most important ones are those that are most necessary for societies to survive. Second, they suggest that people also vary greatly in their terms of their innate abilities, and that there are a strictly limited number of people who possess the natural talents and potential required to fill these strategically important positions and roles. Third, they point out that, in order to become qualified to fill these roles and positions, talented individuals must undergo training to cultivate and develop their inherent abilities and convert them into the skills that they will require as the incumbents of these key roles and positions. These training periods typically involve significant sacrifices, including lengthy and intense periods of study, costly tuition fees and other expenses, and a loss of income and other benefits and opportunities for advancement. Consequently, society must attach much higher rewards to the most critical roles and positions as incentives to attract the most talented people, motivate them to acquire the intense level of training they demand, and compensate them for their sacrifices. Higher rewards are also necessary to ensure that they will continue to perform their tasks conscientiously once they have assumed society's most crucial roles and positions. Finally, borrowing the idea of 'supply and demand' from economic theory, they acknowledge that the level of rewards that society attaches to these strategically important roles and positions will also be affected by the number of people in society who have the talent, training, and desire to fill them; rewards will be higher when there is a scarcity of suitably qualified people who can assume them and decline as their numbers increase. Thus, for Davis and Moore, social inequality (1) comes about naturally in response to society's need to fill crucial roles and positions, (2) serves a very positive function in society, and (3) is inevitable, and hence a universal feature of all modern societies.

Davis and Moore's neo-functionalist account clearly endorses and legitimates the equal-opportunity ideal in modern capitalist societies. From their view, modern capitalist societies are meritocracies; people reach the top positions on the basis of innate talent and training (merit). They are highly rewarded because they are doing important work that few have the capacity to do, and as a means of compensation for the sacrifices they have made to become qualified to fill the top positions. Since their view is the 'common sense' perspective held by many in modern capitalist societies, it is important to critically examine its central propositions more closely.

Like Social Darwinist views, the neo-functionalist perspective has been criticized on several different grounds (Broom and Cushing 1977; Collins 1975; Huaco 1963; Tumin 1953). First, it does not tell us how we can objectively determine, or demonstrate, which social positions are the most functionally important in society. Davis and Moore's original account appears tautological; they state that the positions that are most important for social stability and the survival of societies are the ones that are most highly rewarded, and then cite the high levels of rewards as evidence of their functional importance. This kind of circular reasoning is not very convincing. There are clearly many positions, such as those of farmers, that are critical to the survival of society but not very highly rewarded, while many other positions, such as those held by entertainers and professional athletes, or even lawyers and Supreme Court judges, are considerably less functionally important to society but much more highly rewarded. Moreover, if the rewards attached to various roles and positions are primarily based upon their functional importance, how can we explain the significant variation in rewards for the same roles and positions across the capitalist world? As noted earlier, the total rewards provided to top-level CEOs in the US is dramatically higher than in most other capitalist nations, while the status and rewards provided to most workers in the US is much lower than that enjoyed by workers doing the same work in the Nordic and other nations.[20] This cross-national variation suggests that the level and kinds of rewards attached to positions and roles may have more to do with the balance of power in society than functional importance or scarcity of talents. However, even if the levels and forms of inequality were 'universal' across time and place, this might simply reflect similar constellations of power across them.

In a later version of their theory, Davis and Moore developed the idea that the most functionally important positions are ones that are (1) unique or (2) pivotal, in the sense that many other social positions are highly dependent upon them. But many unique positions, such as translators who are able to decipher and read ancient 'dead' languages, for example, are not so important for the survival of society, however exceptional, impressive, and rare their talents. Similarly, in any system comprised of interdependent roles and positions it can be exceedingly difficult to unambiguously demonstrate that some of them are primary or more pivotal and indispensable than others. Physicians, for example, are often viewed as linchpins, the most central medical practitioners that all others in the health care field greatly rely upon. But doctors are, arguably, just as dependent upon the knowledge, talents, and skills of nurses and a wide range of other health care practitioners who provide or administer an extensive array of essential medicines, services, programs, and training. Finally, even Davis and Moore's attempt to shore up their beleaguered approach by appealing to the notion of 'supply and demand' as an additional determinant of rewards is not problem-free. Indeed, from this economic perspective we might expect to see greater equality, not greater inequality, over time; as increasing numbers of people are attracted to the positions that offer higher rewards, the rewards associated with these positions should decline.

In response to their critics' attack on their central notion that we can objectively determine functional importance, Davis (1948) and Moore (1963) later amended their original theoretical approach. Following Parsons, this revision placed greater emphasis upon the subjective evaluation of roles and positions as functionally important by the members of society. But this opened them up to the same charges that were levelled at their mentor earlier: (1) there is little unambiguous empirical evidence of a general consensus ('shared values') regarding which positions are the most important in society and (2) where there is a consensus, it may have been engineered and imposed from above by the powerful through their control over the media and other organs of the 'means of persuasion'.

A second line of criticism of this approach focuses upon who fills the functional positions in society rather than upon the positions themselves. Davis and Moore argue that there are few people who have the requisite talents to fill the most important positions in society. But even if we accepted their circular premise that the most important positions and roles in society are the ones that are most highly rewarded, it is really the case that there are very few people who can fill these roles? Is there a shortage of people who have the *potential* to become CEOs, doctors, lawyers, and judges, for example? How do we know that these positions require exceptional and rare talents? And how would we objectively determine who is talented enough to fill them? Davis and Moore's approach does not adequately attend to the fact that existing inequalities provide some people with far greater opportunities to become qualified to fill the more highly rewarded positions in society, as noted in the critique of equal opportunity in chapter 2. People from wealthier families, for example, are much more likely to obtain a good education and be connected to people already in the top positions; people from the lower classes and other disadvantaged and excluded groups are far less likely to even aspire to fill these positions, or become motivated to do so. And, even if they do, they are much more likely to drop out of school for a variety of socio-economic reasons.

A third problem with Davis and Moore's thesis has to do with the nature and level of rewards associated with the functionally important positions. They maintain that high rewards must be attached to the most important roles and positions to attract and motivate the most talented people to them. But how high do these rewards have to be? Do CEOs have to earn 200 times or 2,000 times what the average worker earns? Cross-national and cross-temporal variation suggests that it is not necessary to provide such grossly unequal material rewards. In societies that put less emphasis upon material gain, monetary rewards might be less important than social recognition and the intrinsic satisfaction that such roles and positions provide. Davis and Moore also stress the hardships and sacrifices that people endure while training to become qualified to fill the key posts in society. But there are also many benefits associated with this training too, including greater freedom and more opportunities for self-development and self-fulfilment. Moreover, the loss of income that they experience is typically made up for well within their first decade of employment.

Finally, Davis and Moore's central notion that inequality is functional for society is also unproven. In fact, there is great deal of evidence suggesting that inequality can be dysfunctional. As suggested in chapter 3, high levels of material inequality can undermine democracy and lead to higher rates of crime. It may also foster hostility, suspicion, and distrust among those who are not recruited to fill the top positions, undermining integration and social stability. In nations with lower levels of inequality, there is less social unrest. Strike levels, for example, are lower in the Nordic nations, where inequality is lower (and labour movements are much more powerful). Moreover, the unequal access to appropriate motivation, channels of recruitment, and centers of training can greatly limit the possibility of discovering some talented people. The incalculable loss to society that has resulted from the systematic exclusion of women, blacks, gays, people with disabilities, and other groups over the centuries from these positions, and the institutional avenues that lead to them, has only relatively recently been addressed; the loss incurred by the exclusion of those at the bottom of the class system has rarely been acknowledged. The unequal distribution of power and privilege also allows those at the top to rationalize and justify the unequal distribution of material and non-material resources in society.

Like approaches that stress biosocial determinants, functionalist theories suggest that inequality should be fairly uniform across societies. But for functionalists it is the common needs of social systems at similar stages of socio-economic development, rather than genetics, that are responsible for this. And they too are unable to account for significant cross-national variation. Parsons's neo-functionalist approach, however, might be employed to provide an explanation for this cross-national variation as well as the varying policies and other strategies that different countries have introduced to address it. Unlike Davis and Moore, his central argument was not that certain roles or positions *were* actually more important to the survival of social systems than others. Rather, he stressed that the positions at the top in society are the ones that most people in society *believe* to be the most functionally important, and hence the most deserving of the highest rewards. But, like Davis and Moore and most other theorists working within the functionalist tradition, Parsons was primarily concerned with explaining how social order is established and maintained in society, not accounting for cross-national variation in inequality. Indeed, from a functionalist perspective we should again expect a good measure of uniformity, with broadly similar levels of inequality, institutions, and social policies (or their functional equivalents) across the nations of the developed world. But his emphasis upon shared values within societies at least suggests a plausible explanation for the inequality and social policy differences across the nations examined here.

Differences in the levels and kinds of remuneration across social roles and positions from one country to the next, for example, might be a product of cross-nationally different views about which of them are the most important. It could be argued that the considerably higher levels of remuneration that CEOs in the US receive compared to that of their counterparts in most other nations largely reflects widely shared beliefs among Americans that they are performing services *considered* to be among the most invaluable to society. Differing cultures and values may also lead nations to set divergent political goals. The Nordic nations stress a somewhat different set of commitments, concerns, and political goals than those found in the US and the other Anglo-Saxon lands, where equal opportunity and individual performance in the economy appears to be more highly valued. Many researchers have more directly embraced and developed this cultural approach, highlighting a range of cultural and ideological differences as the most central determinants of cross-national variation in social inequality. From this vantage point the nature and level of social inequality in any nation is a direct reflection of the dominant attitudes, beliefs, values, customs, laws, and institutions that constitute its 'national character' and culture. Much attention here has focused upon how and why the Anglo countries differ from most Western European nations.

Cultural Explanations for Inequality

Explanations that focus upon national 'cultures' and dominant values across countries—and the varied forms of institutions they help to generate and shape—are much better placed to explain differences in the character and levels of material and non-material forms of social inequality across the

Anglo and Nordic nations than are theories that emphasize 'universals', such as biological determinants or the needs of social systems. A central consideration in the cultural explanation for cross-national variation in inequality is the varied ways that nations have interpreted and embraced 'liberalism', an important ideological and cultural component in all six of the nations examined here. Rooted in the ideas of Enlightenment philosophers such as Hobbes, Locke, Bentham, and Mill, and in the ongoing struggles for greater religious, political, and social freedoms in Britain and elsewhere in Europe in the late sixteenth and seventeenth centuries, liberalism is considered the first 'modern' political ideology. It developed in reaction to the organic, hierarchical feudal order, with its elaborate network of duties, responsibilities, and for some, innate privilege, and to the authority and arbitrary will of the three key components of the medieval power structure, the monarchy, the aristocracy, and the Church. Today liberalism is the dominant political ideology across all contemporary Western capitalist democracies, stressing individual freedoms and rights. The liberal image of the good society is that of an association of free individuals who have equal rights and equal opportunities to get ahead. However, since the acquisition of most rewards in society should be based upon individual talent and enterprise from the liberal view, people will always have unequal amounts of certain kinds of material and non-material rewards. As noted in chapter 2, inequality is expected and endorsed from a liberal perspective. A central dispute among liberals concerns the kinds and levels of inequality that are viewed as acceptable or unacceptable. While the liberal ideology is broad, and has included several variants and hybrids, encompassing an array of different views and visions concerning the role of government across time and place, it has taken two basic forms, 'classical' liberalism and 'social' liberalism, which have played a greater or lesser role in the cultures of the Anglo-Saxon and Nordic nations.

Classical or 'old' liberalism is the form of liberalism that first emerged to challenge the conservative ideology of the Middle Ages. It emphasized economic freedom against the heavy regulation by Church and state that characterized the late feudal period. The laissez-faire doctrine of minimal government intervention in the marketplace was viewed as central to the establishment of the freedom of individuals. From this perspective, as noted earlier, liberty is conceptualized in largely 'negative' terms, as the absence of coercion, restraint, and interference, stressing 'freedom *from*', especially from the government. However, proponents of laissez-faire typically fail to admit or acknowledge that 'free' market societies did not emerge 'naturally'; rather, they were socio-legally constructed, and are maintained, through a dense network of laws, rules, policies, and other actions taken and enforced by the state. Their construction reflected and facilitated the gradual transfer of power from the feudal nobility and mercantilists, who had benefitted from heavy state regulation of the economy, to the emerging capitalist class. Nevertheless, this interpretation of liberalism, with its emphasis upon curtailing the purview and powers of the state, commonly referred to as 'neo-liberalism' today, has enjoyed a renaissance over the past few decades in virtually every capitalist nation.

Like classical liberalism, *social* liberalism—also called 'radical liberalism' and 'new liberalism'—begins with the same emphasis upon basic individual rights, such as the rights to life, liberty, and property.[21] But from this perspective, the lack of key, indispensable amenities and provisions can be just as threatening to liberty as any form of government coercion and can render individual rights largely impotent or irrelevant. Social liberalism conceptualizes liberty in a much more inclusive and 'positive' way than classical liberalism, placing greater emphasis upon the individual's possibilities of fulfilling his or her potential. Liberty, for social liberals, is not simply a matter of formally or legally establishing equal rights for individuals and protecting them from the state; it includes some emphasis upon 'freedom *to*' and 'freedom *for*', not just 'freedom *from*'. Social liberals maintain that most individual liberties can be secured only under certain economic and social conditions. The freedom *to* exercise individual rights requires a common foundation or starting point for all, and this typically necessitates greater freedoms *for* the state to provide it. This is the position advocated by Rawls, Dworkin, and others who support 'equality of condition', or 'fair equal opportunity'. Although social liberalism supports the capitalist market system, it also acknowledges the need for state intervention in some crucial circumstances and areas. However, adherents to the social liberal perspective can differ markedly in their estimation of what constitute essential material and non-material provisions, and how far the state should go to provide them, as well as the form that this intervention should take. For some social liberals, primary and secondary education, health care, and a few other basic supports are sufficient to secure and promote equal rights and equal opportunities across society. For many others a much wider range of income programs, social services, legal protections, and other measures is required. Some liberals maintain that the necessary supports should be of a uniform quality and available to all as entitlements or rights. They often advocate public sector provision as the most efficient means to meet these requirements. Others maintain that these supports should normally be allocated on the basis of need and furnished through fiscal policies and other measures that promote their provision through the private sector first, and via the public sector only when all other means have been exhausted—an approach that is considerably closer to classical liberalism.

Social liberalism has played an important role in all of the Anglo nations. But in the US—where it has more often been denigrated as 'bleeding heart liberalism' and the views of the 'far left'—it has been much more focused upon addressing discrimination and promoting the rights and causes of minorities and various other underprivileged or socially excluded groups (including women, African Americans, Hispanics, immigrants, and gays), than upon the regulation of the economy and the provision of universal public social programs, benefits, and services for everyone. Indeed, government proposals to introduce comprehensive social programs that would seriously address child poverty and homelessness, or a national public health care system, or several other state programs that are in place across most of the advanced capitalist world, are routinely rejected in the US as socially destructive, and castigated as communist, socialist, Marxist, and even 'un-American', an epithet that has few cross-national parallels. When introduced, social programs and other forms of government intervention have more often been tolerated as a necessary evil (Wills 1999). Few countries, including the other Anglo-Saxon nations, have exhibited the same level of distrust and blatant hostility toward the state as that found in the US. Classical liberalism, combined with a much more restricted interpretation of social liberalism than that found in Canada and the UK, characterizes the political culture in the US. The markedly greater stress on individualism, self-interest, and self-reliance, has been noted in an early study of industrial society and social policy in the US welfare state by two prominent American political scientists:

> Of basic importance to American capitalism is its great emphasis upon the rational, acquisitive, self-interested individual.... Individualism is both a theory of human behavior and a doctrine in justification of laissez faire.... If there is any formula summing up these beliefs it is the one repeated in the American home and school: Everyone has equal *opportunity* to get ahead; everyone has the moral *duty* to *try* to get ahead ('make the most of himself'); if a man fails, it is his own fault and he should feel guilty (and, some would add, his children and his parents should feel ashamed) (Wilensky and Lebeaux 1965: 33, 34, 35).

In the Nordic and other lands, the 'nation' and the 'state' are overlapping concepts; in the US people more commonly draw a very sharp distinction between the two of them. Americans are often considered among the most patriotic of all national citizens, but their intense love for their nation is often matched by an intense public antipathy toward the state. State intervention is typically portrayed as an enemy of freedom from this classical liberal tradition, a position vigorously contested by social liberals. Despite the pronounced emphasis upon 'free speech' in the US, it is often suggested that there can be little room to deviate from these dominant cultural views and values, an observation made over a century and a half ago by Tocqueville, among the first to address 'American exceptionalism':[22]

> I do not know any country where, in general, less independence of mind and genuine freedom of discussion reign than in America....

> In America the majority draws a formidable circle around thought. Inside those limits the writer is free; but unhappiness awaits him if he dares to leave them. It is not that he has to fear an auto-da-fé, but he is the butt of mortifications of all kinds and of persecutions every day. A political career is closed to him: he has offended the only power that has the capacity to open it up. Everything is refused to him, even glory.... He yields, he finally bends under the effort of each day and returns to silence as if he felt remorse for having spoken the truth.... there is no freedom of mind in America.... One sees [other] governments that strive to protect mores by condemning the authors of licentious books. In the United States no one is condemned for these sorts of works; but no one is tempted to write them (Tocqueville 2000 [1835, 1840]: 244–245).

The dominance of 'Americanism', as an ideology, was more recently acknowledged by Seymour Martin Lipset (1996:31), Tocqueville's most eminent successor and a prominent contemporary representative of the culturalist perspective: 'In Europe, nationality is related to community, and thus one cannot become un-English or un-Swedish. Being an American, however, is an ideological commitment. It is not a matter of birth. Those who reject American values are un-American'.

In the Nordic lands, 'social democracy', a more far-reaching, left-wing variant of social liberalism, has played a more dominant role on the political scene for many decades, ideologically and in party politics. Like social liberalism, it highlights individual freedoms and equal opportunity and sees a greater need for state intervention to promote and secure them. But it also stresses some of the values associated with democratic socialism, such as social and economic equality, collectivism, and social solidarity. And it has more explicitly recognized the need to 'humanize' capitalism, seeking to eliminate and prevent poverty, homelessness, and many other excesses and by-products of the market system. Unlike democratic socialism—a less prominent ideological and political tendency present in the Nordic nations—social democracy seeks only to administer and reform capitalism rather than to transcend it by democratizing the economy. Over the past two decades social democratic governments everywhere have often been considerably more willing to shrink from their long-standing reformist commitments. However, the social democratic view of liberty in the Nordic lands has placed greater emphasis upon freedom from those who own and control the capitalist economy than upon freedom from the state. Consequently, their welfare states are more 'decommodifying' than those in the Anglo-Saxon nations (Esping-Andersen 1990; Olsen 2002). The comprehensive networks of universal and relatively generous income supports, social services, and other programs there, often provided as entitlements, render their residents appreciably less dependent upon the market and employers for their well-being. In contrast, residents in the Anglo-Saxon nations are much more commodified; their welfare states are often described as 'residual', comprising a much more restricted range of programs that are considerably less generous and more often provided on the basis of need, rather than as a right. This is especially true in the US. Belatedly and reluctantly built up between the 1930s and 1970s, its rudimentary welfare state is among the least developed in the advanced capitalist world. Many of its programs are measures of 'last resort', designed to promote self-reliance and ensure that the market is not undermined rather than to address inequality, which is viewed as an inevitable and natural outcome of competition. Dependence upon friends and family is strongly endorsed, and dependence upon some public provisions, such as the police and armed forces for security or the schools for education, is viewed as natural and acceptable. But dependence upon the state for economic well-being is widely and passionately viewed as unnatural and objectionable. This was clearly evident in the recasting of Aid to Families with Dependent Children (AFDC) into a workfare program, via the tellingly titled Personal Responsibility and Work Opportunity Reconciliation Act (PRWORA). AFDC, it proclaimed, 'trapped people in dependency'.[23] Staying home to raise children is touted as the ideal for middle-class women but not for poor single mothers, and this reform was designed to push them into the workforce. Businesses and industries that provide commodities for sale in the market can be heavily subsidized by fiscal and tariff polices and other measures, but those who provide children—the future labour force, and producers and purchasers of those same commodities—have few entitlements and little public support.

The different political cultures that these social policy approaches reflect is evident in international surveys of public attitudes concerning inequality and the role of the state. People in the Anglo-Saxon lands, and particularly in the US, are much more likely to accept higher levels of economic inequalities, and to view them more positively, as essential to a dynamic economy. They are generally much less likely to favour government redistribution and many other forms of state intervention (Edlund 1999, Mehrtens 2004; Svallfors 1995, 1998). For many researchers working within the cultural theoretical school, cross-national variation in levels of inequality largely reflects these views and long-standing traditions.[24] Simply put, in the Anglo-Saxon nations the free market, and the inevitably higher levels of inequality associated with it, are more widely accepted as final, and as a necessary byproduct of capitalism, than they are in the Nordic lands. And within the Anglo-Saxon world, inequality is most commonly and most firmly embraced as a social good that need not be offset in the US. There, it is often suggested, 'the State plays a more limited role than elsewhere because Americans, more than other people, want it to play a limited role' (King 1973b:418).

But *why* do Americans want it to play a more limited role than people in the Nordic and other advanced capitalist nations, including Canada and the

UK? *Why* do the attitudes, values, ideologies, and institutions that comprise the cultures across these nations vary so markedly?

For many working within the culturalist tradition, the roots of this cross-national cultural and institutional variation can be found in the unique histories of these nations. The American political scientist Louis Hartz (1955, 1964) sought to explain why the political culture and institutions in a 'new society', such as the US, were notably different from that in Britain, its 'mother country'. When Hartz was writing in the mid-1960s, it had been more than two decades since two British economists and social reformers, John Maynard Keynes and William Beveridge, first captured the public imagination in Britain with their proposals for greater state intervention. Indeed, by this time the institutionalization of their plans for fiscal and monetary policy to mitigate the adverse effects of economic downturns, and for the construction of a 'cradle-to-grave' welfare state, were well underway in the UK. Hartz sought to explain why the US embraced a much more laissez-faire or 'classical' form of liberalism than that found in Britain at the time. The US, he suggested, was a 'fragment culture'. It was largely settled, not by great lords with aristocratic lineages and privileges, but by middle-class emigrants who had few ties to the conservative ('Tory') values and traditions associated with Britain's feudal past. Conservatism, the dominant ideology of the feudal period, supported and legitimated a hierarchical, authoritarian, and traditional social order. But its organic or corporate conception of society also stressed the idea of community and cooperation among the highly unequal orders that comprised the feudal social structure. Feudal society was characterized by a complex network of superordinate and subordinate social ranks and corresponding chains of mutual obligation. Serfs, the largest group at the bottom of the feudal stratification system, were required to work and provide for their lords. But the nobility was also obligated to take care of this lower order—however naturally inferior it was deemed to be—by providing serfs with the means to ensure their subsistence, a tradition known as noblesse oblige. With capitalism came liberalism, a new social and political ideology that contradicted the core values associated with conservatism. The priority of the community and emphasis upon cooperation gave way to the priority of the individual and an emphasis upon competition. The prominence given to tradition and hierarchy was gradually supplanted by new values, such as freedom (the liberties and rights of individuals) and equality (understood as equal opportunity).

In societies that had a feudal past, it has been suggested, the core values stressed by both of these central ideological and socio-cultural traditions—conservatism and liberalism—could merge. This allowed for the formation of new hybrid ideologies, such as socialism, social democracy, and social liberalism, ideological alloys that each embraced some blend of the cooperative, corporate, and collectivist values that conservatism stressed with the individual rights and freedoms associated with liberalism. But the US was largely founded by people who had consciously left feudal conservatism and hierarchy far behind, a development ratified and reinforced by the American Revolution. This absence of any tradition built upon the idea of a corporate community, in which the privileged elite at the top are responsible for those who are less well off, thwarted the possibility for a new ideological hybrid in the US, or even a tempering of the extreme individualism and self-reliance associated with the classical form of liberalism that had taken firm root there.

Hartz was not the first to suggest that a 'purer' form of liberalism could be found in the US because it did not have feudal social classes or traditions to draw upon. As early as the latter part of the nineteenth century, Friedrich Engels (1935 [1892]:25), Karl Marx's close friend and collaborator, had already proposed that the highly individualistic American culture was related to this absence in the US, which he contrasted with the situation in the UK: 'A durable reign of the bourgeoisie has been possible only in countries like America, where feudalism was unknown, and society at the very beginning started from a bourgeois basis. ... In England the bourgeoisie never held undivided sway'. The Italian Marxist Antonio Gramsci and British Fabian socialist and author H.G. Wells also made similar observations long before Hartz (Lipset and Marks 2000). But Hartz developed the idea of 'fragment cultures' furthest and applied his theoretical perspective to several other European colonies—or 'new societies'—including Canada, which he viewed as broadly similar to the US, a position also endorsed by Canadian political scientist Kenneth McRae (1964).[25]

Other researchers working within this same theoretical framework, however, have placed greater emphasis upon the *differences* between these two North American nations, highlighting Canada's greater concern with social inequality, more collectivist orientation, stronger support for some forms of state intervention, and more comprehensive and inclusive welfare state. Canadian history, they suggested, differed in some very important ways from American history, allowing it to maintain much stronger ties to Britain and its feudal traditions and values—cultural ties that gave Canadian liberalism a more conservative and collectivist cast. First, Canada did not support the American Revolution, and the Loyalists and colonial administrators living in the US that had supported Britain moved northward to Canada, bringing their conservative views and greater penchant for political intervention with them. This 'counter-revolutionary' tendency and conservatism in Canada would be reinforced in the War of 1812 and the defeat of the liberal rebellions in Upper Canada (Ontario) and Lower Canada (Quebec) in 1837, as well as through the steady influx of British immigrants and trade unionists over the decades (Horowitz 1968, 1978; Lipset 1986, 1990, 1996). And in Quebec, the seigniorial system—a modified French-Canadian version of feudalism and noblesse oblige—was in place for over two centuries.[26]

The Nordic lands, in contrast, had a longer and much more deeply rooted feudal tradition than French Canada, but one which also differed markedly from its more familiar 'classical' expression in Britain and elsewhere in continental Europe. Outside the Nordic world the relationship between the nobility and the enserfed peasantry was more clearly one of superordinate over subordinate; peasants were highly dependent upon lords for their economic well-being and protection and typically had no formal political voice in the 'Three Estates of the Realm', the monarch's legislative and advisory bodies representing the clergy, the nobility, and the burghers/commoners. In Sweden and Finland (a Swedish province from the 1150s until 1809), however, the peasants had constituted a Fourth Estate since the fifteenth century, when serfdom was officially abolished, and the other three Estates were much weaker than in Britain and on the Continent. Moreover, it was the king who had established the nobility here, and he greatly restricted its members' power by granting them fewer rights, including the right to pass on their estates through inheritance. He also undermined the position of the other traditional rival for power, the Catholic Church, by confiscating all of its land and wealth and establishing the Lutheran state church. And because the nascent bourgeoisie was never as well-established or powerful in the Nordic lands, property rights were not as sacred as in most of the rest of Europe. In this context, kings often allied themselves with the Fourth Estate in order to overrule the other three Diets. In Norway, where feudal structures were less developed, the peasantry was not formally represented as an Estate, but they often played a significant role in local governments. Unlike elsewhere in Europe, the Nordic peasantry was more likely to receive support from the monarchy/state than from the nobility. Thus, organic unity, cooperation, collectivism, and community were more of an outgrowth of state paternalism and the early establishment of a developed public bureaucracy than of noblesse oblige in the Nordic lands (Nilsson 1997; Rojas 1991; Scott 1988; Sørensen and Stråth 1997; Trägårdh 1990a, 1990b).

Despite its considerable insights, the culturalist perspective also has several weaknesses that should be addressed. First, while there is little doubt that individualism and anti-statism are dominant values that are more firmly embraced at a broad, ideological level in the US (and, albeit to a lesser extent, in the other two Anglo-Saxon nations) than in the Nordic nations, there has always been somewhat less value consensus among Americans than is typically acknowledged. There also has been a wide range of competing and often contradictory views that have received considerable support at critical junctures. At the policy level rather than the ideological level, Americans have sometimes overcome their 'anti-statism' and exhibited considerable support for public social programs. This is most obviously reflected in the widespread public support for New Deal social programs of the 1930s, the Great Society measures in the 1960s, and several other instances of government intervention. Americans do not view public education (at the primary and secondary levels at least) as 'un-American'. Some surveys suggest that, as in other nations, there is much greater support for social programs that are more generous and approximate universalism, and greater hostility toward means-tested measures that are viewed as easily and commonly abused (Cook and Barrett 1992; Coughlin 1979; Larsen 2008; Svallfors 1991).[27]

National values and cultures are sometimes neglected, or dismissed as largely irrelevant, to discussions of social inequality. In a period when governments increasingly rely upon focus groups, town hall meetings, and public opinion polls and surveys, cultural considerations must be treated more seriously. Several studies suggest that public attitudes can have an impact on social policy. For example, governments seeking to shore up low approval ratings—especially around election time—may increase social spending, introduce new social programs, or cut back on measures that are deemed unpopular (Burstein 1998; Hicks 1984). But while dominant national values, such as individualism and anti-statism or collectivism and statism, and dominant political ideologies, such as classical liberalism and social liberalism or social democracy, may have deep roots that extend back for centuries, it is important to consider how they are developed, articulated, packaged, and perpetuated over the decades. Before the highly financed and well-orchestrated public attack on and vilification of Canada's universal, tax-financed health care system by the American Medical Association, the insurance industry, the media, and the administration of George H.W. Bush in the 1990s, there was a surprisingly high level of support for it among the American public. Another survey indicated that almost 85% of Americans thought the government should 'definitely or probably' be responsible for providing health care for the sick (Olsen 2002). The way that long-standing and deeply seated national values are interpreted, regenerated, and sustained by powerful interests is often ignored, and existing values are too often accepted as simply indigenous and artlessly generated.

Cultural/historical-institutionalism points to the establishment of institutions as a central way that national values become crystallized and perpetuated over time. They highlight the ways that cultures and institutions foster and sustain each other (Klass 1985; Lockhart 2001).[28] For example, the fragmentation of health care delivery via the creation and maintenance of separate programs in the US, such as Medicaid for the indigent and Medicare for the elderly, has helped to undermine and divert public support among Americans for a more inclusive national health care system in the US. Low and declining levels of funding for government programs and social services undermine their quality and, consequently, the level of support for them among the public. Government intervention has also been much more harsh and intrusive in the US than in most other nations, and not just in the area of social policy. The US penal system, for example, is also much more focused upon retribution than upon rehabilitation or prevention. The labour relations system—the network of norms, regulations, and legislation that set the terms of collective bargaining and govern other worker/management and workplace issues—is notably less supportive or 'worker friendly' in the US too. It would not be surprising to discover that citizens from the Nordic lands and other nations that express strongly favourable attitudes toward the state would feel very differently after immigrating to the US and experiencing its more austere and often brutal approach for a few years. Institutions can clearly privilege and sustain some values and behaviours over others and lock them in tightly.

Institutions may restrict or provide opportunities for collective action and promote or impede opportunities for policy change. But, as with the culturalists that stress values, cultural and historical institutionalists often accept existing institutions and approaches as 'givens', without asking *who* is continually shaping and regenerating them. How do classical liberal values and institutions become re-packaged and sold as neo-liberal values and institutions? The cultural/historical institutionalist approach leaves out any role for agency and purposeful actions. The institutionalization of fiscal measures emphasizing tax breaks, and the character of labour legislation in the US, undermines social programs and the position of workers there. But these institutions are regularly ratified, reinforced, regenerated, repackaged, and re-sold to the public. In the US, for example—where taxes are comparatively low—actors such as the media and the government routinely vilify taxes as unjust, 'socialist', and a restriction on freedom; in Sweden—where taxes are relatively high—they are presented as a central means for upholding the rights, entitlements, and freedoms of residents. The focus on institutions alone, as 'independent variables', obscures the way that they are dependent variables too, and shaped by the 'balance of power' among key actors in a society. An exclusive focus upon institutions gives the approach a deterministic bent. It has difficulty accounting for institutional change—including the elimination of long-standing institutions such as slavery and Jim Crow laws in the US. And it implies that there is little that can be done to reduce existing inequalities. Cultural theorists often suggest that levels of inequality and the character of institutions largely reflect the views and wishes of most residents that are embedded in national value systems. Cultural-institutionalists place greater emphasis upon the institutions themselves, and more commonly bemoan their restrictive character, but they also suggest there is very little room for change. Their emphasis upon the way institutions maintain existing social structures, without consideration of actors or conflict, gives the approach a functionalist cast.

The culturalist perspective on social inequality provides a fascinating and often overlooked take on cross-national variation, which has both uncritical and critical variants. Some adherents to the culturalist perspective exhibit a Panglossian optimism and acceptance of inequality. From their view every nation has exactly the level and kind of social inequality and state intervention that its citizens desire. Those culturalists who are more concerned with the high levels of inequality in the Anglo-Saxon nations, however, are interested in trying to change the dominant culture and practices. They want to foster the development of the collectivist, cooperative, and solidaristic ethic and values that are missing from their 'liberal fragment' societies. But such a strategy necessarily entails careful consideration of the balance of power in society, the focus of the next chapter.

Notes

1. Fourth-century Athens is often considered the zenith of democratic achievement. Here important decisions were made directly, by the collective choice of all citizens ('direct democracy') rather than by elected officials representing the public as in democracies today ('representative democracy'). But it should be remembered that a majority of people who resided there, including women, slaves, and non-Athenians, were not considered citizens and were excluded from participating in its governing. Plato, however, was concerned with its excesses and the social instability he believed it fostered, not with its exclusionary nature.
2. However, some feminist critics, such as Diana Coole (1988: 40–41), argue that Plato was somewhat less egalitarian than is often suggested. Although, following Socrates, he maintained that women's souls and virtue were the same as men's and was willing to allow them into the ruling class, Plato 'never overcame the images identified with the female in Greek culture, and so women's association with dimensions outside the rational political order endured'.
3. The idea of a separation of powers was not original to Locke. It was at least implicit in Aristotle's work and present in medieval political theory. And it was more fully developed by Charles Louis de Secondat Montesquieu (1689–1755) later.
4. The elite theorists—Vilfredo Pareto, Gaetano Mosca (1858–1941), and Roberto Michels (1876–1936)—emphasized conflict within the elite groups and between them and the masses. However, unlike Marx, they were not *critical* conflict theorists. They maintained that elites dominated because of their inherent superiority, although Mosca and Michels also acknowledged their socially advantaged positions. All three elite theorists viewed this situation as natural and inevitable (unalterable).
5. Instincts—the inherent, genetically determined complex patterns of behaviour found in the animal world—should not be confused with reflexes, the automatic or involuntary neuromuscular reactions elicited by some stimulus.
6. Spencer and Sumner were also influenced by the work of the British classical economist and demographer Thomas Malthus (1766–1834). Malthus challenged the dominant conventional view that a large population was synonymous with wealth. He had argued that the natural rate of population growth was geometrical while that of food production was much less, growing only arithmetically. Populations would grow until they met the limitations of the food supply. Unless subject to 'negative' checks that decrease birth (such as birth control, moral restraint, and delayed marriages) or 'positive' checks that increase death (war, famine, or pestilence) there will be social misery and vice. He maintained that increasing the living conditions of the poor and the working class would lead to an increase in the size of the population that, in turn, would reduce the food supply, thereby lowering living standards. Spencer and Sumner, in contrast, were more concerned with the *quality* of the population, rather than its size.
7. Darwin (1982 [1859]:67) talked about the 'struggle for existence' and 'natural selection'. But, in a later edition of his *The Origin of Species*, he referred to Spencer's more

familiar phrase, the 'survival of the fittest', as 'more accurate' and 'sometimes equally convenient'. However, as noted, 'fittest' had a different connotation for Darwin.

8. Of course, the idea that you could improve human populations through genetic policy, promoting reproduction among those deemed superior and discouraging or prohibiting reproduction among those thought to be genetically inferior, was certainly not confined to the US. Forced sterilization policies were in place in virtually every industrialized capitalist nation, including Canada (McLaren 1990) and the Nordic lands (Broberg and Roll-Hansen 1996).

9. Of course, their work built upon that of many others. The first tests to measure mental ability were developed by Alfred Binet in France in 1905 to determine if normal schooling was suitable for students with learning difficulties. It was translated into English in the US by the American psychologist and geneticist Herbert Goddard. Administered on Ellis Island, the test was employed to prevent unwanted groups from immigrating to the US (Rattansi 2007). It was later adopted and developed by the Stanford psychologist Lewis M. Termin into the Stanford-Binet IQ Test, which is still widely used today. The idea that intelligence is a highly heritable trait and that differences in intelligence across races as measured by IQ tests could be genetic can be traced back to the work of Arthur Jensen and William Shockley.

10. They go on to state that 'the government should stop subsidizing births to anyone, rich or poor' (Herrnstein and Murray 1994: 549). However, given their earlier lament that the government is not supporting rich women (i.e., 'encouraging the wrong women'), this add-on appears disingenuous.

11. Charles Murray (1984), a political scientist associated with the right-wing American Enterprise Institute in the US, had published a book a decade earlier that closely followed the Social Darwinist perspective calling for the elimination of social programs on the grounds that they promoted deviant behaviour and immorality among the poor.

12. The 'g' or 'general factor' of cognitive ability identified by the British psychologist Charles Spearman is based upon factor analysis, a family of statistical techniques that are used to reduce or simplify a large number of measured variables into one or a smaller number of factors. It is often employed in the analysis of survey data to identify common underlying dimensions or components (factors) across a range of attitudes. For example, positive attitudes toward social welfare programs, progressive fiscal policies, higher minimum wages, trade unions, and greater government regulation over corporations may all be associated with, or 'load onto', a common or underlying factor. In this case, however, the 'g' is the general factor of intelligence reflecting an individual's performance on tests measuring a range of cognitive tasks.

13. Steven Jay Gould (1995:13) points to the 'central fallacy in using the substantial heritability of within-group IQ (among whites, for example) as an explanation of average differences between groups (whites versus blacks, for example)'.

14. The fact that the British anthropologist and 'father of eugenics' Sir Francis Galton (1822-1911) was Darwin's cousin has no doubt added to the confusion.

15. Although Darwin focused upon individuals in his account of evolution in *The Origin of Species*, in a later work, *The Descent of Man* (1871), he suggested that evolution might also work at the level of groups or species as well, an approach adopted by contemporary researchers such as the ethologist Konrad Lorenz. Thus, while a behaviour such as bravery might not be adaptive or beneficial for individuals, because it puts their lives in danger, it might be selected and retained because it benefits the larger community.

16. John Stuart Mill's account of social order via laissez-faire conditions was somewhat more qualified, pointing to the necessity of trade unions to allow for greater bargaining power parity between employers and workers.

17. Poverty was not a problem in pre-modern societies; indeed, from a Durkheimian perspective, since everyone was equally poor, poverty may have functioned as a source of social integration and equilibrium. Moreover, poverty discourages anomie because limited resources decrease the temptation to indefinitely extend one's range of needs.
18. For Durkheim, central institutions and various roles in society were analogous to the organs of the body; each performs a specific function.
19. Weber's work, it has been noted, has provided a theoretical foundation for functionalists such as Talcott Parsons and Robert Merton, as well as conflict/power theorists such as C. Wright Mills (Horowitz 1999).
20. Studies also show that even within the US, the higher rewards received by some CEOs are not based upon their performance (Broom and Cushing 1977).
21. However, despite its very similar name, 'new liberalism' should not be confused with 'neo-liberalism'. Neo-liberalism reasserts the classical liberal view that the most efficient allocation of resources is achieved by the competitive market and holds that state intervention (usually viewed as 'interference') necessarily tramples the rights of individuals.
22. The term 'American exceptionalism' was first used by Tocqueville to note that, for both good and ill, the US was qualitatively different from other nations. He argued that, in contrast with the class-ridden societies of Europe, American society was egalitarian, because there was no tradition of natural hierarchy at birth; rather, people were seen as intrinsically equal. However, he also worried about the growing power of the new 'industrial aristocracy' (capitalist class) and the 'tyranny of the majority'. Many others, including those working within the functionalist tradition, have viewed the US as an exceptional leader or pathbreaker—the 'first new nation'—that anticipated the future development of the older, more tradition-bound nations of Europe and elsewhere. For others, however, the term American exceptionalism best summarizes the United States' position as one of the most inegalitarian advanced capitalist societies, where income and wealth are very unequally distributed, the welfare state is lean, rudimentary, and more geared toward social control and upholding the market, and there is a relatively weak tradition of socialist values and no viable socialist, social democratic, or even social liberal parties. From this view, the US is a socially backward or stunted society that has not caught up to its European counterparts (Lipset 1996; Pierson 1990).
23. Similar policy changes occurred in Canada and the UK. Proponents of these workfare programs maintain that people need to work *while* they are receiving public assistance. But many other social programs are based upon the idea that the less fortunate and those in need should be supported by the fortunate. Public health care systems, pensions, parental leaves, and child care are financed and supported by everyone through taxation and insurance schemes, and the people who utilize them are not required to work for benefits and services when they need them. 'Workfare encourages both participants and other members of the polity to think of themselves as economic participants rather than as citizens' (King 2005:78; Olsen 2002).
24. It should be stressed that many researchers who acknowledge cross-national attitudinal and value differences do not necessarily accept the cultural view as the only or central explanation for the variation in the levels of inequality and the characters of welfare states across countries. Nor do they necessarily support the notion that these variations simply reflect the 'will of the people'.
25. English Canada and South Africa, Hartz maintained, were also liberal fragment cultures. But the settlement patterns in French Canada and Latin America led to the creation of more conservative political fragment cultures there.
26. Introduced by France to help establish its Empire in North America, the seigniorial system differed from European feudalism in several respects. In the UK and

continental Europe, nobles promised their allegiance and military support to monarchs or overlords in exchange for a piece of land (a fief) that they would exercise dominion over and could pass on to a male heir. In New France the lands (seigniories) were maintained by landlords (seigneurs), who might be members of the clergy or military officers rather than nobles. But while the seigneurs parcelled out the land to their tenants (habitants), the lands remained the property of the King of France and the power to impose penalties and fines to tenants was held by his commissioners. However, there was some notion and tradition of mutual obligation between the seigneurs and habitants. The seigniorial system was in place between 1627 and 1854, long after France had ceded lower Canada to Britain (in 1763). The Quebec Act of 1774 ensured that French Civil law and, hence the seigniorial system, would remain in place after British Conquest (McNaught 1988).

27. Some researchers suggest that hostility toward public assistance programs ('welfare') in the US has been as much a reflection of racist attitudes toward African Americans, who are incorrectly perceived as the largest group of recipients and as system abusers, as it has been a reflection of individualism (Gilens 1999; Neubeck and Cazenave 2001; Quadagno 1994).

28. The emphasis upon the architecture of long-standing institutions in society is also emphasized by state-centred and polity-centred theorists, path-dependency approaches, and historical-institutionalists. All of these closely related theoretical perspectives suggest that the character and design of existing institutions shape and limit future policy developments.

6 Challenging Inequality: Power and Conflict Accounts

Explanations for Inequality Emphasizing Power and Conflict

The two central classical theorists who established the foundations for the contemporary power/conflict tradition were Karl Marx and Max Weber. Both of them rejected the dominant liberal view—variously endorsed by writers across the biosocial and functionalist paradigms—that inequality stems from the inherent predispositions or talents of individuals. However, while both of these theorists are part of the 'conflict tradition' in sociology, and there are some broad similarities in their theoretical positions, Marx was much more interested in changing society, not just understanding or describing it. Unlike the functionalists and other theorists who either endorsed or resigned themselves to the status quo and high levels of inequality, Marx provided a critical perspective. For him, society was not characterized by equilibrium, justice, and social order. Rather, he focused upon the inherent conflict and antagonism between the two central classes present in all stratified, highly unequal societies: a small but very powerful ruling class and a numerically large, potentially powerful subject class. In capitalist societies these were the capitalist class or bourgeoisie (the owners of the means of production; land, factories and other enterprises, tools, and so on), whose major source of income is profits, and the working class, or proletariat, which must sell its labour power and rely upon its wages in order to survive. Writing in the 1800s, Marx and his collaborator Friedrich Engels observed that workers in England, the most industrialized and economically advanced nation in the world at the time, were *oppressed* (i.e., living and working under desperate, miserable, and dehumanizing conditions), *exploited* (because most of the value that they produced was extracted by the capitalist), and *alienated* (deprived of any real control over their work and its fruits and of any sense of 'job satisfaction').

For Marx, the division of labour in society and in the workplace reflected the imbalance in power between these two central classes and could not be the basis for social order and harmony as Durkheim and the functionalist tradition suggested. Despite this critical stance, Marx's approach was also radical, holding much greater possibility for change than the other theoretical traditions reviewed earlier that, implicitly or explicitly, viewed social inequality as inevitable.

For Marx, class was both a condition of social life and an engine for social action and change through class struggle. However, Marx also acknowledged the superior power of the capitalist class, highlighting several barriers that the working class would have to face and overcome. First, the state system—the government and its many branches, including the judiciary (the courts and legal system) and other repressive elements (such as the police and the army)—is economically dependent upon capitalists to finance political parties and candidates and on a dynamic capitalist system for its tax revenue. Consequently, it will largely serve their long-term interests. Second, the dominant ideas, values, and ideologies in capitalist societies will always represent the interests of capitalists and the capitalist system. They will serve to conceal and mystify the true nature of capitalism, making it appear that the specific class interests of capitalists are universal. Unlike many adherents to the cultural-institutional tradition, for Marx the central institutions and related networks of legislation and norms and the dominant values systems and cultures in society were neither neutral nor natural. Finally, workers themselves are economically dependent upon capitalists and capitalism.

Weber had a different and more multi-dimensional account of classes and conflict in society. Unlike Marx, he highlighted broad gradational differences in 'life chances' across classes (and other groups) in society, but his notion of 'market situations' was more relational, emphasizing the differing access that classes (and other groups) have to various kinds of income-generating assets and other organizational resources and how they can use them to enhance their opportunities and power vis-à-vis others in society. Exclusive ownership and control over the means of production provides capitalists with greater wealth and power over other classes and groups. But the latter may employ various other means, such as credentialing, licensing, organizing, or other forms of 'social closure' to improve their position in society.

For both Marx and Weber, then, power plays a very central role. Given the complexity of this concept, it is useful to consider its levels and forms.[1] We can identify three **levels of power**: (1) situational, (2) institutional, and (3) systemic/societal (Alford and Friedland 1985; Wright 1994). We can also identify three central **forms of power**—economic, ideological, and political—each based upon different, but often closely related, types of resources. The balance of power in society largely reflects the access that classes and other groups have to these resources, and their ability to organize, within the context of the capitalist system.

Situational Power: Actors

Situational power refers to the power held by actors in particular situations and settings. As noted in the introductory discussion of power in chapter 1, some actors may be able to impose alternatives to the preferences and goals of their subordinates through the use of physical force, coercion, violence, economic deprivation, or myriad other disincentives. Even the threat of such actions, whether voiced or simply anticipated, can foster cooperation or submission and encourage people to forgo their own desires and interests in favour of those of more powerful interests. However, powerful actors may opt to use the 'carrot' instead of the 'stick', offering a range of rewards to induce people to cooperate with them and compensate them for their compliance and support. Salary increases, promotions, stock options, company cars, bonuses, paid vacations, time off, and numerous other 'fringe benefits' are enticements routinely used by employers. In these cases there need not be any conflict, overt or covert, because subalterns come to internalize and embrace, or at least accept, the views, wishes, purposes, and plans of the powerful.[2] The powerful may also attempt to manipulate or persuade the powerless to accept existing situations, such as extreme inequalities in income and wealth or very high levels of poverty, as a reflection of the 'natural order' of things. This kind of purposeful shaping of the public mind may be covert, relying upon selectively limited or biased information in the manner of most commercial advertising, or it may be more overt and explicit. Lastly, powerful actors may rely upon the state and the legal system to maintain their privileged position.

These various courses of action are not mutually exclusive; indeed, they are most often alternately or concurrently employed by the powerful. The power of actors to take such actions is largely dependent upon their access to key resources and their ability to organize and create a unified front. In capitalist societies the most important resources are (1) material or economic resources (wealth, capital, property, jobs), (2) normative or ideological resources (the media, education), and (3) explicitly political resources (influence over state policy). The capitalist class enjoys significant control over the first two resources directly, through ownership of the means of production and the means of persuasion, and somewhat more indirectly over the third. The working class and other groups in society rely more upon organizational resources to try to influence the state and others in society.

The capitalist class already has a significant degree of inherent, informal organizational unity by virtue of its members' broadly similar economic interests; for example, free trade, lower taxes, fewer and more meagre social programs that leave workers more dependent upon the market, and anti-labour legislation are widely and firmly embraced across the corporate world. But capitalists have significantly increased this 'intrinsic unity' through the proliferation of dense networks of interlocking corporate directorships within and across the manufacturing, financial, and service sectors of the economy.[3] This class unity is further bolstered through the creation of powerful employer federations and business associations. Employers have established federations at the industry or sectoral levels expressly to foster a more united front, allowing them to coordinate common economic and social strategies and work together to shape public opinion in favour of their interests. In Europe these federations, in turn, have often been organized into confederations ('peak federations', or federations of federations). In the Nordic world these include the Confederation of Finnish Industries (*Elinkeinoelämän Keskusliitto*, EK), the Federation of Finnish Enterprises, and the Confederation of Norwegian Enterprise (*Næringslivet Hovedororganisasjon*, NHO), which has a current membership of over 19,800 companies.[4] In Sweden the most prominent and influential employers organization is the Confederation of Swedish Enterprise (*Svenskt Näringsliv*), created via a merger of two long-standing bodies, the Swedish Employers Federation (*Svenska Arbetsgivareföreningen*) and the nation's largest trade association, the Federation of Swedish Industries (*Industriförbundet*), in 2001. This confederation also finances *Timbro*, a libertarian think tank with a candidly declared mission 'to originate, promote and disseminate ideas and issues supporting the principles of free markets, free enterprise, individual liberty and a free society' and work to 'win the hearts and minds of new generations'.[5] In the UK, the Confederation of British Industry (CBI), with a membership of some 200,000 companies, has played a similar role to that of its European counterparts but, in North America—where the labour movements have been relatively weak—such employer confederations have not been necessary. However, the interests of the capitalist class and the business community in North America have been well represented and defended by other associations, such as the Business Council and the Business Roundtable in the US, and in Canada the Fraser Institute and the Canadian Council of Chief Executives (CCCE), composed of the chief executive officers (CEOs) of the 150 largest enterprises.[6] Through the creation of employer federations and business associations, and the funding of dense policy networks comprised of think tanks, foundations, research institutes, discussion groups, and numerous other bodies expressly designed to foster greater consensus on important policy issues, the capitalist class has greatly increased its clout and influence over government policy (Brownlee 2005; Domhoff 1998; Dye 1995; West and Loomis 1998). Moreover, the ideas, accounts, agendas, and policy prescriptions they champion are routinely presented in the mass media as simply 'commonsensical', the only rational and credible way to view and address the social world.

The mass media—the newspapers and magazines, television and radio stations, and other outlets that most citizens rely upon as their central sources of information and means of interpreting and understanding what is going on in the world around them—are themselves, of course, a crucial power resource in capitalist society, constituting the central and perhaps most potent element of the 'means of persuasion'. Since most companies involved in the media are private enterprises, and heavily reliant upon advertising dollars from other corporations for their revenue, they have long been intimately tied to the corporate world's neo-liberal outlook and policy positions. However, through rapid and intense spates of buyouts and acquisitions over the past few decades, media enterprises have become increasingly concentrated into fewer and fewer hands, creating huge 'mixed-media' conglomerates that, in turn, have been purchased by, and become strategic components of, considerably larger and much more economically diverse conglomerates. The media giants sell their most important 'asset'—their readers and audiences—to other, often closely linked corporations, which sell their products and promote their views in the media. Very few other actors have such a cozy set up, with so many resources and opportunities to influence how people think, or shape what they think about (Bagdikian 1992; Chomsky and Herman 1988; McChesney and Nichols 2002; Winter 1997).

The exercise of ideological power often entails the presentation of particular viewpoints or policy options as the only reasonable ones. This can be especially effective when the issues at hand require a specialized expertise and vocabulary that most people may not possess. 'Free trade', for example, was widely and passionately endorsed across the mainstream media in North America in the years prior to the passage of the Free Trade Agreement (FTA) in 1989 and the North American Free Trade Agreement (NAFTA) in 1992. But blatant agenda-shaping was perhaps most glaringly evident in the 1990s in the US when powerful representatives of 'big business' in the insurance and medical fields spent millions of dollars demonizing the public single-payer health care systems in place across much of the advanced capitalist world, thereby virtually ensuring that the only discussions and proposals concerning health care reform that would be seen as credible would have to centre around the creation of some form of market-based, managed care.[7] Similarly, discussions of fiscal policy that dominate in the media in the Anglo-Saxon nations invariably suggest that taxes are only an economic burden and very rarely, if ever, remind people that taxes fund a wide range of valued services and amenities, including our public schools and universities, our hospitals and health care systems, our libraries, and our parks, that make our cities safer and livable. The dominant 'taxes as burden' discourse is explicitly designed to incite and deepen widespread antipathy toward taxation and allow for further tax reductions on the wealthy and powerful. The reduced taxes, in turn, undermine the government's ability to provide high quality services. This encourages those who are better off to search for private alternatives who then demand further tax cuts on the grounds that they do use public services as much, leading to a further deterioration of our roads, bridges, schools, and libraries.

However, agenda-setting more typically entails setting limits around the *range* of issues open for discussion, rather than just the explicit promotion of particular positions. Studies suggesting that the Nordic (or other) nations with developed social programs and significant state intervention have often outperformed the US along several economic indicators *and* have significantly lower levels of poverty and healthier populations, for example, are only very infrequently brought to light in the mainstream US media; articles suggesting that there might be alternatives to the capitalist market system itself are entirely unacceptable and virtually never appear in the mainstream media. Even within the very narrow range of issues that are countenanced, the narrative is always massaged and shaped. Thus, the 'abuse' of social programs by the poor, and the 'threat' posed by the homeless, are more often identified and defined as central issues to be addressed, rather than the desperate poverty, homelessness, and growing inequalities that capitalism generates. This bias is often reflected in the very language we have all come to employ. Fiscal policy and social policy, for example, are usually referred to as '*re*distributive' measures that (1) reflect unfair government coercion or, less commonly, (2) constitute the fabric of protective 'social safety nets'. But either way, the very notion of *re*distribution implies that the prior, market-generated distribution of wealth, income, and opportunities is somehow 'natural', rather than itself a product of state policies that allow the inheritance of great wealth, ensure low taxes for corporations and the wealthy, and uphold private property rights above all others while often endorsing minimum wage levels that families can barely survive on. Similarly, discussions of 'deregulation' suggest that markets have been 'freed' from undue state interference, when in fact they have been *re*-regulated in ways that benefit corporations and the wealthy. The reduction or elimination of corporate and estate taxes and measures that encourage private over public forms of health care and other social programs simply reflect a different form of government intervention. Frequent references to estate taxes as 'death taxes' and 'double taxes' in the mainstream media are also misleading. In fact, estate taxes are progressive and, unlike death and 'death taxes', only affect a very small percentage of the population—wealthy property owners.[8] And since they are levied on stocks, bonds, real estate, and other assets that have increased in value since they were purchased, they are really just deferred taxes on this untaxed appreciation and profit. The reference to welfare states as 'social safety nets' popular in the Anglo-Saxon nations reflects a similar bent. The idea of social rights and entitlements—with some exceptions, such as primary and secondary education and, outside of the US, health care—is eclipsed by this liberal metaphor endorsing the market as the sole or central vehicle to distribute wealth in society. It suggests that social benefits should be only temporary last resort measures for those destitute members of society—if deemed worthy—who fell ('failed') while 'performing' in the market economy (Page and Simmons 2000).

Political power involves an ability to influence what the state—the most central political resource in society—does. Numerous studies have indicated how the capitalist class has been able to do this far more effectively than any other actors. First, the upper reaches of the state have been 'colonized' by the capitalist class in most capitalist nations. Members of the capitalist class have commonly assumed the highest positions of the executive (government), judicial, legislative, and repressive branches of the state in almost all capitalist nations.[9] And even when not directly represented in the state, members of this economic elite are often closely connected to those in the state elite via blood ties, intermarriages, or social origins, often having gone to the same schools and grown up in the same neighbourhoods. These ties and common or similar social origins foster an ideological unity that accepts free market capitalism as beyond question. Thus, when those in government profess to be doing what they believe is in the national interest—just as when those running media enterprises strenuously insist that 'no one tells them what to say'—it is often true. But these ties and common social origins ensure that the positions of state elites (like those of media elites) will not often be appreciably different from those of most other capitalist class members, and that alternative viewpoints will not be well-represented or appear very often, if at all (Domhoff 1998; Miliband 1977).[10] Second, well-heeled business organizations are able to use their intricate networks of policy advisory groups to greatly influence government policy. But they can also directly and markedly shape the political scene and political agendas by underwriting the cost of the electoral campaigns of political parties and candidates. Very wealthy individuals can greatly influence the issues that elections will be fought over, even if they do not gain office, by throwing their financial might behind them (Birnbaum 2000; Center for Public Integrity 1998; Sifry and Watzman 2004). For example, as the presidential candidate for the Reform Party in the US in 1992, Texas billionaire Ross Perot helped to ensure that the federal budget deficit would be a central concern that year, and it has remained a top priority in US politics ever since. Similarly, while billionaire Steve Forbes, the editor-in-chief of a leading US business magazine (*Forbes*), did not succeed in his two bids to become the presidential candidate for the Republican Party in 1996 or 2000, he has been enormously successful as an evangelist for freer markets and lower taxes. In Canada the Conservative Party was assisted in its bid to assume office in 1988 by reversing its long-standing anti-free trade position in order to benefit from the millions of dollars big business was shelling out to promote free trade; in effect, every dollar the business/corporate community spent selling free trade to the Canadian public would help to elect the Conservatives.

While the capitalist class is exceptionally well organized and enjoys unparalleled influence over some of the most important resources in society, power is almost never held exclusively by this class, or by any one group. And power is fluid. That means that it is possible for the balance of power to shift under certain circumstances. Through organization and access to alternative power resources, other actors can increase their strength, altering the balance of power in society. In the Nordic lands, for example, the balance of power among key actors is notably different than in the Anglo-Saxon world. Although no group can rival the power of the capitalist class there, or in any other capitalist society, labour and other groups are much more organized, and labour and women are more widely represented in the state bodies and in parliament. Universal social programs, provided as entitlements, render individuals less dependent upon the market and employers, further bolstering their power. Alternative forms of media have been publicly subsidized to ensure that mainstream media views do not entirely engulf alternative viewpoints; coverage of the debate over membership in the European Union (EU) in the Nordic lands was considerably more even-handed than the free trade debate in North America, partly owing to state policies that helped to keep smaller, alternative media outlets alive.[11] And there has been much greater public funding for electoral campaigns so that private wealth is a less crucial force in the shaping of election issues and the character of political parties.

Institutional Power and Systemic Power

As indicated above, power need not be always actively wielded by actors or manifest in conflicts. It is also inscribed in the dominant institutions in society. The ability of workers to organize, and the kinds of actions they may take, are in large measure determined by institutional rules. In the US, the rights gained by labour through the 1935 federal National Labor Relations Act (NLRA) were soon strictly qualified and constrained with the passage of the Labor-Management Relations Act in 1947.[12] Labour legislation has been considerably stronger in Canada and the UK, and markedly so in the Nordic lands. Rules concerning the funding of election campaigns can also impart a strong bias and shape the balance of power in society. In the US, where the emphasis is upon 'free speech', spending limits are restricted to presidential campaigns only, and even then, only when candidates voluntarily agree to them as a condition for accepting public financing. Outside of these executive-level campaigns there is little public funding available for candidates seeking to gain a seat in the national legislature in the US. Consequently, American voters are presented with candidates who are either wealthy themselves or acceptable to wealthy private funders. In the other Anglo-Saxon nations there is greater emphasis placed upon achieving a more level playing field, with more stringent spending and contribution limits and greater public support for electoral campaigns. The UK, for example, provides public funding for media, and Canada provides public media subsidies and partial funding for individual campaigns. The Nordic lands, in contrast, provide much more generous public support for political parties but, reflecting their greater commitment to issues rather than personalities, do not provide support to individual candidates (Alexander 2005; Mandle 2004). These different institutions and rules significantly alter the nature of politics, shaping electoral agendas, influencing voter turnout, and affecting state policy.[13]

Institutional biases permeate all central social institutions, such as the state, the family, religion, the educational system, and the media, and they are reflected in the dominant 'culture', the popular norms, attitudes, values, practices, and traditions securely in place. Of course, they are obviously not unrelated to what various actors do (or have done in the past) to create, shape, and sustain them—a fact often glossed over by those who support a strictly cultural/institutionalist approach. But unlike situational power exercised by actors, power expressed through institutional biases often goes virtually undetected because such biases are widely accepted as commonsensical, as evident in the pronouncements of the Texas State Board of Education concerning the selection of school textbooks in the 1980s:

> Textbook content shall promote citizenship and the understanding of the free-enterprise system, emphasize patriotism and respect for recognized authority.... Textbook content shall not encourage lifestyles deviating from generally accepted standards of society (quoted in Galbraith 1983:24).

The fact that the 'generally accepted' or dominant standards and values of society are socially constructed, and continually renewed and defended, is not often acknowledged; they are simply taken-for-granted and left unquestioned. In the words of the Italian political theorist Antonio Gramsci, they have become 'hegemonic' and, consequently, serve to help secure the position of the powerful.

At another broader level, power is embedded in the capitalist system itself. Since states largely rely upon taxation and borrowing from the private sector to acquire the financial resources they need to operate, they are greatly dependent upon a dynamic, profitable capitalist economy. Indeed, virtually all major actors in society are economically dependent upon this, as political scientist Adam Przeworski (1985:139) notes: '[the] current realization of material interests of capitalists is a necessary condition for the future realization of the material interests of any group under capitalism'.[14] Moreover, unfavourable conditions for the accumulation of capital in any nation can encourage capitalists to withhold investments of capital there ('investment strikes') and relocate investments and enterprises ('capital flight')—or threaten to do so—if more business-friendly policies are not adopted.

Sociologist Erik Olin Wright effectively captures the three levels of power reviewed here with his analogy to a chess game. Some of the chess pieces, or 'actors', have considerably more power than that held by other pieces (situational power). Their power is enhanced, or weakened, by the 'rules of the game' that determine the various ways the different kinds of chess pieces may move across the board (institutional power). But the structure of the chessboard itself, with its specific arrangement of a finite set of squares of a predetermined size, profoundly shapes and restricts the movements of all pieces, advantaging some of them over others (systemic power).[15]

Given its control or influence over the 'means of production' (economic enterprises), the 'means of persuasion' (the media), and the 'means of coercion' (the state), and the structural biases of the capitalist system itself, the capitalist class will always be the most powerful actor in society. However, drawing on ideas from Marx and Weber, some contemporary theorists suggest that it is possible to significantly shift the power imbalance in society, improving the position of workers and other organized groups vis-à-vis that of the capitalist class. Researchers working within a 'power resources theory' (PRT) tradition, for example, have shown that when workers increase their level of power, they can significantly reduce several forms of social inequality in society both directly in the market and indirectly by establishing comprehensive and supportive welfare institutions, programs, and laws (Esping-Andersen 1985a, 1985b, 1990; Korpi 1978, 1983; Stephens 1980).

Power resources theorists highlight two broad, central types of resources that can enable the working class to begin to shift the power balance in society. The first types of resource that they stress are **organizational/associational resources**. Workers can increase their power and foster greater solidarity by organizing unions. With high levels of union density (the rate of union membership relative to the size of the non-agricultural labour force), many forms of inequality begin to decline. However, in order to more effectively challenge the power of capitalists and address inequality across society, it is also crucial that labour unions, bodies, and federations are united and work closely together. Labour organizations and federations representing workers across various workplaces, occupational lines, and economic sectors must be organized into 'peak' umbrella associations or confederations that foster solidarity and allow them to more effectively work together and speak with 'one voice'—posing a much greater challenge and threat to capital—and bargain on behalf of a much larger group of workers over a wider range of workplace and broader societal issues and concerns. Under such circumstances they can effect changes that will benefit everyone in society, not just their membership. As evident in Table 6.1, union density rates and coverage rates (the percentage of the labour force that is covered by union agreements) have been much higher in the Nordic lands than in the Anglo-Saxon nations for some time. Indeed, the Nordic lands have typically had among the highest rates of unionization and coverage among the capitalist nations, and Sweden has been a world leader in this area for many decades. Moreover, the powerful blue collar confederations and white collar centrals in Norway (LO, YS), Sweden (LO, TCO), and Finland (SAK, STTK)

TABLE 6.1 **Power Resources in Six Nations**

	Anglo-Saxon Nations			Nordic Nations		
	Canada	**UK**	**US**	**Finland**	**Norway**	**Sweden**
Union Density						
1970	31%	45%	27%	51%	57%	68%
1980	34%	51%	22%	69%	58%	78%
1990	33%	39%	15%	72%	58%	80%
2000	30%	30%	13%	75%	54%	79%
2007	29%	28%	12%	70%	54%	71%
Coverage[a]						
2003	32%	33%	12%	92%	72%	93%
Major Labour Confederations	Canadian Labour Congress **(CLC)**	Trades Union Congress **(TUC)**	American Federation of Labor-Congress of Industrial Organizations **(AFL-CIO)**	Central Organization of Trade Unions **(SAK)**	Confederation of Labour **(LO)**	Trade Union Confederation **(LO)**
				Confederation of Salaried Employees **(STTK)**	Confederation of Vocational Unions **(YS)**	Confederation of Professional Employees **(TCO)**
				Confederation of Unions for Academic Professional **(AKAVA)**	Confederation of Professional Associations **(AF)**	Confederation of Professional Associations **(SACO)**
Main Left Party (Social Democratic/ Labour Party)	Cooperative Commonwealth Federation **(CCF)** / New Democratic Party **(NDP)**	Labour Party	———	Finnish Labour Party **(SDP)**	Norwegian Labour Party **(DNA)**	Swedish Social Democratic Labour Party **(SAP)**

[a]Collective bargaining coverage rates

Sources: OECD (nd) Trade Union Density in OECD Countries 1960–2007; OECD (2004b).

have long bargained on behalf of the great majority of the workers in their nations at the national, sectoral, or industry level, often working together to improve wages, working conditions, and benefits for all.[16] While not as high as in the Nordic nations, in the first few decades of the post-World War II period union density in the UK was markedly higher than in Canada and, especially, the US, where it has been exceptionally low.[17] The central labour confederation in the UK, the Trades Union Congress (TUC), has played a much more prominent role there than the Canadian Labour Congress (CLC) has in Canada or its American counterpart, the American Federation of Labor-Congress of Industrial Organizations (AFL-CIO), has in US. At the start of the 1950s, union density was higher in the US than in Canada, but it began a steady decline by the middle of that decade, while Canada's rate continued to climb. However, union density has dropped in all three Anglo-Saxon nations over the past few decades—and especially in the US—attended by higher rates of inequality in these three nations. It has also declined somewhat in the Nordic lands but remains very high by international standards.

In addition to organizational/associational resources, PRT also highlights the importance of **political resources**. The strong presence of a 'left' (social democratic or socialist/labour) party that can represent the interests of workers and other organized groups in the state can also be a central means of reducing inequality. And, of course, the power of the working class will be greatest if these left parties are able to assume power and stay in office for lengthy periods of time. Both types of power resources have been far more developed in the Nordic lands than in the Anglo-Saxon countries for many decades. The social democratic/labour parties in the Nordic lands established roots very early on and have been exceptionally prominent on the political scenes there. Founded in 1889, Sweden's Social Democratic Labour Party, or SAP (*Socialdemokratiska Arbetarpartiet*), won its first seat in parliament (*Riksdag*) in 1896. It was part of a coalition government in 1917 and held power for brief periods in the 1920s but, after assuming office in 1932, it remained in power for a period of 44 years (1932–1976). Given its extensive period of incumbency—it was in power for sixty-six years between 1932–2006—the SAP has long been regarded as Sweden's 'natural party of government'.[18] Few political parties anywhere in the democratic capitalist world of nations, whatever their political stripe, have matched the SAP's success, but Norway's Labour Party, or DNA (*det Norsk Arbeiderparti*), has had a broadly similar electoral history and profile of incumbency. The DNA was established in 1887 and held power for 30 years, between 1935 to 1965. It maintained an absolute majority in parliament (*Storting*) from 1945–1961, and has assumed office on several occasions over the past few decades (e.g., 1973–1981, 1990–1997). Created in 1899, the Social Democratic Party of Finland, or SDP (*Sosialdemokraattinen Puolue*), has also been a central fixture on the political scene and in parliament (*Eduskunta*). It has been almost as dominant in Finnish politics—participating in 70% of the governments between 1945 and 2002—as were its Norwegian (72%) and Swedish (82%) counterparts during the same period (Arter 2003).[19] In all three nations the social democratic/labour parties have been very closely linked to their union movements. In Sweden, for example, LO, the powerful blue-collar central, was actually created by the SAP in 1898; the Norwegian LO was established the following year. They have also often relied upon support from other left, or left-leaning, parties in their nations. The popularity and lengthy periods of incumbency of the Nordic social democratic/labour parties allowed them to develop policies and gradually erect comprehensive welfare states that could address many aspects of social inequality in their countries.

In the Anglo-Saxon nations the power resources of workers have been less developed, and much less secure. In the first few decades following World War II, however, labour's power resources in the UK more closely resembled those in the Nordic nations and were reflected in declining levels of inequality and a greater commitment to the idea of rights and entitlements and a comprehensive 'cradle-to-grave' welfare state. Indeed, during this period the welfare state in the UK was not so unequivocally a member of the 'liberal welfare regime'. Founded in 1900 as an outgrowth of the labour movement, the Labour Party in the UK has played an important role as the major opposition to the Conservative party since the 1920s. However, it has not been nearly as electorally successful as its Nordic counterparts. In Canada, none of the left parties established in the early part of the twentieth century managed to establish secure roots, but a coalition of progressive agrarian, socialist, and labour organizations came together to create the Cooperative Commonwealth Federation (CCF) in 1932. Neither it, nor its successor, the New Democratic Party (NDP) has ever held power at the national level, but CCF/NDP parties have often assumed office at the provincial level, and have played a central role in the development of social programs, including the universal health care system, in Canada. The US stands out yet again as exceptional here; it is the only advanced capitalist nation without an electorally viable socialist, social democratic, or labour party. Even within the Anglo-Saxon world of nations the US is an outlier, with the lowest level of power resources, the highest levels of inequality, and a vestigial and rapidly diminishing welfare state.

By now there are myriad studies demonstrating the significant impact of high levels of power resources on inequality across a range of advanced capitalist nations. Union strength (union density and centralization) greatly reduces levels of pre-tax and transfer income inequality and poverty rates, while left-party governance is closely associated with large reductions in post-tax and post-transfer income inequality. High levels of power resources are also associated with higher levels of social spending and the creation of more comprehensive and generous welfare states, which in turn can further reduce income inequality and poverty and provide numerous other supports (Björn 1979; Bradley et al. 2003; Brady 2003a, 2003b; Dryzek 1978; Gustafsson and Johansson 1999; Hewitt 1977; Hicks 1991, 1999; Hicks and Swank 1984; Huber and Stephens 2001; Korpi 1989; Korpi and Palme 1998; Moller et al. 2003; Rueda 2008).

A complementary, and rapidly growing, body of research also suggests that inequality goes down, and welfare states are built up, in nations that have higher levels of female participation in the paid labour force and greater representation of women in parliament. It also highlights the important role of women's agency in these developments (Bolzendahl and Brooks 2007; Hobson 1993; Hobson and Lindholm 1997; Huber and Stephens 2000; Lewis and Åström 1992; Lindholm 1991; Lovenduski 2005; Ruggie 1984; Sandqvist 1992; Wängnerud 2000). These kinds of organizational and political resources have also been much more evident in the Nordic nations than in the Anglo-Saxon nations, and in the Nordic lands they have been very closely associated with social democratic/labour movements.[20]

Researchers and theorists often seek to demonstrate that it is the distribution of power resources (the balance of power) in society, *or* the nature of institutions, *or* the character of the dominant culture, that is *the* central determinant of the nature and levels of social inequality in society. But the separation of these three variables is an entirely artificial one. In fact, they are inextricably and symbiotically linked to one another, as schematically illustrated in Figure 6.1. Nations with powerful labour movements and high levels of female representation in parliament develop comprehensive, supportive welfare states (institutions) that generate public support for such collective measures, including a willingness to pay higher taxes in order to maintain and extend them (culture). The industrial relations systems in all six nations integrate, regulate, and institutionalize their labour movements, providing union rights and restrictions on union activities. But labour's far greater strength in the Nordic nations allowed it to establish more supportive labour laws and cultivate a more collectivist culture. Compared to the Anglo-Saxon nations, people across a broad spectrum of the economy are more likely to identify themselves as part of the working class, and to support unions in the Nordic nations (Clement and Myles 1994; Johnston and Baer 1993). The Nordic unions have more often operated as parts of broader social movements than as discrete institutions with narrow concerns.[21] In the US, the greater power of capital undermined labour's attempts to

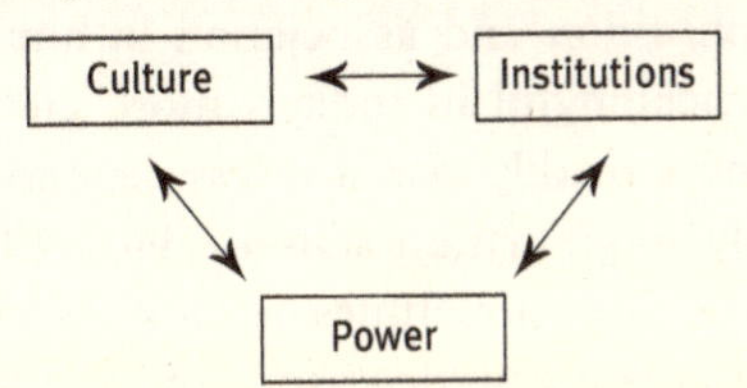

FIGURE 6.1 The Reciprocal Influence of Key Socio-Political Forces

develop its power resources and strategies from the start. Capital fought to implant laws and institutions that would maintain this power imbalance, foster individualism, and forge a more highly atomized consumer culture (Goldfield 1989; Griffin et al. 1986; Voss 1993).

Marx thought that the working class would be the 'gravedigger of capitalism', and that its manifestations in the most economically developed nations, such as the US and the UK, would be among the first to be interred. But many today, including many Marxists, would argue that there has been no need for working-class shovels to break ground yet; capitalism is alive and well, especially in advanced capitalist nations. Indeed, with increasing global integration, its life expectancy has been extended. From this view, the 'gains' made by labour, women's groups, and other instances of organized agency, are often presented as illusory. Lower levels of inequality and the development of welfare states and other social and legal supports are viewed as minor and largely empty concessions. This is clearly not the perspective presented here. The lower and 'shallower' levels of poverty, larger middle classes, better health and longer life expectancies, and the panoply of high quality social programs and services, including child care, health care, post-secondary education and a wider range of protective rights and legislation, make life in these nations qualitatively better than in the Anglo-Saxon lands. Of course, these gains have not eliminated—or even addressed—all forms of social inequality in these societies. Indeed, some of its most central forms are intrinsic to capitalism. They will never be eliminated until this free market system—built upon a particular form of class relations that places control over the means of production, and hence, power, in the hands of so few—is superseded by an alternative social arrangement based upon some form of economic democracy. Moreover, while some of the impressive achievements made in the Nordic lands are quite secure now—relatively few interests or actors would care to challenge long-standing bans on corporal punishment or many of the rights achieved by women, gays/lesbians, and other groups in these nations, for example—other achievements, including the comprehensive, generous, and decommodifying welfare states and social programs in these nations, might be incrementally transformed, and support for them undermined. The balance of power in these societies has been slowly shifting back toward capital over the past two decades, concomitant with rising levels of material inequality, greater polarization, and at least some levels and types of welfare retrenchment. Power resources, such as high levels of unionization and association in any one nation are, arguably, somewhat less meaningful in today's more globally integrated world. Because capital can more readily exit, it is less dependent upon labour forces or governments in any single nation (Olsen 1991, 1992). Incumbent social democratic/labour parties can sometimes be difficult to distinguish from some of their liberal or conservative predecessors and successors in many nations today. But the lessons the Nordic nations provide for us should not be lost or discounted. Too many accounts of inequality link their invaluable critical diagnoses to an ultimately fatalistic political stance. The greater solidarity and political organization, development of alternative institutions, restrictions on some of the powers of capital, and fostering of more collectivist cultures that have had considerable success at the national level in the Nordic lands provide a road map for developments that must be fostered at the international level in order to secure and transcend their considerable achievements.

Notes

1. In addition to the classic sociological works by Marx and Weber, many other contemporary theorists, such as Galbraith (1983), Lukes (2005), Scott (2001), and Wrong (1988), thoroughly explore the concept of power.
2. Two Italian theorists, the Florentine political advisor and historian, Niccolò Machiavelli and the sociologist and economist Vilfredo Pareto, made similar observations about the exercise of power in politics. Some political elites and leaders were like 'foxes', relying upon cunning, inducements, and rewards to obtain compliance, while others were like 'lions', employing force and coercion. They maintained that both types of elite strategies were necessary for political stability.
3. Private corporations (industries, commercial, and financial enterprises) are governed by boards of directors (elected by shareholders) who exercise proprietary (ownership) functions; setting goals, agendas, and policies; and making all crucial decisions. Interlocking directorates exist when the same directors sit on the boards of directors of multiple corporations. Studies of interlocking directorates demonstrate that the largest enterprises are closely linked through dense networks of such directorships. This not only leads to conflicts of interest and undermines the 'competitive spirit' that is supposed to be the life blood of capitalism, it also creates a greater concentration of corporate power, allowing the directors to promote the broad interests of their class as a whole, rather than just that of a particular enterprise (Domhoff 1998; Schwartz 1987).
4. Finland's EK was established in 2005 through the merger of the large industry and service employer federations; Norway's NHO was created in 1989 through the merger of three employer associations, the Federation of Norwegian Industries, the Norwegian Employers' Confederation, and the Federation of Norwegian Craftsmen.
5. Its website is http://www.timbro.se.
6. The Business Council on National Issues, or BCNI, was created in 1976 but changed its name to the Canadian Council of Chief Executives in 2001.
7. On the role of employers and business and organizations in the struggle over health care in the US see Mintz (1998), Quadagno (2005), and West and Loomis (1998). Some representatives of 'big business', however, such as the large American automobile manufacturers, were much more open to a public health care system if only because they believed it could lower their health care costs, improve corporate profitability, and allow them to compete on more equal footing with their counterparts in Europe, where auto workers are included in public health care programs.
8. A progressive tax is one in which the tax rate increases in line with the tax base. It is based upon the ability-to-pay principle, so wealthier people pay a higher tax rate. Estate taxes and income taxes are the most familiar progressive taxes. However, in practice, 'progressive' taxation systems typically provide the wealthy with more and greater tax deductions too.
9. Historically, members of the capitalist class have often assumed positions as presidents and prime ministers and held key cabinet positions and other positions of power while also serving as heads of companies and holding other important posts in

the economic sphere. Legislation in most advanced capitalist nations now requires them to put their holdings in a 'blind trust' when they assume high level political positions, but their economic interests, ideological biases, and connections with those in the corporate/economic world remain firmly in place.

10. For an overview of this 'instrumentalist' perspective see Olsen (2002), chapter 6.
11. After serious deliberations Finland joined the EU and adopted the Euro as its currency. With a slim majority of public support in favour, Sweden opted to join the EU, but it has not adopted the Euro. (Thus, like the UK and Denmark, it remains outside the 'Eurozone'.) Norway decided not to join the EU.
12. The National Labor Relations Act (informally known as the 'Wagner Act' after its principal drafter, Senator Robert Wagner) was introduced in 1935 by the federal government. It was designed to protect the rights of workers, allow them to engage in collective bargaining, and take part in strikes and other forms of concerted activity. However, these rights were undermined or weakened with the passage of the National Labor-Management Relations Act (informally known as the 'Taft-Hartley Act' after its sponsors, Senator Robert Taft and Representative Fred Hartley) in 1947.
13. Average voter turnouts across all elections since 1945 were as follows for the six nations examined here: 83.3% in Sweden, 79.5% in Norway, 79.1% in Finland, 74.9% in the UK, 68.4% in Canada, and 48.3% in the US.
14. Labour movements are best placed for bargaining when the capitalist economy is booming and all of their members are employed. Under such conditions, employers are more reliant upon them; they have no 'reserve army of labour' (the unemployed and underemployed) to draw upon and cannot as easily threaten or cow their workers.
15. This analogy illustrates the structural aspects of capitalism and the ways it can even place limits upon what capitalists—the most powerful 'pieces'—can do. For example, companies that opt to pay good wages, offer good social programs and benefits, and demonstrate serious concern and leadership over health and safety and other environmental issues might find it very difficult to successfully compete with other enterprises that are not following suit. From a 'structuralist' perspective, closely associated with the work of neo-Marxists such as Nicos Poultantzas, the state will always act to secure the capitalist system and the *long-term* interests of all capitalists. However, in doing so, it will sometimes frustrate the wishes or demands of particular capitalists (see Olsen 2002, chapter 4 for an overview of this perspective).
16. The associations and unions representing academics and professional workers have also been part of powerful union centrals in Norway (AF), Sweden (SACO), and Finland (AKAVA). In the Anglo-Saxon nations professionals are less likely to consider themselves part of the working class and view labour organizations as appropriate bodies to represent them.
17. France is the only advanced capitalist nation with a lower union density level (10%) than that in the US (13%) but it has an exceptionally high coverage rate; over 93% of workers in France are covered by union agreements while only 14% of US workers are covered.
18. Although the SAP has not typically held an absolute majority, it has not entered a coalition government with another party since 1957 (when it was part of a coalition government with the Agrarian party). Rather, it has forged agreements with, and relied on support from, other parties on particular issues.
19. Finland's party was established in 1899 as the Finnish Labour Party but changed its name to the Finnish Social Democratic Party in 1903.
20. The women's movement has often had to frame its demands in terms that were consonant with those of the social democratic/labour movements in the Nordic lands, but they have also been able to shape them.
21. However, public sector unions in the Anglo-Saxon nations have been more willing to engage their members in broader issues, such as campaigning against neoliberal policies.

References

Aaberge, Rolf, Anders Björklund, Markus Jäntti, Mårten Palme, Peder J. Pedersen, Nina Smith, and Tom Wennemo. 2002. Income Inequality and Income Mobility in the Scandinavian Countries Compared to the United States. *Review of Income and Wealth* 48:443–469.

Acker, Joan. 2000. Revisiting Class: Thinking from Gender, Race and Organizations. *Social Politics* 7(2):192–214.

Adam, Barry. 2007. Why Be Queer? *Questioning Sociology*. George Pavlich and Myra Hird, eds. Toronto: Oxford University Press. 71–79.

AFL-CIO. 1998. *Too Close For Comfort: How Corporate Boardrooms are Rigged to Overpay CEOs*. Washington, DC: AFL-CIO.

Alcock, John. 2001. *The Triumph of Sociobiology*. Oxford: Oxford University Press.

Alesina, Alberto, and Robert Perotti. 1994. The Political Economy of Growth: A Critical Survey of Recent Literature. *World Bank Economic Review* 8(3):351–371.

Alexander, Herbert E. 2005. Comparative Analysis of Political Party and Campaign Financing in the United States and Canada. *The Delicate Balance Between Political Equity and Freedom of Expression: Political Party Financing in Canada and the United States*. Steven Griner and Daniel Zovatto, eds. Washington, DC: Organization of American States (OAS) International IDEA. 7–21.

Alford, Robert R., and Roger Friedland. 1985. *Powers of Theory: Capitalism, the State and Democracy*. Cambridge: Cambridge University Press.

Alford, Lee J., and Joseph P. Ferrie. 1999. *Southern Paternalism and the American Welfare State*. New York: Cambridge University Press

Alston, Phillip, and James Crawford, eds. 2000. *The Future of Human Rights Treaty Monitoring*. Cambridge: Cambridge University Press.

Anderson, Sarah, John Cavanagh, Chuck Collins, Sam Pizzigati, and Mike Lapham. 2007. *Executive Excess 2007: The Staggering Cost of U.S. Business Leadership*. Washington, DC: Institute for Policy Studies; Boston, MA: United For a Fair Economy.

Andersson, Roger. 2007. Ethnic Residential Segregation and Integration Processes in Sweden. *Residential Segregation and the Integration of Immigrants: Britain, the Netherlands and Sweden*. Karen Schönwälder, ed. Berlin: Wissenschaftszentrum Berlin für Sozialforschung gGmbH.

Appiah, K. Anthony, and Amy Gutman. 1996. *Color Consciousness: The Political Morality of Race*. Princeton: Princeton University Press.

Aristotle. 2000 (350 BCE). *Politics*. New York: Dover Publications.

______. 2004 (350 BCE). *The Nichomachean Ethics*. London: Penguin Books.

Arjona, Roman, Maxime Ladaique, and Mark Pearson. 2001. *Growth, Inequality and Social Protection: Labour Market and Social Policy Occasional Paper No. 51*. Paris: OECD.

______. 2002. Social Protection and Growth. *OECD Economic Studies* 35:7–45.

Arneson, Richard J. 2002. Equality. *The Blackwell Guide to Social and Political Philosophy*. Robert L. Simon, ed. Oxford: Blackwell Publishers. 85–105.

Arrow, Kenneth J. 1979. The Tradeoff Between Growth and Equity. *Theory for Economic Efficiency: Essays in Honour of Abba P. Lerner*. Harry I. Greenfield, ed. Cambridge: MIT Press. 1–11.

Arrow, Kenneth, Samuel Bowles, and Steven Darlauf, eds. 2000. *Meritocracy and Economic Inequality*. Princeton: Princeton University Press.

Arter, David. 2003. Scandinavia: What's Left is the Social Democratic Consensus. *Parliamentary Government* 56(1):75–98.

Atkinson, Anthony B., Lee Rainwater, and Timothy M. Smeeding. 1995. *Income Distribution in OECD Countries: Evidence from the Luxembourg Income Study*. Paris: OECD.

Auerbach, James A., and Barbara Kivimae Krimgold, eds. 2001. *Income, Socioeconomic Status, and Health: Exploring the Relationships*. Washington, DC: Academy for Health Services Research and Health Policy.

Bagdikian, Ben. 1992. *The Media Monopoly*. 4th ed. Boston: Beacon Press.

Baldus, Bernd. 2004. *Inequality's Inner Secrets: Theories of Social Inequality*. Unpublished manuscript.

Baxter, Janeen. 1997. Gender Equality and Participation in Housework: A Cross-national Perspective. *Journal of Comparative Family Studies* 28(3):220–247.

Bayefsky, Anne F. 2001. *The UN Human Rights Treaty System: Universality at a Crossroads*. Ardsley, NY: Transnational.

Bebchuck, Lucian, and Yaniv Grinstein. 2005. The Growth of Executive Pay. *Oxford Review of Economic Policy* 21(2):283–303.

Beckfield, Jason. 2004. Does Income Inequality Harm Health? *Journal of Health and Social Behavior* 45(3):231–248.

Berlin, Isaiah. 1969. Four Essays on Liberty. London: Oxford University Press.

Berven, Nina. 2002. National Politics and Global Ideas? Welfare Work and Legitimacy in Norway and the United States. Working Paper 12–2002. Bergen, Norway: Stein Rokkan Centre for Social Studies, University of Bergen.

Birdsall, Nancy, David Ross, and Richard Sabot. 1995. Inequality and Growth Reconsidered. *World Bank Economic Review* 9(3):477–508.

Birnbaum, Jeffrey. 2000. *The Money Men: The Real Story of Fund-Raising's Influence on Political Power in America*. New York: Crown.

Björn, Lars. 1979. Labour Parties, Economic Growth, and the Redistribution of Income in Capitalist Democracies. *Comparative Social Research* 2:93–128.

Blanden, Jo, Paul Gregg, and Stephen Machin. 2005. Intergenerational Mobility in Europe and North America. London: Centre for Economic Performance, London School of Economics.

Bolzendahl, Catherine, and Clem Brooks. 2007. Women's Political Representation and Welfare Spending in 12 Capitalist Democracies. *Social Forces* 85(4):1509–1534.

Booth, Charles. 1897. *Life and Labour of the People of London*. London: Macmillan

Bowles, Samuel, and Herbert Gintis. 2002. The Inheritance of Inequality. *Journal of Economic Perspectives* 16(3):3–30.

Bradbury, Bruce, Stephen P. Jenkins, and John Micklewright, eds. 2001. *The Dynamics of Poverty in Industrialized Countries*. Cambridge: Cambridge University Press.

Bradley, David, Evelyne Huber, Stephanie Moller, François Nielsen, and John D. Stephens. 2003. Distribution and Redistribution in Post-Industrial Democracies. *World Politics* 55(2):193–228.

Brady, David. 2003a. Rethinking the Sociological Measurement of Poverty. *Social Forces* 81(3):715–752.

———. 2003b. The Politics of Poverty: Left Political Institutions, the Welfare State and Poverty. *Social Forces* 82(2):557–588.

Broberg, Gunnar, and Nils Roll-Hansen. 1996. *Eugenics and the Welfare State: Sterilization Policy in Denmark, Sweden, Norway and Finland*. East Lansing, MI: Michigan State University.

Broom, Leonard, and Robert G. Cushing. 1977. A Modest Test of an Immodest Theory: The Functional Theory of Stratification. *American Sociological Review* 42(2):157–169.

Brown, Michael K. 1999. *Race, Money and the American Welfare State*. Ithaca, NY: Cornell University Press.

Brownlee, Jamie. 2005. *Ruling Canada: Corporate Cohesion and Democracy*. Halifax: Fernwood Publishing.

Browning, Edgar K., and William R. Johnson. 1984. The Trade-off Between Equality and Efficiency. *Journal of Political Economy* 92(2):175–203.

Bulmer, Martin, and Anthony M. Rees, eds. 1996. *Citizenship Today: The Contemporary Relevance of T. H. Marshall*. London: UCL Press.

Burstein, Paul. 1998. Bringing the Public Back In: Should Sociologists Consider the Impact of Public Opinion on Public Policy. *Social Forces* 77(1):27–62.

Burton, John Alexander, and Christian E. Weller. 2005. *Supersize This: How CEO Pay Took Off While America's Middle Class Struggled*. Center for American Progress.

Caplovitz, David. 1963. *The Poor Pay More*. New York: The Free Press.

Carens, Joseph. 1981. *Equality, Moral Incentives and the Market: An Essay in Utopian Politico-Economic Theory*. Chicago: University of Chicago Press.

Center for Public Integrity. 1998. *The Buying of Congress*. New York: Avon Books.

Chan, Chak Kwan, and Graham Bowpitt. 2005. *Human Dignity and Welfare Systems*. Bristol: Policy Press.

Charlton, James I. 1998. *Nothing About Us Without Us: Disability Oppression and Empowerment*. Berkeley: University of California Press.

Chomsky, Noam, and Edward Herman. 1988. *Manufacturing Consent: The Political Economy of the Mass Media*. New York: Pantheon Books.

Chung, Haejoo, and Carles Muntaner. 2007. Welfare State Matters: A Typological Multilevel Analysis of Wealthy Countries. *Health Policy* 80(2):328–339.

Clayton, Matthew, and Andrew Williams, eds. 2000. *The Ideal of Equality*. London: Macmillan Press.

Clearinghouse on International Developments in Child, Youth and Family Policies at Columbia University. http://www.childpolicyintl.org.

Clement, Wallace, and John Myles. 1994. *Relations of Ruling: Class and Gender in*

Postindustrial Societies. Montreal and Kingston: McGill-Queen's University Press.

Cobb, Clifford, Ted Halstead, and Jonathon Rowe. 1995. If the GDP is Up, Why is America Down? *The Atlantic Monthly* (October).

Coburn, David. 2000. Income Inequality, Social Cohesion and the Health Status of Populations: The Role of Neo-liberalism. *Social Science and Medicine* 51(1):135–146.

Collins, Patricia Hill. 1993. Toward a New Vision: Race, Class and Gender as Categories of Analysis and Connection. *Race, Sex & Class* 1(1):25–45.

Collins, Randall. 1975. Functional and Conflict Theories of Educational Stratification. *American Sociological Review* 36(6):1002–1019.

Conference Board of Canada. 2004. *Understanding Health Care Cost Drivers and Escalators*. Ottawa: Conference Board of Canada.

Conley, Dalton. 1999. *Being Black, Living in the Red: Race, Wealth and Social Policy in America*. Berkeley: University of California Press.

Cook, Fay Lomax, and Edith J. Barrett. 1992. *Support for the American Welfare State: The Views of Congress and the Public*. New York: Columbia University Press.

Cooke, Martin, Daniel Beavon, and Mindy McHardy. 2003. Measuring the Wellbeing of Aboriginal People: An Application of the United Nations Human Development Index to Registered Indians in Canada, 1981–2001. *Aboriginal Policy Research: Setting the Agenda for Change* 1. Jerry P. White, Paul Maxim, and Daniel Beavon, eds. Toronto: Thompson Educational Publishing.

Coole, Diana H. 1988. *Women in Political Theory: From Ancient Misogyny to Contemporary Feminism*. Brighton, UK: Wheatsheaf Books.

Corak, Miles, ed. 2004. *Generational Income Mobility in North American and Europe*. Cambridge: Cambridge University Press.

Coughlin, Richard. 1979. Social Policy and Ideology: Public Opinion in Eight Rich Nations. *Comparative Studies in Sociology* 2:3–40.

Crystal, Graef S. 1992. *In Search of Excess: The Overcompensation of American Executives*. New York: W.W. Norton & Company, Inc.

Currie, Elliott. 1998. *Crime and Punishment in America*. New York: Metropolitan Books.

Cutright, Phillips. 1965. Political Structure, Economic Development, and National Security Programs. *American Journal or Sociology* 70(4):537–550.

______. 1967. Inequality: A Cross-National Analysis. *American Sociological Review* 32:562–578.

Dahl, Robert. 1957. The Concept of Power. *Behavioral Science* 2(3):201–215.

Darwin, Charles. 1982 (1859). *The Origin of Species*. London: Dent.

Davies, James B., Susanna Sandström, Anthony Shorrocks, and Edward N. Wolff. 2008. The World Distribution of Household Wealth. Helsinki, Finland: United Nations University, World Institute for Economic Development Economics Research. (Discussion Paper No. 2008/03).

Davis, Kingsley. 1948. *Human Society*. New York: McGraw-Hill.

Davis, Kingsley, and Wilbert E. Moore. 1945. Some Principles of Stratification. *American Sociological Review* 10(2):243–249.

Dawkins, Richard. 2006 (1976). *The Selfish Gene*. Oxford: Oxford University Press.

Domhoff, G. William. 1998. *Who Rules America? Power and Politics in the Year 2000*. 3rd ed. Mountain View, CA: Mayfield Publishing.

Donnelly, Jack. 2003. *Universal Human Rights in Theory and Practice*. 2nd ed. Ithaca, NY: Cornell University Press.

Draper, Patricia. 1975. !Kung Women: Contrasts in Sexual Egalitarianism in Foraging and Sedentary Contexts. *Toward an Anthropology of Women*. Rayna Reiter, ed. New York: Monthly Review Press. 77–109.

Dryzek, John. 1978. Politics, Economics and Inequality: A Cross-National Analysis. *European Journal of Political Research* 6(4):399–410.

Durkheim, Émile. 1964 (1893). *The Division of Labor in Society*. New York: Free Press.

______. 1982 (1895). *The Rules of Sociological Method*. New York: Free Press.

Durrant, Joan E. 1995. Culture, Cognition and Child Abuse. *Readings in Child and Adolescent Development: A Canadian Perspective*. Katherine Covell, ed. Toronto: Nelson Canada. 28–48.

Durrant, Joan E., and Gregg M. Olsen. 1997. Parenting and Public Policy: Contextualizing the Swedish Corporal Punishment Ban. *The Journal of Social Welfare and Family Law* 19(4):443–461.

Dworkin, Ronald. 2000. *Sovereign Virtue: The Theory and Practice of Equality*. Cambridge: Harvard University Press.

Dye, Thomas R. 1995. *Who's Running America? The Clinton Years*. 6th ed. Englewood Cliffs, NJ: Prentice Hall.

Edlund, Jonas. 1999. Trust in Government and Welfare Regimes: Attitudes To Redistribution and Financial Cheating in the USA and Norway. *European Journal of Political Research* 35(3):341–370.

Ekberg, Gunilla. 2004. The Swedish Law that Prohibits the Purchase of Sexual Services: Best Practices for Prevention of Prostitution and Trafficking in Human Beings. *Violence Against Women* 10(10):1187–1218.

Elman, R. Amy. 2001. Unprotected by the Swedish Welfare State Revisited: Assessing a Decade of Reform for Battered Women. *Women's Studies International Forum* 24(1):39–52.

Endicott, Karen L. 2006. Gender Relations in Hunter-Gather Societies. *The Cambridge Encyclopedia of Hunters and Gatherers*. Richard B. Lee and Richard Daly, eds. Cambridge: Cambridge University Press. 411–418.

Engels, Frederick. 1935 (1892). *Socialism Utopian and Scientific*. New York: International Publishers.

Erikson, Robert. 1993. Descriptions of Inequality: The Swedish Approach to Welfare Research. *The Quality of Life*. Martha Nussbaum and Amartya Sen, eds. Oxford: Clarendon Press. 67–83.

Erikson, Robert, and Rune Åberg. 1987. *Welfare in Transition: A Survey of Living Conditions in Sweden 1968–1981*. Oxford: Oxford University Press.

Erikson, Robert, and John H. Goldthorpe. 1992. *The Constant Flux: A Study of Class Mobility in Industrial Societies*. Oxford: Clarendon Press.

Esping-Andersen, Gøsta. 1985a. Power and Distributional Regimes. *Politics and Society* 14(2):223–56.

———. 1985b. *Politics Against Markets: The Social Democratic Road to Power*. Princeton: Princeton University Press.

———. 1990. *The Three Worlds of Welfare Capitalism*. Princeton: Princeton University Press.

Estes, Richard J. 2004a. *At the Crossroads: Dilemmas in International Development*. Dordrecht: Kluwer Academic Publishers.

———. 2004b. Development Challenges of the 'New Europe'. *Social Indicators Research* 1–44.

Evans, Robert G., Morris L. Barer, and Theodore R. Marmor, eds. 1994. *Why are Some People Healthy and Others Not?* New York: Aldine de Gruyter.

Fellegi, Ivan P. 1997. *On Poverty and Low Income*. Ottawa: Statistics Canada.

Ferguson, Ann. 1990. The Intersection of Race, Gender and Class in the United States Today. *Rethinking Marxism* 3(3/4):45–64.

Fields, Barbara Jeanne. 1990. Slavery, Race and Ideology in the United States of America. *New Left Review* 1(181):95–118.

Fischer, Claude S., Michael Hout, Martin Sanchez Jankowski, Samuel R. Lucas, Ann Swidler, and Kim Voss, eds. 1996. *Inequality By Design: Cracking the Bell Curve Myth*. Princeton: Princeton University Press.

Fleras, Augie, and Jean Leonard Elliott. 2000. *Unequal Relations: An Introduction to Race, Ethnic, and Aboriginal Relations in Canada*. 3rd ed. Scarborough: Prentice Hall Allyn & Bacon Canada.

Forbes. 2005. The Forbes 400. *Forbes: The 400 Richest People in America* 176(7):89.

———. 2008a. Entertainment All Stars. *Forbes: Money, Power, Influence*. 20 October 2008.

———. 2008b. Lives of the Very Rich. *Forbes: Money, Power, Influence*. 24 March 2008.

———. 2008c. The Richest People in the World: 1,125 Billionaires. *Forbes: Special Issue*. 24 March 2008.

Frank, Robert. 2000. *Luxury Fever: Money and Happiness in an Era of Excess*. Princeton: Princeton University Press.

Fraser, Steven, ed. 1995. *The Bell Curve Wars: Race, Intelligence and the Future of America*. New York: Basic Books.

Freeman, Richard. 1995. The Labor Market. *Crime*. James Wilson and Joan Petersilia, eds. San Francisco: Institute for Contemporary Studies. 171–191.

Fürst, Gunilla. 1999. *Sweden—The Equal Way*. Stockholm: Swedish Institute.

Fuwa, Makiko. 2004. Macro-level Gender Inequality and the Division of Household Labor in 22 Countries. *American Sociological Review* 69(6):751–767.

Galbraith, John K. 1971. *The New Industrial State*. Boston: Houghton Mifflin.

———. 1983. *The Anatomy of Power*. Boston: Houghton Mifflin.

Gangl, Markus. 2005. Income, Permanent Incomes and Income Dynamics: Comparing Europe to the United States. *Work and Occupations* 32:140–162.

Gardner, Howard. 1999. *Intelligence Reframed: Multiple Intelligences for the 21st Century*. New York: Basic Books.

Geist, Claudia. 2005. The Welfare State and the Home: Regime Differences in the Domestic Division of Labour. *European Sociological Review* 21(1):23–41.

Giddens, Anthony. 1978. *Durkheim: His Life, Work, Writings and Ideas*. Sussex: Harvester Press.

Gilens, Martin. 1999. *Why Americans Hate Welfare*. Chicago: University of Chicago Press.

Glenn, Evelyn Nakano. 2002. *Unequal Freedom: How Race and Gender Shaped American Citizenship and Labor*. Cambridge: Harvard University Press.

Global Initiative to End All Corporal Punishment of Children. 2005a. Ending Legalised Violence Against Children: Report for East Asia & Pacific Regional Consultation–UN Secretary General's Study on Violence Against Children. Bangkok: Global Initiative to End All Corporal Punishment of Children.

______. 2005b. Ending Legalised Violence Against Children: Report for Europe & Central Regional Consultation–UN Secretary General's Study on Violence Against Children. Ljubljana: Global Initiative to End All Corporal Punishment of Children.

______. 2005c. Ending Legalised Violence Against Children: Report for North America Regional Consultation–UN Secretary General's Study on Violence Against Children. Toronto: Global Initiative to End All Corporal Punishment of Children.

Goldfield, Michael. 1989. Worker Insurgency, Radical Organization and New Deal Labor Legislation. *American Political Science Review* 83(4):1257–1282.

Gould, Stephen Jay. 1995. Curveball. *The Bell Curve Wars: Race, Intelligence and the Future of America*. Steven Fraser, ed. New York: Basic Books. 11–22.

Gravelle, Hugh, John Wildman, and Matthew Sutton. 2002. Income Inequality and Health: What Can We Learn From Aggregate Data? *Social Science and Medicine* 54(4):577–589.

Graves, Joseph. 2004. *The Race Myth*. New York: Penguin.

Griffin, Larry J., Michael E. Wallace, and Beth A. Rubin. 1986. Capitalist Resistance to the Organization of Labor Before the New Deal: Why? How? Success? *American Sociological Review* 51(April):147–167.

Gustafsson, Björn, and Mats Johansson. 1999. In Search of Smoking Guns: What Makes Income Inequality Vary of Time in Different Countries? *American Sociological Review* 64(4):585–605.

Halleröd, Björn. 1996. Deprivation and Poverty: A Comparative Analysis of Sweden and Great Britain. *Acta Sociologica* 39(2):141–168.

Halstead, Ted, and Clifford Cobb. 1996. The Need for New Measurements of Progress. *The Case Against the Global Economy and For a Turn Toward the Local*. Jerry Mander and Edward Goldsmith, eds. San Francisco: Sierra Club Books. 197–206.

Harman, Chris. 1999. *A People's History of the World*. London: Bookmarks.

Harris, Nigel. 1995. *The New Untouchable: Immigration and the New World Order*. London, Penguin Books.

Hartz, Louis. 1955. *The Liberal Tradition in America: An Interpretation of American Political Thought since the Revolution*. New York: Harcourt Brace.

______. 1964. *The Founding of New Societies*. New York: Harcourt, Brace & World, Inc.

Hauhart, Robert C. 2003. The Davis-Moore Theory of Stratification: The Life Course of a Socially Constructed Classic. *American Sociologist* 34(4):5–24.

Hedström, Peter, and Stein Ringen. 1987. Age and Income in Contemporary Society: A Research Note. *Journal of Social Policy* 16(2):227–239.

Herrnstein, Richard, and Charles Murray. 1994. *The Bell Curve: Intelligence and Class Structure in American Life*. New York: Free Press.

Hewitt, Christopher. 1977. The Effect of Political Democracy and Social Democracy on Equality in Industrial Societies: A Cross-National Comparison. *American Sociological Review* 42(June):450–464.

Hicks, Alexander. 1984. Elections, Keynes, Bureaucracy, and Class: Explaining US Budget Deficits, 1961–1978. *American Sociological Review* 49(2):165–181.

______. 1991. Unions, Social Democracy, Welfare and Growth. *Research in Political Sociology* 5:209–234.

______. 1999. *Social Democracy and Welfare Capitalism*. Ithaca, NY: Cornell University Press.

Hicks, Alexander, and Duane Swank. 1984. On the Political Economy of Welfare Expansion: A Comparative Analysis of 18 Advanced Capitalist Democracies. *Comparative Political Studies* 17(1):81–119.

Hiilamo, Heikki. 2004. Changing Family Policy in Sweden and Finland During the 1990s. *Social Policy and Administration* 38(1):21–40.

Hird, Myra J. 2007. Am I a Woman? *Questioning Sociology*. George Pavlich and Myra Hird, eds. Toronto: Oxford University Press. 56–70.

Hobbes, Thomas. 1985 (1651). *Leviathan*. London: Penguin Books.

Hobson, Barbara. 1993. Feminist Strategies and Gendered Discourses in Welfare States: Married Women's Right to Work in the United States and Sweden. *Mothers of a New World: Maternalist Politics and the Origins of Welfare States*. Seth Koven and Sonya Michel, eds. New York: Routledge. 396–429.

Hobson, Barbara, and Marika Lindholm. 1997. Collective Identities, Women's Power Resources, and the Construction of Citizenship Rights in Welfare States. *Theory and Society* 26:475–508.

Hocking, Barbara A., and Barbara J. Hocking. 1999. Colonialism, Constitutionalism, Costs and Compensation: A Contemporary Comparison of Legal Rights and Obligations of and towards the Scandinavian Sami and Indigenous Australians. *Nordic Journal of International Law* 68:31–52.

Hofstadter, Richard. 1955. *Social Darwinism in American Thought*. Boston: Beacon Press.

Horowitz, Gad. 1968. *Canadian Labour in Politics*. Toronto: University of Toronto Press.

———. 1978. Notes on 'Conservatism, Liberalism and Socialism in Canada'. *Canadian Journal of Political Science* 11(2):383–399.

Horowitz, Irving. 1999. *Behemoth: Main Currents in the History and Theory of Political Sociology*. London: Transaction Publishers.

Huaco, George A. 1963. A Logical Analysis of the Davis-Moore Theory of Stratification. *American Sociological Review* 28(5):801–804.

Huber, Evelyne, and John D. Stephens. 2000. Partisan Governance, Women's Employment and the Social Democratic Service State. *American Sociological Review* 65(3):323–342.

———. 2001. *Development and Crisis of the Welfare State*. Chicago: University of Chicago Press.

Hudson, Michael. 1996a. Cashing in on Poverty. *The Nation* 262(20):11–14.

———, ed. 1996b. *Merchants of Misery: How Corporate America Profits from Poverty*. Monroe: Common Courage Press.

Huston, Aletha C., ed. 1994. *Children in Poverty*. Cambridge: Cambridge University Press.

Huston, Aletha C., Vonnie C. McLoyd, and Cynthia Garcia Coll. 1994. Children and Poverty: Issues in Contemporary Research. *Child Development* 65(2):275–282.

Hvinden, Bjørn. 2004. Nordic Disability Policies in a Changing Europe: Is There Still a Distinct Nordic Model? *Social Policy and Administration* 38(2):170–189.

İmrohoroğlu, Ayse, Antonio Merlo, and Peter Rupert. 2001. What Accounts for the Decline in Crime? Working Paper No. 01–15. Penn Institute for Economic Research.

Inter-Parliamentary Union. 2009. *Women in National Parliaments*. 31 October 2009. http://www.ipu.org.wmn-e/classif.htm.

Isaacs, Julia B. 2007. Economic Mobility of Black and White Families. Washington, DC: Brookings Institution.

Jacobson, Matthew Frye. 1998. *Whiteness of a Different Color: European Immigrants and the Alchemy of Race*. Cambridge: Harvard University Press.

Jäntti, Markus, Knut Røed, Robin Naylor, Anders Björklund, Bernt Bratsberg, Oddbjørn Raaum, Eva Österbacka, and Tor Eriksson. 2006. American Exceptionalism in a New Light: Earnings Mobility in the Nordic Countries, the United Kingdom and the United States. Discussion Paper No. 1938. Bonn, Germany: Institute for the Study of Labor (IZA).

Johnston, William, and Douglas Baer. 1993. Class Consciousness and National Contexts: Canada, Sweden and the United States in Historical Perspective. *Canadian Review of Sociology and Anthropology* 30(2):271–295.

Judge, Ken. 1995. Income Distribution and Life Expectancy: A Critical Appraisal. *British Medical Journal* 311(7015):1282–1285.

Kangas, Olli, Urban Lundberg, and Niels Ploug. 2006. Three Routes to a Pension Reform. Stockholm: Institute for Future Studies.

Kaplan, George A., Elise R. Pamuk, John W. Lynch, Richard D. Cohen, and Jennifer L. Balfour. 1996. Income Inequality in the United States: Analysis of Mortality Potential Pathways. *British Medical Journal* 312(7037):999–1003.

Kawachi, Ichiro, and Bruce P. Kennedy. 2002. *The Health of Nations: Why Inequality is Harmful to Your Health*. New York: The New Press.

Keister, Lisa A. 2000. *Wealth in America: Trends in Wealth Inequality*. Cambridge: Cambridge University Press.

Kennedy, David. 1996. The Decline of the Socialist Party of America, 1901–1919. *Socialist History* (9):8–22.

Kennedy, Bruce P., Ichiro Kawachi, and Deborah Prothrow-Stith. 1996. Income Distribution and Mortality: Cross Sectional Ecological Study of the Robin Hood

Index in the United States. *British Medical Journal* 312(7037):1004–1007.

Kenworthy, Lane. 1995. Equality and Efficiency: The Illusory Tradeoff. *European Journal of Political Research* 27(2):225–254.

______. 2004. *Egalitarian Capitalism: Jobs, Incomes and Equality in Affluent Countries.* New York: American Sociological Association Rose Series, Russell Sage Foundation.

King, Anthony. 1973a. Ideas, Institutions and the Policies of Governments: A Comparative Analysis: Parts I and II. *British Journal of Political Science* 3(3):291–313.

______. 1973b. Ideas, Institutions and the Policies of Governments: A Comparative Analysis: Part III. *British Journal of Political Science* 3(4):409–423.

King, Desmond. 2005. Making People Work: Democratic Consequences of Workfare. *Welfare Reform and Political Theory.* Lawrence M. Mead and Christopher Beem, eds. New York: Russell Sage Foudation. 65–81.

Kjeldstad, Randi. 2001. Gender Policies and Gender Equality. *Nordic Welfare Policies in European Context.* Mikko Kautto, Johan Fritzell, Bjørn Hvinden, Jon Kvist, and Hannu Uusitalo, eds. London: Routledge.

Klass, Gary M. 1985. Explaining America and the Welfare State: An Alternative Theory. *British Journal of Political Science* 15(4):427–450.

Korpi, Walter. 1978. *The Working Class in Welfare Capitalism: Work, Unions and Politics in Sweden.* London: Routledge & Kegan Paul.

______. 1980. Approaches to the Study of Poverty in the United States: Critical Notes From a European Perspective. *Poverty and Public Policy: An Evaluation of Social Science Research.* Vincent T. Covello, ed. Cambridge: Schenkman. 287–314.

______. 1983. *The Democratic Class Struggle.* London: Routledge & Kegan Paul.

______. 1989. Power, Politics and State Autonomy in the Development of Social Citizenship: Social Rights During Sickness in Eighteen OECD Countries Since 1939. *American Sociological Review* 54(3):309–328.

Korpi, Walter, and Joakim Palme. 1998. The Paradox of Redistribution and Strategies of Equality: Welfare State Institutions, Inequality, and Poverty in Western Countries. *American Sociological Review* 63:661–687.

Korsmo, Fae L. 1993. Swedish Policy and Saami Rights. *The Northern Review* 11:32–55.

Kramer, Joyce M. 1995. Social Welfare of the Indigenous Peoples Within the United States of America. *Social Welfare with Indigenous Peoples.* John Dixon and Robert Scheurell, eds. London: Routledge.

Krugman, Paul R. 2007. *The Conscience of a Liberal.* New York: W.W. Norton & Company, Inc.

Kuznets, Simon. 1955. Economic Growth and Income Inequality. *The American Economic Review* 45(1):1–28.

______. 1965. *Economic Growth and Structure.* New York: Norton.

Kvist, Roger. 1994. The Racist Legacy in Modern Swedish Saami Policy. *The Canadian Journal of Native Studies* XIV(2):203–220.

Larsen, Christian Albrekt. 2008. The Institutional Logic of Welfare Attitudes: How Welfare Regimes Influence Public Support. *Comparative Political Studies* 41(2):145–168.

Lee, Richard B., and Richard Daly. 2006. Introduction: Foragers and Others. *The Cambridge Encyclopedia of Hunters and Gatherers.* Richard B. Lee and Richard Daly, eds. Cambridge: Cambridge University Press.

Lenski, Gerhard, and Jean Lenski. 1982. *Human Societies: An Introduction to Human Societies.* 4th ed. New York: McGraw-Hill.

Leon, David A., Denny Vågerö, and P. Olausson Otterblad. 1992. Social Class Differences in Infant Mortality in Sweden: A Comparison with England and Wales. *British Medical Journal* 305(6855):687–691.

Lewis, Jane, and Gertrude Åström. 1992. Equality, Difference and State Welfare: Labor Market and Family Policies in Sweden. *Feminist Studies* 18(1):59–87.

Lieberman, Robert C. 1998. *Shifting the Color Line: Race and the American Welfare State.* Cambridge: Harvard University Press.

Lilja, Margaret, Ingela Månsson, Leif Jahlenius, and Maryanne Sacco-Peterson. 2003. Disability Policy in Sweden. *Journal of Disability Policy Studies* 14(3):130–135.

Lindholm, Marika. 1991. Swedish Feminism, 1835–1945: A Conservative Revolution. *Journal of Historical Sociology* 4(2):121–142.

Lindqvist, Rafael. 2000. Swedish Disability Policy: From Universal Welfare to Civil Rights? *European Journal of Social Security* 2(4):399–418.

Lipset, Seymour M. 1986. Historical Traditions and National Characteristics: A Comparative Analysis of Canada and the United States. *Canadian Journal of Sociology* 11(2):113–155.

———. 1990. *Continental Divide: The Values and Institutions of the United States and Canada*, New York: Routledge.

———. 1996. *American Exceptionalism: A Double-Edged Sword*. New York: W.W. Norton & Company, Inc.

Lipset, Seymour M., and Gary Marks. 2000. *It Didn't Happen Here: Why Socialism Failed in the United States*. New York: W.W. Norton & Company, Inc.

Locke, John. 1988 (1688). *Two Treatises of Government*. Cambridge: Cambridge University Press.

Lockhart, Charles. 1984. Explaining Social Policy Differences Among Advanced Industrial Societies. *Comparative Politics* 16(3):335–350.

———. 2001. *Protecting the Elderly: How Culture Shapes Social Policy*. Pennsylvania: Pennsylvania State University Press.

Lopreato, Joseph, and Timothy Crippen. 1999. *Crisis in Sociology: The Need For Darwin*. London: Transaction Publishers.

Lovenduski, Joni. 2005. *Feminizing Politics*. Cambridge: Polity Press.

Lovenduski, Joni, and Jill Hills. 1981. *The Politics of the Second Electorate: Women and Public Participation*. London: Routledge & Kegan Paul.

Lukes, Steven. 2005. *Power: A Radical View*. 2nd ed. New York: Palgrave Macmillan.

Luxembourg Income Study. 2000. LIS Database: Key Figures. http://www.lisproject.org.

Mackenzie, Hugh. 2007. *The Great CEO Pay Race: Over Before it Begins*. Toronto: Canadian Centre for Policy Alternatives.

Mackie, Thomas T., and Richard Rose. 1982. *The International Almanac of Electoral History*. 2nd ed. New York: Facts on File, Inc.

Mandle, Jay. 2004. The Politics of Democracy. *Challenge* 47(1):53–63.

Margalit, Avishai. 1996. *The Decent Society*. Cambridge: Harvard University Press.

Marmot, Michael. 2004. *The Status Syndrome: How Social Standing Affects Our Health and Longevity*. New York: Owl Books.

Marshall, T.H. 1950. *Citizenship and Social Class and Other Essays*. Cambridge: Cambridge University Press.

———. 1964. *Class, Citizenship and Social Development*. New York: Doubleday.

Marx, Karl. 1934 (1852). *The Eighteenth Brumaire of Louis Bonaparte*. Moscow: Progress Publishers.

———. 1978. On the Jewish Question. *The Marx-Engels Reader*. 2nd ed. Robert C. Tucker, ed. New York: W.W. Norton & Company, Inc. 26–52.

Marx, Karl, and Frederick Engels. 1960. *The German Ideology*. New York: International Publishers.

Mason, Andrew. 1998. *Ideals of Equality*. Oxford: Blackwell.

McChesney, Robert W., and John Nichols. 2002. *Our Media, Not Theirs: The Democratic Struggle Against Corporate Media*. New York: Seven Stories Press.

McLaren, Angus. 1990. *Our Own Master Race: Eugenics in Canada, 1885–1945*. Toronto: McClelland & Stewart.

McNaught, Kenneth. 1988. *The Penguin History of Canada*. London: Penguin Books.

McRae, Kenneth D. 1964. The Structure of Canadian History. *The Founding of New Societies: Studies in the History of the United States, Latin America, South Africa, Canada and Australia*. Louis Hartz, ed. New York: Harcourt, Brace & World, Inc.

Mead, Margaret. 1963 (1935). *Sex and Temperament in Three Primitive Societies*. New York: William Morrow.

Mehrtens, F. John. 2004. Three Worlds of Public Opinion? Values, Variation and the Effect on Social Policy. *International Journal of Public Opinion Research* 16(2):115–143.

Mellor, Jennifer M., and Jeffrey Milyo. 2003. Is Exposure to Income Inequality a Public Health Concern? Lagged Effects of Income Inequality on Individual and Population Health. *Health Services Research* 38(1.1):137–151.

Miliband, Ralph. 1977. *The State in Capitalist Society: The Analysis of the Western System of Power*. London: Quartet Books.

Minde, Henry. 2001. Sami Land Rights in Norway: A Test Case for Indigenous Peoples. *International Journal on Minority and Group Rights* 8(107):107–125.

Mintz, Beth. 1998. The Failure of Health Care Reform: The Role of Big Business in Policy Formation. *Social Policy and the Conservative Agenda*. Clarence Y.H. Lo and Michael Schwartz, eds. Massachusetts: Blackwell. 210–224.

Miringoff, Marc, and Marque-Luisa Miringoff. 1999. *The Social Health of a Nation: How America is Really Doing*. New York: Oxford University Press.

Mishel, Lawrence, Jared Bernstein, and Sylvia Allegretto. 2005. *The State of Working America 2004/2004*. Ithaca, NY: Cornell University Press.

Mishel, Lawrence, Jared Bernstein, and Heidi Shierholz. 2008. *The State of Working America 2008/2009*. Ithaca, NY: Cornell University Press.

Moller, Stephanie, David Bradley, Evelyne Huber, François Nielsen, and John D. Stephens. 2003. Determinants of Relative Poverty in Advanced Capitalist Democracies. *American Sociological Review* 68(1):22–51.

Moore, Wilbert E. 1963. But Some are More Equal than Others. *American Sociological Review* 28(1):13–28.

Moscovitch, Allan, and Andrew Webster. 1995. Aboriginal Social Assistance Expenditures. *How Ottawa Spends 1995–1996: Mid-Life Crises*. Susan D. Phillips, ed. Ottawa: Carleton University Press. 209–235.

Murray, Charles. 1984. *Losing Ground: American Social Policy,1950–1980*. New York: Basic Books.

National Council of Welfare. 2007. *First Nations, Métis and Inuit Children and Youth: Time to Act*. Ottawa: National Council of Welfare.

Navarro, Vicente, Carles Muntaner, Carme Borrell, Joan Benach, Maica Rodríguez-Sanz, Núria Vérges, and M. Isabel Pasarín. 2006. Politics and Health Outcomes. *The Lancet* 368(9540):1033-1037.

Nermo, Magnus. 1999. *Structured By Gender: Patterns of Sex Segregation in the Swedish Labour Market*. Stockholm: Stockholms Universitet.

Neubeck, Kenneth J., and Noel A. Cazenave. 2001. *Welfare Racism: Playing the Race Card Against America's Poor*. New York: Routledge.

Newell, Peter. 2005. The Human Rights Imperative for Ending All Corporate Punishment of Children. *Eliminating Corporal Punishment: The Way Forward to Constructive Child Discipline*. Stuart Hart, ed. Paris: UNESCO.

Nilsson, Torbjörn. 1997. Scandinavian Liberalism–Prophets Instead of Profits. *The Cultural Construction of Norden*. Østein Sørensen and Bo Stråth, eds. Stockholm: Scandinavian University Press.

Nolte, Ellen, and Martin McKee. 2003. Measuring the Health of Nations: Analysis of Mortality Amenable to Health Care. *British Medical Journal* 327(7424):1129–1133.

Nozick, Robert. 1974. *Anarchy, State and Utopia*. New York: Basic Books.

O'Connor, Julia, Ann Shola Orloff, and Sheila Shaver. 1999. *States, Markets, Families: Gender, Liberalism and Social Policy in Australia, Canada, Great Britain and the United States*. Cambridge: Cambridge University Press.

Organisation for Economic Co-operation and Development. (nd). Trade Unions Density in OECD Countries 1960–2007. Paris: OECD.

______. 1996. *OECD Employment Outlook*. Paris: OECD.

______. 2004a. Corporate Data Environment. Paris: OECD.

______. 2004b. *Economic Outlook* 76(2). Paris: OECD.

______. 2005. *Pensions at a Glance*. Paris: OECD.

______. 2007. *Society at a Glance: OECD Social Indicators*. Paris: OECD.

______. 2008. Online OECD Employment Database. http://www.oecd.org/document.

Okun, Arthur M. 1975. *Equality and Efficiency: The Big Tradeoff*. Washington, DC: Brookings Institution.

Oliver, Melvin L., and Thomas Shapiro. 1989. Race and Wealth. *Review of Black Political Economy* 17(4):5–25.

______. 2006. *Black Wealth/White Wealth*. 2nd ed. New York: Routledge.

Olsen, Gregg M., ed. 1988. *Industrial Change and Labour Adjustment in Sweden and Canada*. Toronto: Garamond.

______. 1991. Labour Mobilization and the Strength of Capital: The Rise and Stall of Economic Democracy in Sweden. *Studies in Political Economy* (34):109–45.

______. 1992. *The Struggle for Economic Democracy in Sweden*. Aldershot, England: Avebury/Gower.

______. 1994. Locating the Canadian Welfare State: Family Policy and Health Care in Canada, Sweden and the United States. *The Canadian Journal of Sociology* 19(1):1–20.

______. 1995. The Search for a New Model: Industrial Relations in Sweden. *Labour Gains, Labour Pains: 50 Years of PC 1003*. Cy Gonick, Paul Phillips, and Jesse Vorst, eds. Winnipeg/Halifax: Society for Socialist Studies/Fernwood. 383–404.

______. 1996. Re-modeling Sweden: The Rise and Demise of the Compromise in a Global Economy. *Social Problems* 43(1):1–20.

______. 1999. Half Full or Half Empty? The Swedish Welfare State in Transition. *Canadian Review of Sociology and Anthropology* 36(2):241–267.

______. 2002. *The Politics of the Welfare State: Canada, Sweden and the United States*. Don Mills, ON: Oxford University Press.

______. 2007. Toward Global Welfare State Convergence? Family Policy and Health Care in Sweden, Canada and the United

States. *Journal of Sociology and Social Welfare* XXXIV(2):143–164.

———. 2008 Labour Market Policy in the United States, Canada and Sweden: Addressing the Issue of Convergence. *Social Policy and Administration* 42(4):323–341.

Olsen, Gregg M., and Robert J. Brym. 1996. Between American Exceptionalism and Social Democracy: Public and Private Pensions in Canada. *The Privatization of Social Policy: Occupational Welfare and the Welfare State in America, Scandinavia and Japan*. Michael Shalev, ed. London: Macmillan Press. 261–279.

Olsen, Gregg M., and Julia S. O'Connor, eds. 1998. Understanding the Welfare State: Power Resources Theory and its Critics. *Power Resources Theory and the Welfare State: A Critical Approach*. Toronto: University of Toronto Press. 3–33.

Olsson, Sven E., and David Lewis. 1995. Welfare Rules and Indigenous Rights: the Sami People and the Nordic Welfare States. *Social Welfare with Indigenous Peoples*. John Dixon and Robert P. Scheurell, eds. London: Routledge. 141–185.

Orr, Amy J. 2003. Black-White Differences in Achievement: The Importance of Wealth. *Sociology of Education* 17(4):281–304.

Page, Edward C. 1985. *Political Authority and Bureaucratic Power: A Comparative Analysis*. 2nd ed. Brighton, UK: Wheatsheaf.

Page, Benjamin I., and James R. Simmons. 2000. *What Governments Do: Dealing with Poverty and Inequality*. Chicago: University of Chicago Press.

Parsons, Talcott. 1964. *Essays in Sociological Theory*. New York: Free Press.

Perotti, Roberto. 1996. Growth, Income Distribution and Democracy: What the Data Say. *Journal of Economic Growth* 1(2):149–187.

Persson, Torsten, and Guido Tabellini. 1994. Is Inequality Harmful for Growth? *American Economic Review* 84(3):600–621.

Peter, Tracey. 2006. Domestic Violence in the United States and Sweden: A Welfare State Typology Comparison within a Power Resources Framework. *Women's Studies International Forum* 29(1):96–107.

Pettit, Becky, and Bruce Western. 2004. Mass Imprisonment and the Life Course: Race and Class Inequality in US Incarceration. *American Sociological Review* 69:151–169.

Phillips, Anne. 1995. *The Politics of Presence*. Oxford: Oxford University Press.

Phillips, Kevin. 2002. *Wealth and Democracy: A Political History of the American Rich*. New York: Random House.

Pierson, Christopher. 1990. The 'Exceptional' United States: First New Nation or Last Welfare State? *Social Policy and Administration* 24(3):186–198.

Pontusson, Jonas. 2005. *Inequality and Prosperity: Social Europe Vs. Liberal America*. Ithaca, NY: Cornell University Press.

———. 2006. Whither Social Europe. *Challenge* 49(6):35–54.

Przeworksi, Adam. 1985. *Capitalism and Social Democracy*. Cambridge: Cambridge University Press.

Quadagno, Jill. 1994. *The Color of Welfare: How Racism Undermined the War on Poverty*. Oxford: Oxford University Press.

———. 2005. *One Nation Uninsured: Why the US has No National Health Insurance*. Oxford: Oxford University Press.

Raphael, Dennis, ed. 2004. *Social Determinants of Health: Canadian Perspectives*. Toronto: Canadian Scholars' Press.

———. 2008. Shaping Public Policy and Population Health in the United States: Why Is the Public Health Community Missing in Action. *International Journal of Health Services*, 38(1):63–94.

Rattansi, Ali. 2007. *Racism: A Very Short Introduction*. Oxford: Oxford University Press.

Rawls, John. 1971. *A Theory of Justice*. Cambridge: Harvard University Press.

Ray, Rebecca, and John Schmitt. 2007. No Vacation Nation. Center for Economic and Policy Research, Washington, DC.

Rees, Anthony M. 1996. T.H. Marshall and the Progress of Citizenship. *Citizenship Today: The Contemporary Relevance of T.H. Marshall*. Martin Bulmer and Anthony M. Rees, eds. London: University College London Press.

Rimlinger, Gaston V. 1971. *Welfare Policy and Industrialization in Europe, America and Russia*. New York: John Wiley & Sons, Inc.

Ringen, Stein. 1988 Direct and Indirect Measures of Poverty. *Journal of Social Policy* 17(3):351–365.

Rivera, Amaad, Brenda Cotto-Escalera, Anisha Desai, Jeannette Huezo, and Dedrick Muhammad. 2008. *Foreclosed: State of the Dream 2008*. Boston, MA: United For a Fair Economy.

Rojas, Mauricio. 1991. The 'Swedish Model' in Historical Perspective. *Scandinavian Economic History Review* XXXIX(2):64–74.

Rose, Richard. 1991. Is American Public Policy Exceptional? *Is America Different: A New Look at American Exceptionalism*. Byron E. Shafer, ed. Oxford: Clarendon Press. 187–221.

Ross, David P., E. Richard Shillington, and Clarence Lochhead. 1994. *The Canadian Fact Book on Poverty*. Ottawa: The Canadian Council on Social Development.

Rousseau, Jean-Jacques. 1984 (1755). *A Discourse on Inequality*. London: Penguin Books.

Rowntree, Seebohm. 1901. *Poverty: A Study of Town Life*. London: Macmillan.

Ruddick, Susan. 1996. Constructing Differences in Public Spaces: Race, Class and Gender as Interlocking Systems. *Urban Geography* 17(2):132–151.

Rueda, David. 2008. Left Government, Policy and Corporatism: Explaining the Influence of Partisanship on Inequality. *World Politics* 60(3):349–389.

Ruggie, Mary. 1984. *The State and Working Women: A Comparative Study of Britain and Sweden*. Princeton: Princeton University Press.

Ruggles, Patricia. 1990. *Drawing the Line: Alternative Poverty Measures and Their Implications for Public Policy*. Washington, DC: The Urban Institute.

Runblom, Harald. 1998. Sweden as a Multicultural Society. *Current Sweden* 418:1–10.

Russell, Bertrand. 1938. *Power: A New Social Analysis*. London: George Allen and Unwin.

Sahlins, Marshall. 1972. *Stone Age Economics*. Chicago: Aldine.

———. 2006. The Original Affluent Society. *The Politics of Egalitarianism: Theory and Practice*. Jacqueline Solway, ed. New York: Berghahn Books. 79–98.

Sainsbury, Diane. 2006. Immigrants' Social Rights in Comparative Perspective: Welfare Regimes, Forms of Immigration and Immigration Policy Regimes. *Journal of European Social Policy* 16(3):229–244.

Sandqvist, Karin. 1992. Sweden's Sex-Role Scheme and Commitment to Gender Equality. *Dual-Earner Families: International Perspectives*. Suzan Lewis, Dafne N. Izraeli, and Helen Hootsmans, eds. Newbury Park: Sage. 80–98.

Sarlo, Christopher. 1992. *Poverty in Canada*. Vancouver: The Fraser Institute.

Scholz, John Karl, and Kara Levine. 2004. U.S. Black-White Wealth Inequality. *Social Inequality*. Kathryn M. Neckerman, ed. New York: Russell Sage Foundation.

Schwartz, Michael. 1987. *The Structure of Power in America: The Corporate Elite as a Ruling Class*. New York: Holmes & Meier.

Scott, Franklin D. 1988. *Sweden: The Nation's History*. Carbondale and Edwardsville: Southern Illinois University Press.

Scott, John. 2001. *Power*. Cambridge: Polity Press.

Sen, Amartya. 1997. Inequality, Unemployment and Contemporary Europe. *International Labour Review* 136(2):155–72.

———. 2006. Conceptualizing and Measuring Poverty. *Poverty and Inequality*. David B. Grusky and Ravi Kanbur, eds. Stanford California: Stanford University Press. 30–46.

Sennett, Richard. 2003. *Respect in a World of Inequality*. New York: W.W. Norton & Company, Inc.

Shewell, Hugh. 2004. *Enough to Keep Them Alive: Indian Welfare in Canada, 1873–1965*. Toronto: University of Toronto Press.

Sierminska, Eva, Andrea Brandolini, and Timothy Smeeding. 2006. Comparing Wealth Distribution Across Rich Countries: First Results from the Luxembourg Wealth Study. Working Paper No. 1. Luxembourg: Luxembourg Income Study.

Sifry, Micah, and Nancy Watzman. 2004. *Is That a Politician in Your Pocket? Washington on $2 Million a Day*. Hoboken, NJ: John Wiley & Sons, Inc.

Smelser, Neil J. 1973. Alexis de Tocqueville as Comparative Analyst. *Comparative Methods in Sociology*. Ivan Vallier, ed. Los Angeles: University of California Press. 19–47.

Smith, Adam. 2003 (1776). *The Wealth of Nations*. New York: Bantam Dell.

Smith, Kevin B. 2002. Typologies, Taxonomies, and the Benefits of Policy Classification. *Policy Studies Journal* 30(3):379–395.

Socialstyrelsen. 2004. *Prostitution in Sweden 2003: Knowledge, Beliefs and Attitudes of Key Informants*. Stockholm: Socialstyrelsen.

Soininen, Maritta. 1999. The 'Swedish Model' as an Institutional Framework for Immigrant Membership Rights. *Journal of Ethnic and Migration Studies* 25(4):685–702.

Solon, Gary. 2002. Cross-national Differences in Intergenerational Earnings Mobility. *Journal of Economic Perspectives* 16(3):59–66.

Solway, Jacqueline, ed. 2006. *The Politics of Egalitarianism: Theory and Practice*. New York: Berghahn Books.

Sörensen, Kerstin, and Christina Bergqvist. 2002. *Gender and the Social Democratic Welfare Regime: A Comparison of Gender-Equality Friendly Policies in Sweden and Norway*. Stockholm: Arbetslivinstitut.

Sørensen, Øysten, and Bo Stråth, eds. 1997. Introduction: The Cultural Construction of Norden. *Cultural Construction of Norden*. Oslo: Scandinavian University Press. 1–24.

Spencer, Herbert. 1929 (1873). *The Study of Sociology*. New York & London: Appleton and Company.

———. 1969 (1851). *Social Statics*. New York: Augustus M. Kelley.

Spilerman, Seymour. 2000. Wealth and Stratification Processes. *Annual Review of Sociology* 26:497–524.

Spricker, Paul. 1993. *Poverty and Social Security: Concepts and Principles*. London: Routledge.

Stephens, John D. 1980. *The Transition from Capitalism to Socialism*. Atlantic Highlands: Humanities Press.

Stromwell, Layne K., Stephanie Brzuzy, Polly Sharp, and Celina Andersen. 1998. The Implications of Welfare Reform for American Indian Families and Communities. *Journal of Poverty* 2(4):1–15.

Svallfors, Stefan. 1991. The Politics of Welfare Policy in Sweden: Structural Determinants and Attitudinal Cleavages. *British Journal of Sociology* 42(4):609–634.

———. 1995. Institutions and the Comparative Study of Beliefs about Justice. *In the Eye of the Beholder: Opinions on Welfare and Justice in Comparative Perspective*. Stefan Svallfors, ed. Umeå: Impello Säljsupport AB. 116–126.

———. 1998. Worlds of Welfare and Attitudes Toward Distribution: A Comparison of Eight Western Nations. *European Sociological Review* 13(3):283–304.

Swank, Duane. 1992. Politics and the Structural Dependence of the State in Democratic Capitalist Nations. *American Political Science Review* 86(1):38–54.

———. 2002. *Global Capital, Political Institutions and Policy Change in Developed Welfare States*. Cambridge: Cambridge University Press.

Swedish Association of Local Authorities and Regions. 2005. *Swedish Health Care in an International Context*. Stockholm: Swedish Association of Local Authorities and Regions.

Swedish Institute. 2000. Disability Policies in Sweden. Stockholm: Swedish Institute.

Talberth, John, Clifford Cobb, and Noah Slattery. 2006. *The Genuine Progress Indicator 2006: A Tool for Sustainable Development*. Oakland, CA: Redefining Progress.

Tawney, Richard Henry. 1952 (1931). *Equality*. London: George Allen and Unwin.

Teeple, Gary. 2005. *The Riddle of Human Rights*. New York: Humanity Books.

Tham, Henrik. 1993. Trends Among Social Assistance Recipients in Sweden Since 1945. *Scandinavian Journal of Social Welfare*. 2(3):158–166.

Thelen, David P. 1970. Rutherford B. Hayes and the Reform Tradition in the Gilded Age. *American Quarterly* 22(2):150–165.

Tiger, Lionel, and Robin Fox. 1972. *The Imperial Animal*. London: Secker & Warburg.

Tocqueville, Alexis de. 2000 (1835, 1840). *Democracy in America*. Chicago: University of Chicago Press.

Towers Perrin. 1998. *Worldwide Total Rewards 1998*. New York: Towers Perrin.

Townsend, Peter. 1979. *Poverty in the United Kingdom: A Survey of Household Resources and Standards of Living*. Berkeley: University of California Press.

Townson, Monica. 1999. *Health and Wealth: How Social and Economic Factors Affect our Well Being*. Ottawa: Canadian Centre for Policy Alternatives.

Trägårdh, Lars. 1990a. Swedish Model or Swedish Culture? *Critical Review* 4(4):569–590.

———. 1990b. Varieties of Volkish Ideologies: Sweden and Germany 1848–1933. *Language and the Construction of Class Identities*. Bo Stråth, ed. Gothenburg: Gothenburg University Press. 25–54.

Trigger, Bruce G. 1990. Maintaining Economic Equality in Opposition to Complexity: An Iroquoian Case Study. *The Evolution of Political Systems: Sociopolitics in Small-scale Sedentary Societies*. Steadman Upham, ed. Cambridge: Cambridge University Press. 119–145.

Tumin, Melvin M. 1953. Some Principles of Stratification: A Critical Analysis. *American Sociological Review* 28(4):387–394.

———, ed. 1970. *Readings on Social Stratification*. Englewood Cliffs, NJ: Prentice Hall.

UNICEF. 2007. *Child Poverty in Perspective: An Overview of Child Well-being in Rich Countries*. Report Card No. 7. Florence, Italy: UNICEF Innocenti Research Centre.

United Nations. nd. Declarations and Conventions Contained in General Assembly Resolutions. http://www.un.org/documents/instruments/docs_en.asp.

———. nd. Office of the United Nations High Commissioner for Human Rights. http://www2.ohchr.org/english/law/cescr.htom.

———. nd. United Nations Treaty Collection: Chapter IV: Human Rights. http://treaties.un.org.

———. nd. Universal Declaration of Human Rights. http://www.un.org/Overview/rights.html.

______. 2009. Human Development Report 2009. New York: United Nations.

Vallier, Ivan, ed. 1973. *Comparative Methods in Sociology: Essays on Trends and Applications*. Los Angeles: University of California Press.

van den Berghe, Pierre L. 1974. Bringing Beasts Back In: Toward a Biosocial Theory of Aggression. *American Sociological Review* 39(6):777–788.

Vågerö, Denny, and Olle Lundberg. 1989. Health Inequalities in Britain and Sweden. *The Lancet* 334(8653):35–36.

Veit-Wilson, John H. 1987. Consensual Approaches to Poverty Lines and Social Security. *Journal of Social Policy* 16(2):183–211.

Venetoulis, Jason, and Cliff Cobb. 2004. *The Genuine Progress Indicator 1950–2002 (2004 Update)*. Oakland, CA: Redefining Progress.

Vincent, Susan. 2003. *Dressing the Elite: Clothes in Early Modern England*. Oxford: Berg.

Vogel, Joachim. 1997. Living Conditions and Inequality in the European Union 1997. Eurostat Working Papers.

Voss, Kim. 1993. *The Making of American Exceptionalism: The Knights of Labor and Class Formation in the Nineteenth Century*. Ithaca, NY: Cornell University Press.

Walmsley, Roy. 2007. *World Prison Population*. 6th ed. London: International Centre for Prison Studies, King's College London.

Wängnerud, Lena. 2000. Testing the Politics of Presence: Women's Representation in the Swedish Riksdag. *Scandinavian Political Studies* 23(1):67–91.

Weber, Max. 1947. *The Theory of Social and Economic Organization*. New York: Oxford University Press.

______. 1958. *From Max Weber: Essays in Sociology*. New York: Oxford University Press.

Weeden, Kim A. 2002. Why Do Some Occupations Pay More than Others? Social Closure and Earnings Inequality in the United States. *American Journal of Sociology* 108(2):55–101.

Wennemo, Irene. 1993. Infant Mortality, Public Policy and Inequality: A Comparison of 18 Industrialised Countries, 1950–85. *Sociology of Health and Illness* 15(4):429–446.

West, Darrell M., and Burdett A. Loomis. 1998. *The Sound of Money: How Political Interests Get What They Want*. New York: W.W. Norton & Company, Inc.

Western, Bruce, and Katherine Beckett. 1999. How Unregulated is the US Labor Market? The Penal System as a Labor Market Institution. *American Journal of Sociology* 104(4):1030–1060.

Whitehouse, Edward. 2007. *Pensions Panorama: Retirement Income Systems in 53 Countries*. Washington, DC: World Bank.

Whitman, James Q. 2003. *Harsh Justice: Criminal Punishment and the Widening Divide Between America and Europe*. New York: Oxford University Press.

Wilensky, Harold L. 1975. *The Welfare State and Equality*. Berkeley: University of California Press.

Wilensky, Harold L., and Charles N. Lebeaux. 1965. *Industrial Society and Social Welfare*. New York: The Free Press.

Wilkinson, Richard G. 1996. *Unhealthy Societies: The Afflictions of Inequality*. London: Routledge.

______. 2005. *The Impact of Inequality: How to Make Sick Societies Healthier*. New York: The New Press.

Wilkinson, Richard G., and Kate E. Pickett. 2006. Income Inequality and Population Health: A Review and Explanation of the Evidence. *Social Science and Medicine* 62(7):1768–1784.

Wills, Gary. 1999. *A Necessary Evil: A History of American Distrust of Government*. New York: Simon & Schuster.

Wilson, Edward O. 1975. *Sociobiology: The New Synthesis*. Cambridge, MA: Harvard University Press.

______. 2004 (1978). *On Human Nature*. Cambridge, MA: Harvard University Press.

Winter, James. 1997. *Democracy's Oxygen: How Corporations Control the News*. New York: Black Rose Books.

Wolff, Edward N., ed. 1996. International Comparisons of Wealth Inequality. *Review of Income and Wealth* 42(4):433–451.

______. 2002. *Top Heavy: The Increasing Inequality of Wealth in America and What Can Be Done About It*. New York: The New Press.

______. 2006. *International Perspectives on Household Wealth*. Cheltenham, UK: Edward Elgar.

World Health Organization. 2000. *The World Health Report 2000—Health Systems: Improving Performance*. Geneva: WHO.

Wright, Erik Olin. 1994. *Interrogating Inequality*. London: Verso.

______. 2000. Working-Class Power, Capitalist Class Interests and Class Compromise. *American Journal of Sociology* 105(4):957–1002.

______. 2002. The Shadow of Exploitation in Weber's Class Analysis. *American Sociological Review* 67(6):832–853.

Wrong, Dennis. 1988. *Power: Its Forms, Bases and Uses*. Chicago: University of Chicago Press.

Yalnizyan, Armine. 2007. *The Rich and the Rest of Us: The Changing Face of Canada's Growing Gap*. Toronto: Canadian Centre for Policy Alternatives.

Zawilski, Valerie, and Cynthia Levine-Rasky. 2005. *Inequality in Canada: A Reader on the Intersections of Gender, Race, and Class*. Don Mills: Oxford University Press.

Index